MW00815340

# Believing, Caring, and Doing in the United Church of Christ

# Believing, *Caring, and* Doing

IN THE UNITED CHURCH OF CHRIST

## An Interpretation

*Gabriel Fackre*

United Church Press
Cleveland

*To Dorothy*
*Believer, Carer, Doer*

United Church Press, 700 Prospect Avenue, Cleveland, Ohio 44115-1100

unitedchurchpress.com

© 2005 by Gabriel Fackre

All rights reserved. Published 2005

Printed in the United States of America on acid-free paper

10  09  08  07  06  05      5  4  3  2  1

**Library of Congress Cataloging-in-Publication Data**

Fackre, Gabriel J.
    Believing, caring, and doing in the United Church of Christ : an interpretation/
    Gabriel Fackre.
        p.   cm.
    Includes bibliographical references.
    ISBN 0-8298-1641-0 (paper : alk. paper)
    1. United Church of Christ. I. Title.
BX9885.F33 2005
285.8'34—dc22                                              2005047698

# Contents

# Prologue

UCC FOLK WILL RECOGNIZE IN the title of this book the words of a familiar bumper sticker: "To Believe is to Care is to Do." I have seen it frequently on student cars on our Andover Newton campus, and others will find it now and then in the parking lots of UCC congregations. What does it mean?

For some it entails the conflation of the three verbs. What else is the believing that church people do but caring and doing? The second and third terms are what the first term is all about, the caring for others being the attitude and the doing the action. Another interpretation is more sequential with believing having a role of its own, one that must issue in the attitude and action. Both construals stress the end point, the doing that is expressed in another descriptor of the UCC as a "just peace Church." The stress on "doing" comes to us naturally, as the UCC stands in the "world-formative" Reformed stream of church history, as Nicholas Wolterstorff identifies that heritage in his book, *When Justice and Peace Embrace*.[1] From Geneva forward, our tradition has lifted up "sanctification" as fundamental to the Christian faith, the witness to a grace that makes for holiness in self and society. This is a point the United Church of Christ delegation made regularly in its recent conversations with Lutherans as we moved toward the Formula of Agreement signed in 1997 in which each party declared itself open to both mutual affirmation and mutual admonition, the Reformed stressing the divine sovereignty and growth in sanctification and the Lutherans accenting divine solidarity with us in the church and the simultaneity of sin and justification (*simul iustus et peccator*).[2]

There is a third interpretation of the signature sticker. In this reading, each of the verbs is seen to have an integrity of its own, albeit inseparable from one another. This unity without the loss of distinctions reflects the intent of the founders of the United Church of Christ, a pioneering effort in bringing together the gifts of four streams of Christian history in what is called today in ecumenical circles a "reconciled diversity." Thus with regard to our three terms, believing is not reducible to caring, nor is caring just the interiority of doing. As it will be interpreted in the pages that follow, believing has to do with beliefs, basic convictions, articles of faith for which we live and are ready to die. As inseparable from the others, believing of this sort cannot help but issue in caring and doing. And caring? As noted, what launched the United Church of Christ was our care for the unity of the universal Church, making us a Church self-described as "united and uniting." Caring so understood in this book has to do with our ecumenical passion and its companion, interfaith outreach. As such, it has a meaning in its own right, not reducible to a facet of doing, but inseparable from doing, as it is with believing. And doing? Of course, as noted above, this is a special charism we bring to the church universal, and why we are known for our activist stance in the affairs of day, in continuity with our long-standing world-formative Reformed tradition.

The organization of the book follows the triple accents. Part I views UCC beliefs from various perspectives, initially current convictions, and subsequently, our formative heritage: chapter one is an effort to distill the essence of teachings from our defining documents; chapter two deals with the way our beliefs are expressed; chapter three is a response to a denominational emphasis on the question of authority; chapter four deals with the historic roots of our belief; chapter five is a review of a UCC series of volumes titled *Living Theological Heritage*; chapter six is an examination of an influential declaration of belief from the Congregational wing of the UCC, the Kansas City Statement of Faith. Part II takes up the theme of "caring" as it relates, principally to our ecumenical passion with chapter seven as an argument for the theme of mutual affirmation and admonition on the eve of the vote for the Formula of Agreement; chapter eight as an examination from our Reformed perspective of the breakthrough 1999 accord between

Lutherans and Catholics on the doctrine of justification, the divisive issue in the foreground of the Reformation; chapter nine is a UCC take on one of the key issues, the groundbreaking ecumenical document, *Baptism, Eucharist and Ministry;* chapter ten as an interfaith perspective, a background paper to the "antisupersessionist resolution of General Synod on Jewish-Christian relations and its sequel theological panel on which I served. Part III deals, mainly, with the "doing" of the UCC, but also struggles with the interrelationship of believing and doing which has been a persistent tension in UCC history; chapter eleven is a presentation given at a General Synod on a biennial UCC emphasis focused on how local churches can engage in mission in and for the world, a dominant accent of the 1960s; chapter twelve describes the birth of an alternative newspaper in a small city founded through UCC leadership; chapter thirteen takes up another UCC inspired effort in social justice in the midst of the civil rights revolution; chapter fourteen is a general theory about making social-ethical decisions in the United Church of Christ; chapter fifteen is the application of such a theory to a UCC posture on the attack of September 11, 2001; chapter sixteen challenges the familiar polarization of social action and evangelism; chapter seventeen echoes the same concern, reinterpreting witness as "action evangelism" drawing, as does the previous chapter on my time as consultant in evangelism to the Board for Homeland Ministries. Part IV is a gathering of the three threads of believing, caring and doing, with special attention to the integration of the first and the last by a short history of the beginnings of movements concerned to retrieve the believing foundations for caring and doing in chapter eighteen, and attention to two of them in chapters nineteen and twenty.

As can be seen, the essays in this volume are each a commentary on a particular era's accent from within the lived half-century history of the United Church of Christ. Each chapter, therefore, is a period piece tied to a specific occasion, reflecting the mandate of that time, and thus part of that journey of this denomination, although representative—perhaps in the extreme—of other mainline Churches. The observant UCC reader will soon discover the contextuality of a given essay, as when reference is made to "the New York" offices of the Church, now in Cleveland, older boards of the Church now replaced by new "restructuring," earlier numeration of the UCC Constitution's articles, and like matters of difference over the decades, including a more sanguine view of our Church's future in earlier essays rather than later ones. Then too, there are repetitions such as a return from time to time of notable events that bring together believing, caring, and doing as in the case of Craigville colloquies, similar refrains and documents such as the UCC Statement of Faith and its "story" that emerge in different eras but with varied colorations and shaped in fresh ways by new contexts. In not a few chapters, some aspect of the theological history of the United Church of Christ not generally known will appear.

The treatment of the three accents in the title will follow the sequence of the themes in that aphorism-first believing, then caring, than doing. However, in the history of UCC, the order was otherwise. Shaped by civil rights and peace struggles, "doing" was to the fore in its formative years, as evidence the dating of most of the essays in Part III, followed by ecumenical and interfaith caring in Part II, and finally the accent on believing and theological grounding in Part IV and anticipatications thereof in Part I. The learning, throughout, for this pastor and teacher who has been part of UCC since its inception is that sound teaching and deep believing are basic to durable doing and faithful caring.

Gabriel Fackre

## NOTES

1. Nicholas Wolterstorff, *When Justice and Peace Embrace* (Grand Rapids: Wm. B. Eerdmans Pub. Co., 1983).

2. See the document that laid the groundwork for the agreement, Keith F. Nickle and Timothy F. Lull, eds. *A Common Calling: The Witness of Our Reformation Churches in North America Today* (Minneapolis: Augsburg Fortress, 1993), and the elaboration of the mutuality theme in Gabriel Fackre and Michael Root, *Affirmations and Admonitions* (Grand Rapids: Wm. B. Eerdmans Pub. Co., 1998). I was a UCC representative with Beth Nordbeck on the team of theologians that produced the first volume.

# PART ONE

# Believing

## BELIEVING THE BASICS TODAY

## CHAPTER I

# What Does the United Church
# of Christ Believe

C HURCH NEWSLETTERS TELL US about things on the mind of folk in the United Church of Christ. An article in a newsletter from a lively East coast congregation has this caption: "What Makes for an Ideal Local Church?"

> Does it matter if the UCC projects a common identity of beliefs and doctrine? If a congregation wants to grow, the answer is "yes." According to a Barna Research Group study, what matters most to mainline folk are common identity issues.

Interesting. What a church *believes* matters?

In the fall of 1987, 25 persons gathered in a New York meeting room to make some important decisions. It was a trial of sorts. Who was on trial? The United Church of Christ. Twenty years before that meeting the UCC had entered into an official dialogue with some Lutheran Churches and some Reformed Churches, looking toward "full communion." When such seemed about to happen, the Lutheran denominations involved merged to form the present Evangelical Lutheran Church in America (ELCA), rendering prior developments on full communion moot and requiring renegotiation. . . . However, a part of that new Lutheran Church had developed serious doubts about the UCC. Its leaders questioned whether we really knew what we believed, or if we even had any shared convictions. "After all, you people put on your bumper sticker, 'To believe is to care is to do,' meaning that you see yourself in the business of doing...doing good works, and that's it. You call yourself the 'Just Peace Church.' So you feature good works, right? Sounds like what the Reformation was opposed to: 'works-righteousness.' Besides, your polity doesn't allow for any over-all UCC point of view. You're made up of 6300 congregations (now 6000 or so) each doing its own thing. We Lutherans can talk to the Presbyterians and the Reformed Church in America, for they have creeds and confessions. But the UCC we've known for these past few years doesn't. Why should we be in full communion with you?"

"Not so fast," said our Presbyterian and Reformed comrades. "Let's just see if these charges are true before we eject the UCC." So came the "trial" in November 1987 in a downtown New York boardroom. On hand were key Lutheran theologians, UCC ecumenists Diane Kessler and Thomas (Tom) Dipko, some observers from our fellow Reformed Churches, and three UCC theologians up to bat to say whether and what the UCC taught about the faith. Charles Hambrick-Stowe (pastor of the Church of the Apostles, Lancaster, Pennsylvania, and an adjunct on the Lancaster Seminary faculty) led off with a paper requested by the Lutherans on UCC teaching about "justification by faith." He meticulously went over the UCC historical texts and traditions on justification by faith. Louis Gunnemann, of sainted memory and author of the definitive work on UCC history, *The Shaping of the United Church of Christ* spoke about the UCC's hybrid presbyteral-congregational polity, a "covenantal congregationalism." I was the third presenter, speaking on "The Confessional Nature of The United Church of Christ."

The upshot? The Winter/Spring 1988 issue of *New Conversations* has the papers from the event (Lutheran statements as well as the UCC papers). In that issue, Tom Dipko observes that the "forum has already borne fruit. There are assurances that the Evangelical Lutheran Church in America wishes to continue conversation with the United Church of Christ. . . . "[1] And you know the subsequent history—four more years of dialogue, the production of a volume by a team of Reformed and Lutheran theologians, *A Common Calling*,[2] (which includes a special section on the UCC) that laid the groundwork for more discussions, and then the historic vote in 1997 that brought the UCC and the other Reformed Churches into full communion with the ELCA.

The challenge to the UCC to show that we do have a coherent "UCC belief" and a "confessional heritage" continues to this day. Isn't there a slipped "i" in our name, not the United Church of Christ, but the *Untied* Church of Christ?

Where do we go to find out what a church believes? The Leuenberg Agreement that has brought 80 national churches, Lutheran and Reformed, into full communion says that you can tell by two things: a denomination's written "confessions" and its unwritten "traditions." We show what we believe by the *things written down* and the *things handed on.* The "things handed on" are the practices that express and shape who we are: how we worship, the hymns we sing and prayers we offer, the way we interpret Scripture, the sermons preached, the confirmation and church school classes taught, what happens when we baptize, or serve communion, the architecture of our churches, the stained glass windows, the symbols that surround us, the decisions we make, the committees we appoint, the deeds we do. . . . This is the *ethos* of a church that gets passed on to the next generation. This is the living reality of what we in the UCC are, and what we believe.

From time to time, an effort is made to put on paper what the essentials of these practices and patterns boil down to. These are the "texts" that go along with the aforementioned "traditions," our confessions, creeds and covenants. Do we have them in the UCC? Yes!

Let's start first with our basic covenant, the UCC Constitution. It's gotten a lot of attention lately, having gone through an important revision. The interesting thing about this new Constitution is that while it altered some of the corporate structures of our Church, it did not change one iota of the theology set forth in the theological Preamble of the Constitution or in the section on the basic trinitarian belief of a UCC congregation (Article V, Paragraph 10). The message here is that, in these theological matters, the UCC officially continues to be what our founders said we are. Let's look at the Preamble.

The first thing we notice is what we call ourselves. We are a capital C, "Church." Not the United Churches of Christ, but the United *Church*[4] of Christ. That's different from, let us say, the denomination called the "American Baptist Churches," who are more purely "congregational" in polity. We are not just an association of local congregations. All who have chosen to bear the UCC name are in deep covenant to be together in the fundamental ways expressed in our name and in our Constitution. We make a place for the *corporate* in our ecclesiology, an element of the "organic" in our doctrine of the church, as our Mercersburg forebears would have described it. We are not "all by our lonesome" in separate congregations, but members—organs and limbs—of a larger body of Christ.

But let's get to the particulars. What does the Preamble say about our UCC theology? Not much actually. Why? Because it is more interested in the method of getting at our beliefs than it is in laying out their details. There are a few, of course, as in the passing reference to Christ as "Son of God and Savior," and "two sacraments, Baptism and the Lord's Supper." But the Preamble is more concerned with the question of where we go for our beliefs, that is, the matter of what authorizes them. In theology this is called the concept of authority, of authorization. The Preamble of the UCC Constitution lays out UCC assumptions about authorization this way:

> The United Church of Christ acknowledges as its sole Head, Jesus Christ. . . . It looks to the Word of God in the Scriptures. . . . It claims as its own the faith of the historic Church expressed in the ancient creeds and reclaimed in the basic insights of the Protestant Reformers. It affirms the responsibility of the Church in each generation to make this faith its own in reality of worship, in honesty of thought and expression, and in purity of heart before God.

These are the places we go for our beliefs, the where of the matter. We can portray this "where" as a series of concentric circles. At the center of the circles is "Christ, the sole Head." "This confession," as the Preamble calls it, sets forth our supreme loyalty. The UCC, by definition, is a "confessing Christ" movement. Christ is "the one Word" we have to trust and obey, as the Barmen Declaration of 1934 of Germany's "Confessing Church" that fought Hitler's blood and soil philosophy puts it (a document that influenced our UCC founders and this formulation). The image of Christ as "head" is also found in early Congregational credos—the Cambridge Platform and Savoy Declaration. Our central loyalty is in our very name, the United Church of *Christ*.

Where do we get our knowledge of this sole Head and one Word? The Preamble answers: our Church "looks to the Word of God in the Scriptures," again echoing Barmen that speaks of Jesus Christ, the one Word, "as he is attested for us in Holy Scripture." Scripture is the inner circle of which Christ is the center. Scripture is the *source* of our beliefs, but Scripture as interpreted through the lens of Christ. Scripture is authoritative to the extent that it bears witness to Christ, as it "preaches Christ" as Martin Luther put it.

If the first circle is biblical, then the next circle out is ecclesial. The UCC, "claims as its own the faith of the historic Church expressed in its ancient creeds and the insights of the Protestant Reformers," the latter making us what the Reformers and the Preamble call "evangelical Christians." The church and its historic teachings have a place in our authority structure, a secondary one. They are not the source or center of our belief, but are a resource in interpreting the biblical source and its christological center. The UCC makes an important place for them, but one always held accountable to Jesus Christ as attested by Scripture.

The third circle of authority: the UCC "affirms the responsibility of the Church in each generation to make this faith its own . . ." The ancient faith needs to be made contemporary in terms of the issues and the idiom of the day in which we live. The Preamble charges the UCC to restate and reinterpret our faith in ever-fresh ways, a move made possible by the "presence and power of the Holy Spirit" at work right now. This is a characteristic of our Reformed tradition with its watchword, *semper reformanda!*, always reforming. The ever-active Holy Spirit makes a place for the current *setting* in which the beliefs of the resource, the source and the center are to be made our own, with "more truth and light" waiting to break forth from God's "holy Word."[5]

The challenge for us in our Church is to hold all these elements of authority together, and in the priorities and roles they belong. The temptation is to reduce the circles to our favorite one. The people who stress the setting, eager to make the faith relevant, are tempted to latch on to the latest cultural trends and forget that it is the historic faith of the church, biblically grounded and Christ-centered, that is the substance of what we render contemporary. Others are tempted to reduce the circles to just the Bible and fall into biblicism, or just the historic faith and its ancient formulations and fall into traditionalism. If we are what we say we are, a Church united and uniting, we have to honor the inclusivity and the ordering of the UCC Constitution, no small challenge in this day in which factionalism and fragmentation are everywhere to be found.

What then are the actual UCC beliefs about God, Christ, the church, the world and salvation that are based on our center, our source, our resource and our setting? For an answer we must turn to the official corporate texts of the UCC. How much people in any church, in fact pay attention to official stands is another matter. For example, a recent survey of Roman Catholic parishioners coming out of their church after mass discovered that half of them either did not know, or did not believe, what the Roman Catholic church teaches about the mass. In fact, their views were quite "Zwinglian!" Theological confusion is everywhere. We are all in the same boat, and there is no safe ecclesiastical harbor. So to find what a church believes, we must go by a church's corporate texts, not by anecdotes. We go, therefore, to UCC texts on the what of the matter, sweated over and prayed over for a lengthy period, then, officially decided upon, and corporately declared.

The first time the UCC had to answer the "what" question was at the moment of our founding. The official document that preceded the Constitution is called "The Basis of Union," which made possible the union of Evangelical and Reformed and Congregational Christian Churches. It set forth what it called "a confession," one that "expresses the content and meaning of the faith held generally by the members of the two uniting communions."[6] This declaration "writes down" in terse fashion the essentials of what we've called the "things handed on." After stating them, the Basis of Union goes on to charge the new United Church-to-be to formulate the beliefs found in this confession in what it called "an ampler statement." That happened in 1959 in "the United Church of Christ Statement of Faith." The history of how this came to be, and how it can be interpreted, is found in this splendid small book by the Statement's principal drafter, Roger Shinn, *Confessing the Faith*.[7]

The Basis also makes clear *how* the written-down Church-wide formulation of the pattern of our belief is to be taken. It is "a testimony not a test, of faith," in the famous phrase found in the footnote (II, 2). The reason? It is because in the covenantal congregationalism that we say we are, the way the pattern of belief held among us all is formulated for a congregation is a right granted to the congregation. Thus the Statement of Faith testifies to the world at large of the pattern of our corporate belief, and to UCC congregations what elements should be honored in their own local formulations.

The first thing one notices about UCC belief in this mode is the literary form it takes, the genre in which it speaks. It is a *narrative* genre, a *story* form. Roger Shinn calls our Statement of Faith the recounting of "The Great Story." In this respect it follows the way of Scripture, taking us from the beginning of the world, to its center, Jesus Christ, through its outworking in the church and its mission, and finally to the consummation of all things. This way of doing church credos is not so new, for the early creeds were something like that, a drama in three acts: Act I, creation, God the Maker of heaven and earth; Act II, Christ the redeemer of a fallen creation; Act III, the Holy Spirit, the sanctifier and consummator of God's purposes.

Let's see what those UCC beliefs are that rise out of the storyline, the unfolding drama, the biography of God, so to speak. The Basis of Union begins:

> We believe in God the Father Almighty, Creator and Sustainer of
> heaven and earth.

Sounds just like one of those "ancient creeds" referred to in the UCC Constitution, in this case, the Apostles:

> I believe in God the Father Almighty, Creator of heaven and earth

Or the other one so honored and included in the UCC *Book of Worship,* the Nicene:

> We believe in one God, the Father, the Almighty, maker of heaven and
> earth, of all that is seen and unseen

And the doxological version of the UCC Statement of Faith says it this way with its own elaboration and interpretation:

We believe in you, O God, Eternal Spirit, God of our Savior Jesus
Christ and our God, and to your deeds we testify. You call the worlds
into being, create persons in your own image, and set before each one
the ways of life and death.

We have here "chapter 1" of the Great Story. It boils down to this. This
big world all around us did not happen by accident. Nor is it junk. No
matter how bad it may look, it's good stuff because it is made by a good
Maker. Therefore, don't run away from it into the otherworldly spirituality so popular today. And don't abuse it, as too many forces at work in it
do. Rather, honor it, love it, build it up. And since the world didn't happen by accident, don't buy into the scientism or secularism of the day that
says it all came to be by chance. There is a purpose to it, and a divine
Purposer at work right now, calling the cosmos into being every second
and sustaining it this very minute, as well as creating it at the beginning.
Underneath are the everlasting arms! This is the Christian doctrine of
creation packed into the simple sentences of our UCC credos.

Note all the pieces of this creation: a) the solid earth is one of them.
God made nature, so treat it right, good ecology and environmental
ethics; b) human nature is another part of creation, made in the very
image of God as the UCC Statement asserts, the apple of God's eye—
it's sacrosanct, so fight for its dignity; and c) the Maker made the "heav-
en" as well as the earth. Karl Barth points out that "heaven" refers to the
region of angelic powers, spiritual realities, principalities—that is super-
nature, part of the created order along with nature and human nature.
We better have clear UCC thinking on this with all the other talk
around of angels and New Age religion. (I recommend the October
1994 issue of *Theology Today* as a resource for mainline church people to
think about the angelic powers.)

There's more here in chapter one, but I want to hold off a bit on that,
the reference to the kind of God who made heaven and earth. As in any
story, we only know who the main character is when the story is finished. So the doctrine of God really belongs in the epilogue.

But now back to . . . chapter two. What comes after creation? The
Statement of Faith says out loud what is presupposed in the creeds,
pointing to "aimlessness and sin," "sin and death," and the God who

judges people and nations by a righteous will. In these terms we have the biblical chapter on the fall. Put it this way: God calls the world into being and invites us into friendship, a life together with God. The hand of God reaches out to us, just as Michelangelo portrays it on the ceiling of the Sistine Chapel. But what do we do, from the very beginning of time to this moment? We make a fist and shake it in the face of God. We say "No!" to God's "Yes."

But as the African-American poet, Weldon Johnson, says it, "Young man, young man, your arm is too short to box with God!" So comes the stumble and fall away from God's invitation. This is the sad second chapter of the Great Story. It's why we have a confession of sin in our chief service, the Eucharist, and often in every Sunday service. This is the realism of Christian faith, and a vital part of UCC belief.

Chapter three in Scripture is described in the language of "covenant." First, the covenant with Noah in chapter nine of Genesis, God's persevering love for the world in spite of our fall and the judgment on us, a rainbow promise to stick with us and keep calling us. It's there in the Statement of Faith in the allusion to God seeking us out, and continuing to set before us the ways of life and death. Can we say that wherever there are signs of the good, the true, the beautiful and the holy in this fallen world, there are the indications of God's continuing rainbow giving and seeking? This is an important belief in the discussion today of religious pluralism, and the good in people who are not even religious. There is a "common grace" out there as our Reformed tradition puts it, not yet at the center of the Story, but a part of it. We can portray this universal covenant as the God hand arching over the fallen world in a rainbow preservation, call and promise.

But then there is another gracious covenant in Scripture. The rainbow lands, so to speak, at one point . . . a special covenant with a chosen people, the covenant with Israel. Two-thirds of Christian Scripture is about that special relationship God has with the Jewish people. In spite of that, it is a missing piece in the ancient creeds, a fact which may have contributed to the tragic history of Christian anti-Semitism. This absence is a reminder that all our received creeds and current statements of faith are short of perfection, subject to correction and enlargement in the light of a christologically re-read Scripture. The Statement of Faith does make passing reference to "the prophets," but the need for more clarity on this is reflected in the later General Synod resolution on the covenant with the Jewish people and the two-year theological panel later called to study and interpret it.

Now, to chapter four in the biography of God. This is the big one, and why it is the largest paragraph in the two ancient creeds, and the one on which the whole Tale turns in the Statement of Faith:

> In Jesus Christ the man of Nazareth . . . you have come to us and shared our common lot.

Incredible! The Maker of this world loves it so much, and wants to redeem it so passionately, that the good God comes right into our messy situation. In the words of the gospel of John:

> In the beginning was the Word, and the Word was with God and the Word was God . . . and the Word became flesh and dwelt among us . . .

God up close, God in our midst, God in the flesh! In our hand motions, the God hand now intersects the world at one decisive point, "the *scandal* of particularity," for it is only on Hebrew landscape, only in one tiny Jewish baby. This is why Christians speak of Jesus as divine, or as in Preamble language, the "Son of God," following the Apostles' creed reference to "his only Son" and the Nicene Creed's more developed assertion:

> the only Son of God, eternally begotten of the Father, God from God, light from Light, true God from true God, begotten not made, of one being with the Father.

This is the doctrine of incarnation to which all Christian churches subscribe, key for the UCC in our ecumenical agreements, from the FOA, through COCU to membership in the World Council of Churches whose statement of faith confesses Christ to be "God and Savior."

In a time of religious pluralism there is a great temptation to drop this scandalous particularity from our teaching. If we did that, we would cease to be who we are. There are better ways to honor other religions.[8] Ironically, as my colleague Mark Heim points out, to diminish our own claims to unique truth by saying there is no difference in world religions is to diminish other religions as well, with their right to make that same claim for their own faith.[9]

The accent in historic confessions is on the deity of Christ because God's unique coming among us is the turning point of the Story. But if the incarnation is a real enfleshment, Jesus has to be real flesh and blood, not just a spiritual ghostly-like human garment, a Jesus who did not really share our common lot. The Statement of Faith makes no bones about Jesus' true humanity for God is among us as "the man of Nazareth," a real carpenter from a real town, Nazareth, with a body like ours that bled when cut with a tool or crucified on a cross, a mind that did not know everything all at once but, according to Scripture had to "grow in wisdom," as his body grew in stature from crib to cross, and a spirit like ours that had its doubts and anguish just like ours, right up to and on the cross.

The cross. An empty cross, announcing the risen Lord and savior. At the center of our sanctuaries, the heart of the Christian faith. We confess this centrality when we thank God for:

> Our crucified and risen savior . . . conquering sin and death and reconciling the world to yourself echoing the Basis of Union,
> Our Lord and Saviour, who for us and our salvation lived and died and rose again which in turn summarizes the creeds,
> He suffered under Pontius Pilate, was crucified, died and was buried. On the third day he rose again. (Apostles' Creed)

Why are the cross and the resurrection so central? Of course, the Passion and Easter narratives are the largest sections in the Gospels and the focus of St. Paul's teaching and many of the other books of the New Testament. The reason they give it such high profile is because the plot of the Great Story—how alienation becomes reconciliation—is focused on these events in Christ's life. If our basic problem is this, a fist shaken in the face of the loving, beckoning God, then just how do we get those two hands together? Does God just ignore our malice? Not if God is a *tough* love that holds us accountable for who we are. God is *holy* love not an indulgent sentimentality, as P.T. Forsyth, one of our Reformed forebears put it in the face of what he saw bandied about in his day as a sloppy form of *agape*. The consequences of our action, our No!, have to be suffered. And just who will do that? As a great hymn writer put it, "There is a cross in the heart of God." That's right, it is the good and loving God who steps down into our world in Jesus and onto a cross. In a sense, God's body was broken on Golgotha, God's heart broken on the cross. We have to do here, not just with the suffering of the human Jesus, but with "the crucified God" as Jürgen Moltmann expressed it in his unforgettable book of that title. Or in the language of Martin Luther, on the cross the mercy of God took into itself the judgment of God. When the cross is understood in this way, then we don't make the mistake of thinking of it as God punishing Jesus, but rather, as Paul puts it in 1 Cor. 5:19, as God who was *in* Christ reconciling the world. God's own pathos, a love suffering on Golgotha and victorious at Easter, turns the tide. It also means that wherever there is a sufferer as well as a sinner God is in solidarity with that person, and calls us to be so present as well with the deed of justice as well as the word of justification. So the assertion of the Statement of Faith: You, God, have come to us in Jesus "conquering sin and death and reconciling the world to yourself!" What a Word!

As central as are the cross and resurrection, we can't forget that chapter 4 includes the events leading up to the denouement—Jesus' life and teachings. The Statement of Faith alludes to that in its reference to this "man of Nazareth" sharing our common lot, though it could have said more, as could the ancient creeds have included more of the importance of Jesus' life and teaching. Actually, our Reformed tradition, as in the Heidelberg Catechism, does have an encompassing view of what Christ did for our reconciliation, speaking of his three-fold office—prophetic, priestly, and royal—which is to say, all three phases of Christ's presence among us—his life, his death, and his resurrection. But at its center is what is at the center of our sanctuaries—the intersection of God and the world, the incarnate deity in reconciling at-one-ment, or as the Preamble to the UCC Constitution says it, Jesus Christ, "Son of God and Savior."

When so intersected, the two hands begin to come together. And as such, they constitute the remaining chapters of the Great Narrative:

chapter five—the church; chapter six—salvation; chapter seven—consummation. They are all there, beautifully expressed in the UCC Statement of Faith.

The sentences on the church are more detailed than in the creeds, as our founders were trying to suggest what this new denomination should look like:

> You bestow upon us your Holy Spirit, creating and renewing the church of Jesus Christ, binding in covenant people of all ages, tongues and races. You call us into your church to accept the cost and joy of discipleship, to be your servants in the service of others, to proclaim the gospel to all the world and resist the powers of evil, to share in Christ's baptism and eat at his table, to join him in his passion and victory.

The church here is a diverse covenant community, Paul's Corinthian body of Christ with many parts, born of the Holy Spirit in the sacramental waters of baptism and sustained at the holy table where we veritably share in Christ himself, called to both tell the story, that is "proclaim the gospel," and to do the story, a costly and joyful discipleship (the phrase from the martyr, Dietrich Bonhoeffer) in the service of others, joined thereby to Christ in his passion and victory in both the church and the world. The Statement lays out the framework that UCC thinking and doing (at their best) have followed over the years: inclusivity, or better, catholicity: be holistic, don't settle for reductionism. Catholicity means: in interchurch relations, a passionate ecumenism; in ethics, courage in a struggle for justice for all the forgotten and rejected and for "peace," shalom among peoples and nations; in mission, be sure to do both word and deed; in nurture, both proclamation in word and celebration in sacrament.

Chapter six—salvation! Here again holism, the full gospel, catholicity, is at work, what the Statement of Faith calls the "fullness of grace." That means salvation entails both forgiveness of sins and courage in the struggle for justice and peace, in our Reformation lingo, both justification and sanctification. Redemption of both soul and society, and in each case both "trial" and "rejoicing."

And the grand finale, the last chapter of the Story? The Statement says in terse form . . . eternal life in his kingdom which has no end.

What the *Basis of Union* speaks of as the consummation of the Kingdom of God, the triumph of righteousness and the life everlasting. The creeds are in back of both with four specifics. I think of them not as clear glass letting us see exactly what the final future will be, but as stained glass windows with stunning images that hint of what is to come, letting in enough light for us to read our hymnbooks and praise God for the good End to be: the resurrection of the body, the return of Christ, the final judgment and the life everlasting.

As we move through these chapters of the UCC's telling of the Great Story, a picture of its main character emerges. Who is the God of this narrative? If we translate the seven chapters of the Statement's story into a play, it turns into a three-act drama, the creation of the world with its covenants, the reconciliation of an alienated world in Christ, the Holy Spirit's work of sanctifying the world. The ancient creeds have three paragraphs expressing those three missions. Thus a trinitarian picture of God emerges: God the Father, Creator; God the Son, reconciler: God the Holy Spirit, sanctifier. Christians name God from that drama, as when the *Book of Worship* prescribes baptism "in the name of the Father, and the Son and the Holy Spirit." And why in the UCC, our Constitution defines a local church as the gathering in which persons "who, believing in God as heavenly Father, and accepting Jesus Christ as Lord and Saviour, and depending on the guidance of the Holy Spirit, are organized for . . . worship . . . fellowship . . . and witness"(V. 10)

Surely the Trinity, the unique Christian belief in God, is a mystery. We search for analogies in our experience to explain it. Like $H_2O$ in its three forms—water as liquid, solid, vapor? Three people in a family? A person wearing three hats or having three roles? Not exactly, as there is some flaw in each analogy. It can't be explained. But it can be explored. Today its social meaning is being emphasized, in UCC circles and elsewhere. That is, if God is three Persons so intimately related to each other that these Persons are not a "They" but a "Thou," the one triune God, then that is a model for how the church and the world should be! If God is a Life Together, then we should be a life together: a church, united and uniting, and a world reconciled and reconciling. Isn't that what the UCC is all about?

That Bethany Church newsletter was right. It makes a difference when a church knows what it believes. And as we showed to our critics, appearances to the contrary notwithstanding, the UCC does have convictions that make us who we are. We have a story to tell! Pray God every congregation knows its story, so it can fling that faith joyfully in the air for all to see.

## NOTES

1. Thomas E. Dipko, "Conversation Piece: The Lutheran-Reformed Bilateral and the United Church of Christ," *New Conversations* Vol.10, No. 2 (Winter–Spring, 1988), 6.

2. Keith F. Nickle and Timothy F. Lull, eds., *A Common Calling: The Witness of Our Reformation Churches in North America Today* (Minneapolis: Augsburg Fortress, 1993). The UCC section is pages 75–80.

3. "Leuenberg Agreement," in *An Invitation to Action: The Lutheran-Reformed Dialogue,* Series III, 1981–1983, James E. Andrews and Joseph A. Burgess, eds. (Philadelphia: Fortress Press, 1984), 63, 70.

4. Critics of the UCC at its beginnings who charged it with departure from standard-brand congregationalism sniffed this out right away. See James Deforest Murch, "The 'United Church' of Christ," Christianity Today (May 23, 1959), 10–14.

5. So Pastor Robinson's counsel to the departing pilgrims with its Reformed expectation that Christ the Word has fresh things to say through Scripture.

6. "Basis of Union, II, Faith," in Louis H. Gunnemann, *The Shaping of the United Church of Christ* (New York: United Church Press, 1977), 208.

7. Roger Shinn. *Confessing the Faith: An Interpretation of the United Church of Christ Statement of Faith* (New York: United Church Press, 1990).

8. See Gabriel Fackre, "Christ and Religious Pluralism: the Current Debate," Pro Ecclesia Vol. VII, No. 4 (Fall 1998), 389–397.

9. S. Mark Heim, *Salvations: Truth and Difference in Religion* (Maryknoll: Orbis, 1995), 13–98.

What Does the United Church of Christ Believe?, Prism, Vol.16, No. 2, (Fall 2001). Used by permission.

## CHAPTER 2

# Theology and Forms of Confession in the United Church of Christ

Is THERE A THEOLOGY *of*, or even *in*, the United Church of Christ?" I have heard this question put time and again by seminary students during my years of teaching in two institutions of that faith community over most of its twenty-year life span. It often comes at the end of a basic course in systematic theology, or upon return from an intern year in a local congregation. The students' struggles with twenty-page papers on Nicaea and Chalcedon or the eschatologies of Jürgen Moltmann and Gustavo Gutierrez, juxtaposed to what they perceive as either theological incoherent or hopelessly confused and contradictory tendencies in the parish or denomination, contribute to the world-weary cynicism of the seminary middlers. While this passes, for the most part, as the questioners become engrossed in the search for a job in this same institution, the question raised is worth thinking about, and even worrying about. Especially, is this so as the UCC enters into conversation with the Disciples of Christ.

It is entirely possible that some will greet the implied judgment that there is theology neither in nor of the UCC with thanksgiving. "That's just what we want, on both counts. Faith flourishes in total freedom. And faith is basically not theology but richness of feeling or firmness of moral commitment." Or, from another source, "Beliefs do matter, but they are self-evident to the Bible-believing Christian." Or again, "The Spirit works best when the heavy arm of dogma is restrained."

Surely there is truth in these assertions. Most of us are in the United Church of Christ because we do not believe in theological straitjackets. But finally, freedom is not anarchy, and the notion that faith is only *fidu-*

*cia* is a half truth. There is no fundamental orientation to existence, no ultimate concern, that is devoid of defining ideas, and therefore in some sense of theology. And there is no lasting Christian community without perimeters, however soft their edges and open their lines. The early centuries of the church understood that very well when in their initial identity quest codes of behavior and cultic life took form, and ultimately a belief tradition arose, first in the apostolic writings, and then in the apostolic "rule of faith" and its successors.

In my own wrestle with the students' question I have become increasingly convinced that doubts about the existence of theological patterns, either in or of the UCC, have something to do with *what* is being sought and *where* it is being sought. UCC theology, given its history and direction will not look like the doctrinal loci of the Westminster Confession, or even the chapter headings in Gordon Kaufman's *Systematic Theology*. There are no universally binding Symbols or architectonic theological design to establish doctrinal identity or guard its purity. Given the UCC commitment to the liberty and mystery of the Holy Spirit's working, traditional modes of self-definition are absent.

Are we then left with theological anarchy? I do not believe that for a minute. Theology in and of the UCC is discoverable, but it is to be found in a manner and in forms commensurate with that theology, and the particular kind of faith community with which we are dealing. You must know what to look for and where to look for it. Kierkegaard's dictum is right: an object (or Subject) can only be known in a fashion befitting its nature.[1] While the medium is not itself the message, the message can be heard best in a medium hospitable to it. Therefore, in addressing the subject of the theology and forms of confession in the United Church of Christ, we shall put aside the methodology of the systematics classroom and take instead a cue from John Bunyan. In his "Author's apology" to *Pilgrim's Progress*, this nonconformist theologian—who captures the spirit of that tradition in his writing—declares (indeed, in the less than inclusive language of his time):

> "Solidity indeed becomes the Pen
> Of him that writeth things Divine to men;
> But must I needs want solidness, because

By Metaphors I speak? Were not God's Laws,
His Gospel-Laws, in olden time held forth
By Types, Shadows, and Metaphors? Yet loth
Will any sober man be to find fault
With them, lest he be found for to assault
The highest Wisdom. No, he rather stoops,
And seeks to find out what by Pins and Loops,
By Calves, and Sheep, by Heifers, and by Rams,
Birds, and Herbs, and by the blood of Lambs,
God speaketh to him. And happy is he
That finds the light and grace that in them be.
Dark Figures, Allegories? Yet there springs
From that same Book lustre, and those rays
Of light, that turns our darkest nights to clays."[2]

—The Journey

The United Church of Christ is a voyaging company, on the way as surely as Pilgrim makes the trek to the Celestial City. It follows a trail cut through the wilderness by One who goes before, Jesus Christ, the Pioneer of Hebrews 12. It lives by the Faith that the journey's major perils have already been dealt with by him, making its own travel possible, and the hope that this will also be so on the uncertain terrain before it. For finding its way this band has an old Map which it regularly consults. The lines on it are faded and the paper is fragile, made so by the wear and tear of weather and much handling, and the print is itself hard to read. But the Pioneer has provided it and the people would not be without it.

Around the Map there has grown up a lore. It consists of songs and stories about the feats of the Pioneer and the One who sent him from the Celestial City.

The resources of this company distinguish it from other groups of travelers moving in the same direction but on separate paths. Some have much more detailed charts, complete with AAA-like magic marker lines. Moreover, they carry considerable luggage filled with guide books and travel gear. Yet others are furnished with special communication apparatus which they say puts them in direct touch with the Scout up ahead.

The particular company of pilgrims in question is cognizant of all these parallel trails and travelers and is sometimes envious of their equipment. But for better or worse, these voyagers seem to be destined to travel light with their Map, their songs, and their stories.

What are these songs and stories? They are ways of discerning and declaring the direction of the journey, "forms of confession" in which the theology of the United Church of Christ is to be found. In them are the controlling visions and affirmations of this community *in via*. First let us listen to some of their songs.

## SONGS

In the early centuries of the Church when doctrinal clarity was yet to be had on certain fundamental christological questions, the classic affirmations about the deity, humanity, and unity of Jesus Christ had a life of their own within the *cult: lex orandi, lex credendi*. The law of praying is the law of believing. The central Christian claim that the Word became flesh was sustained and transmitted to the next generation in the worship of the Christian community. Orthodoxy was understood in the more fundamental of its two meanings, pure praise rather than pure doctrine. Or more exactly, right praise was the vehicle of basic theological identity.

In the United Church of Christ one of the important confessional forms is the life of the cult. This is brought forcefully home to us when we suffer through a sermon which parades before a congregation almost every tenet of the current culture-Christianity. Yet even in such depressing circumstances, the Word is not altogether unhearable, for there is the singing of hymns, the reading of Scripture, prayer in the name of Jesus, the great liturgical rhythms of adoration, confession, thanksgiving, intercession, instruction, commitment, and on regular occasion, the event described by one of our Communion liturgies as "the innermost sanctuary of the whole Christian worship."

Elements of basic Christian belief are always available in this life of worship. But more than just random teaching, there is a fundamental thread of Christian conviction that appears in this life of worship, these "songs we sing," that defines the United Church of Christ and marks it as a Christian community. This essential identity has to do with the deeds of God that move from creation to consummation, with their center point in the Person and Work of Christ. That saga is at the very heart of this worship life, as evidence the eucharistic prayer of the UCC service of Word and Sacrament:

> We give you thanks, O Holy Lord, almighty and everlasting God, for the universe you have created, for the heavens and the earth, and for every living thing. We thank you that you have formed us in your image and made us for yourself. We bless you that when we rebelled against you, you did not forsake us, but delivered us from bondage, and revealed your righteous will and steadfast love by the law and the prophets.
>
> Above all, we thank you for the gift of your Son, the Redeemer of all people, who was born of Mary, lived on earth in obedience to you, died on the cross for our sins, and rose again from the dead in victory; who rules over us, Lord above all, who prays for us continually, and will come again in triumph.
>
> We thank you for your Holy Spirit and for your holy church, for the means of grace and for the promise of eternal life. With patriarchs and prophets, apostles and martyrs, with your church on earth and with all the company of heaven, we magnify and praise you, we worship and adore you, O Lord Most Holy.[3]

The saga is in the song. These songs are found not only in our hymnody but, as here, in the great liturgical cadences and sacramental encounters. They live on, however adapted to new language, new environments of thought and sensibility, and however modified in one way or another in the varied congregational life of this pluralistic denomination. So on its journey, this community gathers of an evening around its campfires to sing its songs. Through them, vision is fired. Can we even say that it is so by the mystical Presence of its pioneer Visionary? I do not doubt it.

## STORIES

Campfires are made as well for swapping stories. At the center of its liturgical life is the telling of tales.

The most obvious tales told are to be found in the preaching events of the community. But is it not precisely here that our subjectivity runs wild? Is it not here that our seminary middlers' charge amasses the most persuasive evidence that there is no theology in or of the UCC? Since we have no Missouri Synod-like dogmatic norms, it would appear that a theological rugged individualism surely must rule.

But when we say good-bye to the boiler-plated theologies of some Christian neighbors does this mean that anything goes in our pulpits? Once again we will have to look for outlines of the forms of confession in less obvious places in this particular ecclesial family. One such contour of preaching is, of course, the attention paid to our old Map. There it is on every lectern. And there in the study is the pastor's desk calendar with its lectionaries. And in the chancel hang the paraments, and around the neck of the Storyteller the stole whose colors often change according to the seasons of the church year. And along the study bookshelves are to be found works, sometimes underlined awhile ago, but not as ignored as some denigrators of pastoral theological interest and acumen believe. Yes, from these pulpits we will get immense variety according to the individual sociologies and theologies of these stewards of the Christian mysteries. This freedom is the context in which we have chosen to be, traveling light. But in and through all the autobiographical and situational discontinuities of this preaching there can be heard, I believe, the great continuity, the biography of God.

Of course not all the stories in this company are told from individual pulpits. In fact, we are here seeking the universals, the ecclesial commonalities. Are there general forms of confession which express, in some sense, a UCC point of view? All attempts to answer that question must be prefaced of course with a reminder of Article IV, paragraph 15 of the United Church of Christ constitution:

> The autonomy of the local church is inherent and modifiable only by its own action. Nothing in this Constitution and By-laws of the United Church of Christ shall destroy or limit the right of each local church to continue to operate in the way customary to it; nor shall be construed as giving to the General Synod, or to any Conference or Association now, or at any future time, the power to abridge or impair the autono-

my of any local church in the management of its own affairs, which include, but are not limited to the right to retain or adopt its own methods of organization worship and education . . . to formulate its own covenants and confessions of faith. . . .[4]

"Well, what did I tell you," says our skeptic again. "There it is in print. The UCC says, 'Do your own thing.' "

I can remember vividly the debates around this paragraph in the years when the United Church of Christ was struggling to be born, especially the profound misgivings of many in the Evangelical and Reformed constituency. The presbyteral polity, and corporate and historic commitments of that tradition appeared to be imperiled by this seemingly rank independency. But now we have over twenty years of experience with this paragraph. I have noticed several things in that time. For one, some of the very folk who bewailed it have been only too glad to make subsequent use of it as a weapon against the "New York bureaucracy." But more significantly for the purposes of our subject, it must be noted that the state of theology in the United Church of Christ *de jure* is not the same as its state *de facto*. The living theology of the songs sung around our fires is one sign of this. And now must be added to that the working theology of the stories told among us. These stories are constituted by a network of implicit forms of confession constituted by: the church school curricula, the confirmation manuals and materials, the posture and offerings of the United Church of Christ periodicals, the program materials of various agencies and judicatories, the preparation of clergy in its affiliated seminaries, its ordination procedures, the positions taken by the General Synod, even the "identity ads" of the Office of Communication.[5] In addition to the implicit but formative ethos of belief, there are the explicit confessional testimonies of the United Church of Christ: the one general Symbol, the Statement of Faith, and a variety of other particular doctrinal affirmations inherited from the uniting traditions of this Church. All these theological forms are "without authority." They are resources offered to us, not sources imposed upon us, stories told among us, not directions given to us. But the interesting thing is that now after two decades of life together with them, there is a common set of visions that emerges out of them, which constitute what I would dare to call the theological identity of the United Church of Christ.

Let us look first at an example of some of the unofficial lore of the Church. Now and then, especially in moments of aggressive mission when we are pushed to say what we are really up to, there appears an effort at theological self-identification which gathers together the many colored threads of conviction into something that looks like a whole cloth. Robert Moss drew the attention of the readers of *Evangelism for a New Day*[6] to such a theological sortie, which he said captured the spirit of the denomination. He referred to the "Deering Statement of Commitment" developed as a grassroot effort to say what UCC-style evangelism means. A portion of it reads:

> The Deering Conference on Faith and its Expression calls the United Church of Christ to a joyful sharing of the Christian Story in the decade of the '70s. . . .

At the heart of that heritage there is a drama of what God has done, is doing, and will do. The chief Actor "calls the worlds into being, creates us in his own image, and sets before us the ways of life and death." From the beginning, the creature with the human face falters, and curves inward away from Maker and neighbor. The pull of conscience, the laws of nature, and the lessons of history do not turn the world around. A patient God calls a people, Israel, to share this dream of *shalom*, a vision of peace and freedom among God, humankind, and nature. In the exodus from Egypt God enacts liberation, and in the pointing of prophets God beckons toward reconciliation. We continue as killers of the dream.

"In Jesus Christ the man of Nazareth, our crucified and risen Lord, he has come to us and shared our common lot." In him, hope happens and shalom comes to be. The powers of evil meet their match, mercy covers our guilt, and the future is opened. A new people is born to celebrate the deeds of God and to participate in the Spirit's ever-fresh stirrings of liberation and reconciliation. That Body is turned toward the future looking for the new things God will do, and the time when His full Kingdom will be. 'Blessing and honor, glory and power be unto God!' "[7]

Here is the same kind of figural imagination discernible in the Great Thanksgiving of the Communion service. Here also is the same saga. Thus the "genetic code" of the UCC seems to assert in these key organs of the Body of Christ, liturgy and mission.

## THE STATEMENT OF FAITH

Of course the reader will recognize the influence of a more official confessional form in this Statement, for the latter unashamedly borrows its imagery and movement. The Statement of Faith of the United Church of Christ is the closest thing the UCC has to an explicit general form of confession. Approved by the General Synod of 1959 and commended to the churches for their study and use, it has found an honored place in the theological lore of this community. As Roger Shinn points out in his insightful overview of it in the book written about it by him and Daniel Day Williams, it is "not a standard of objective authority in the United Church."[8] Article IV, paragraph 15 makes impossible any such doctrinal norm as that. While not a "test" of faith, it is, however, a "testimony" of faith, to change the weighting of the words of this familiar slogan. That is, the Statement has somehow caught the theological vision that informs this pilgrim company, and in turn, has shaped it. This is so, not only because of its strategic location at the inception of the United Church of Christ, but because of what is said in it and the way it is said.

For one, the Statement is made in the lyrical and figurative modality that marks this company that lives by its songs and stories. There is liturgical grace here in the way the great affirmations are made, not unlike the cadences of the eucharistic prayer. It is doxological not propositional, a creed sung rather than said. That is why the important and necessary effort to render the language of the Statement more inclusive has had such hard going to date. Many people committed themselves to this characteristic UCC concern of inclusiveness are not ready to sacrifice the metaphorical beauty and power of expression to any heavy-handed efforts at ideological purity. But these concerns need not be mutually exclusive, and some day we will have such a doxologically meaningful inclusive Statement.

But the significance of the Statement lies deeper than the mode of expression. It has to do with faithfulness to the narrative approach to, and substance of, theology, as that has been believed and testified to in our tradition. In this short testimony, as in the eucharistic prayer and evangelistic call, are to be found the great acts of the biblical drama. Indeed, they are not in abstract formulations but in historical concretions. How easily this substantive theology is missed by both presumed friends and foes! Harold Lindsell's citation of the Statement of Faith in his recent diatribe against those who do not espouse the plenary verbal inspiration of the Bible illustrates both of these misunderstandings. Quoting an author writing in the *Unitarian Register* who declares that he finds no conflict with his own theology, Lindsell observes that this is the end result of efforts to dilute the Christian faith.[9]

It is certainly true that there is no explicit reference to the Trinity in the Statement. And if we wanted to dig deeper into levels of classical Christian faith than Lindsell's superficial judgments enable him to go, we could raise some of our own questions: For example, the implied modalistic tendencies (God as such becomes incarnate rather than the Logos, the second Person of the Trinity), the distinction between aimlessness and sin (*accedia*—lassitude, torpor, aimlessness—has always been considered a form of sin), the overly churchly understanding of the age of the Spirit (the Statement does not do justice to the incognito Christ of Matthew 25 who by the power of the Spirit is at work in the world as well as in the Church).

From some quarters there will be a predictable response to this theological probing: "You are turning the Statement into a set of propositions which is precisely what it is not. Rather it is poesy that expresses deep faith and cannot be so dissected. Take it for what it is and do not try to find things in it that are not intended." This is a glittering and beguiling half truth. Indeed, as we have argued earlier, there is a metaphorical way of saying things that gets at them in a fashion that no straight talk can. That has been an important way of speaking in this community, and the Statement of Faith carries on the tradition. But we have a responsibility to say what we mean as well as sing what we say. Or to put it in the words of the philosopher of language, Wilbur Urban, there is in a religious symbol both "symbolic truth" and the "truth of the symbol." The former points to the existential rightness of the mythic. The latter has to do with the belief about the nature of things that is inherent in matters articulated in the figurative mode. I am convinced that the wide and deep usage of the Statement in the United Church of Christ has something to do not only with its lyrical and figurative power that expresses the faith *with which* we believe, but also because it contains the crucial faith *in which* we believe. (Note the classic distinction between *fides qua creditur and fides quae creditur*). Faith is both the trust of the heart and the assent of the mind. We neglect either at our peril.

If these things are true, are not those right who want to embrace us or condemn us for the timidity of this declaration of faith? No, they have missed something basic both in this particular explicit form of confession, and the other range of implicit forms of confession of our Church of which we have been speaking. What they have overlooked is the Storyline that threads its way through this fabric. This fundamental narrative is the framework on which all our songs and tales hang. It furnishes the reference points for our journey. It is the road we are following on our Map. This is the biblical kerygma that has to do with the deeds of liberation and reconciliation, and the Doer of those deeds.

The Storyline is right at the heart of the Statement of Faith, just as it is in its eucharistic and mission counterparts. Thus this Church reads the meaning of life as a drama whose beginning and end are in the will and work of Another with whom we have to do. Our world comes to be out of the purposes of this Eternal Spirit. Creation proceeds by the power of this free and personal God to the fulfillment of its goal. Purpose, Purposer, Power. A version of Augustine's psychological analogy of the Trinity is embedded in the very narrative structure of faith. And this "immanent Trinity" expresses itself in the saga in the missions of the "economic Trinity"; the coming to be of the good creation at whose crown is the creature with the human face called to respond to the purpose of life together in freedom and Peace that is God's own deepest being. Then, the Great Refusal, the No! said by a rebel creation, the resistance of the powers of sin and evil. But that Love that will not let us go claims a particular people for special engagement, displays the vision of Shalom in their release from bondage, their history of promise and judgment, the mandates of the law and the hopes and warnings of the prophets. Then the central act: Shalom incarnate, sharing our common lot. In and through this solidarity with us there is at-one-ment of the estranged. In the life of this Nazarene, in his death and resurrection, there is liberation from the powers of sin and evil and their issue death, and the reconciliation of the world and God. In the final act of the Spirit, there is the birth of the Church, the gift of forgiveness of sins and the cost and joy of discipleship, signed and sealed to us in bread, wine, water, and the Word, the time be the Times of struggle for justice and peace, evangelical proclamation, the divine Presence in trial and rejoicing, and finally the fulfillment of these portents in the end of the things of death, the coming of the God who shall be all in all, to whom be every blessing, honor, power and glory! This Great Story, this Storyline as we have put it, is heard the length and breadth of the United Church of Christ in the many and various ways we have sought to identify, forms of confession implicit and explicit. It gives some warrant to our name, the United Church of Christ:

United—with all its enriching diversity, our different tunes and tales, there is in our Storyline unity of vision and direction; Church—for all our local autonomy, we are the United Church, not the united Churches, pilgrims in common covenant and community; of Christ—it is the Christian Story we have to tell, which common language and saga makes it possible for us to keep company with others going the same way.

Our exploration of the Storyline found in the Statement puts in context some of the questions we raised earlier about the theology of and in this Symbol. Yes, there are weaknesses as earlier indicated. But they are not structural weaknesses. The fundamental framework of Christian belief is there, the narrative structure with all its chapters. Because this is so, the Statement can be interpreted and enriched by a larger ethos of faith. Aimlessness can be understood as the twin sin of arrogance. The mission of God in the world can be kept in company with the work of God in the church, especially in the light of the significant present tenses of the Statement: creates, calls, seeks, judges. The other classical affirmations of the End—resurrection, return, judgment—can keep company with the declarations of eternal life and everlasting Kingdom. Further, precisely because it is offered to and understood by its constituency as a story told and a testimony given, rather than a computer read-out of the divine economy, its relative and corrigible nature is indisputable, and the possibility of revision is always there. (The masculine control of language can be challenged, the implicit trinitarianism can be made more explicit.)

## SUBCOMMUNITIES OF FAITH

So far our inquiry into the theological identity of the United Church of Christ is concentrated on elements of catholicity. We have tried to locate the universals within this community, the songs and stories everyone gets to hear somewhere, somehow within the pilgrim company. But what about the particularities? What of those folk within the United Church of Christ for whom "forms of confession" mean—"Question: What is thy only hope in life and in death? Answer: That I, with body and soul, both in life and in death, am not my own, but belong to my faithful Saviour Jesus Christ, who with his precious blood has fully satisfied for all my sins, and redeemed me from all the power of the Devil ... "[10] Here is the specificity of Question One of the Heidelberg Catechism, memorized by thousands in some parts of the United Church of Christ. Here are not only the great Whys and Wherefores of the Statement of Faith, but the Hows and Whens of the penal substitutionary theory of the Atonement, and more.

To follow our pilgrim church metaphor, there are after the hours of common campfire, late-night gatherings of parts of our company, family clusters which assemble in this or that corner to tell a few of their own bloodline tales and sing some of their own native songs. Sometimes these are very long stories, Norse-like sagas that go on and on, or very intricate songs with many verses. Sometimes they are short tales spoken in accents that are not immediately intelligible. Thus, there is in the UCC lore handed down to us from our ancestors on this journey, remembered with affection and respect, from which we still learn important things. In fact, these traditions enrich our common songs and stories and provide many of the materials for them. These root traditions are constituted by the creeds, confessions, catechisms, and covenants to which the Constitution alludes in the preamble: "It claims as its own the faith of the historic Church expressed in the ancient creeds and reclaimed in the basic insights of the Protestant Reformers."[11] While this commitment is very carefully stated so as not to conflict with Article IV, Paragraph 15, and is further modified by a succeeding sentence which speaks of the need to appropriate this faith in contemporary modes of thought and expression, it would be a mistake to ignore the power of these historical deposits in the life of many congregations.

In parts of Pennsylvania, Ohio, and the Shenandoah Valley, the Heidelberg Catechism or sections of it, is very much a resource in confirmation training. The same thing is true about the Evangelical Catechism[12] in the Missouri Valley and to a less extent the two other inherited confessional Symbols, Luther's Small Catechism and the Augsburg Confession. Indeed, there is also a Hungarian Reformed Catechism used in the Magyar churches. I have never seen the Cambridge Platform of 1648, or the Kansas City Statement of Faith of 1913 as centerpieces of Congregational pedagogy, but I have read enough New England church covenants pasted in the back of Congregational hymnals to know that some of their major themes are still very much with us.[13] And in those same hymn books, along with the Evangelical and Reformed Hymnal, and the new UCC Hymnal, there appear the Apostles' Creed and the Nicene Creed, used sparingly or not at all in many places, but used quite regularly in many others. Family clusters do indeed gather in the corners of church life to remember and honor their heritage.

Several things must he said about these continuing cells of particularity within the larger Body. After twenty years' experience of evenings at both the larger campfire and the smaller enclaves, there does not seem to be any overwhelming evidence of the impossibility of coexistence. What this means, in part, is that some UCC members would feel their faith impoverished if they did not hear it in the language of their forebears, for their identity is bound up with the singularities of their history. This should come as no surprise to a decade that is discovering the formative power of roots. A witness to this important but modest identity function of these traditions is that there is no move on the part of one or another of these after-hour communities to insist that the songs and stories of the great common campfire be replaced by the Heidelberg Catechism, the Cambridge Platform, or the Nicene Creed.

Is this then a case of UCC culture-Christianity and theological indifferentism? It may well be in some cases. But for the most part, there is another explanation. For one, the common affirmations and visions that set the direction for the UCC are sufficiently faithful to the Storyline not to require imperialistic sorties by the subcommunity and its formulations. That is, the old slogan in the E & R tradition applies here: "In essentials unity, in nonessentials liberty, in all things charity." The use of the propositional and catechetical lore of one tradition fits the liberty-charity declaration, for the essentials are secured in other ways. But for others, the catechisms, creeds and covenants of particularity *are* essentials: they are deposits that are felt to secure the theological reference points. It is assumed by those who hold this view that in any Christian Church organized according to the principle of Article IV, paragraph 15 there will be found somewhere confessional norms, at least in the congregation, and perhaps in some larger ecclesial environment in which the congregation makes its home. Therefore, the larger shared declarations of faith, implicit and explicit, will be interpreted in the light of the more specific family norms. The songs and stories around the great campfire will be sung with the accent of those who speak the native tongue.

But there may be a more decisive reason than these two, for the fact that the particularities are held with conviction but not imperialism. It is suggested by the rest of the answer to Question One of the Heidelberg Catechism: "(Jesus Christ) so preserves me that without the will of my Father in heaven not a hair can fall from my head, yea that all things must work together for my salvation. Wherefore, by his Holy Spirit, He also assures me of eternal life and makes me heartily willing and ready henceforth to live unto Him." These assertions, like all the forms of confession we have mentioned so far, have more the character of personal testimony than public test. The Heidelberg Catechism is marked by just that characteristic. It is an existential testimony more than a propositional grid. The other doctrinal deposits in the UCC also function this way, whether they be individual church covenants or the broader creedal or catechetical articulations of faith. These are also "songs and stories" sung and told around smaller campfires, ones that *define* but do not *confine*.

## SEEING AND DOING ALONG THE WAY

Up to now we have dealt with what is to be found in the said and sung lore of the UCC. A final comment must be made about the important context in which these faith statements are made. Put in the Bunyan metaphor we are using, we are dealing now with the manner in which the pilgrim company relates to its surroundings along the way, the people it meets and the places through which it passes. These relationships affect the meaning of its songs and stories, how they must be heard. What are these relationships? First, all our songs and stories tell of the God of long marches who leads out of the lands of bondage, who opens the eyes of the traveler to see the unseen victim by the wayside. The God of the Story bestirs the seer of the invisible poor, hungry, oppressed and forgotten to reach out to them, to share in their struggle, to bind up wounds, to do justice and make peace. There can be no movement toward the Celestial City unless it includes this reaching out in servanthood, and the engagement of the principalities and powers along the way that leave the trail of Jericho Road victims. For the UCC, to f ollow in the footsteps of the Pioneer, to see this Light of world that leads it, is at one and the same time to see *by* and *in* that Light the wretched of the earth, and seeing, to serve.

While this mark of the UCC does not, strictly speaking, constitute a form of confessional identity, it nevertheless functions in just that way. "By their fruits you will know them." From the tendency of a local UCC congregation in its community to be known because of its catalytic role in some important human task, or perhaps its stand on a controversial issue, to the overseas ministries of the Church characterized by the same initiatives, to the well-known denominational forays into one or another critical issue of justice, this pilgrim people is known for its determination to translate the Story of the deeds of God into contemporary historical action. Of course this community regularly falters and fails in its outreach. But its self-definition is one in which the journey cannot be faithfully undertaken unless it goes on in awareness of, and ministry to, those in need along the public way.

This UCC company also keeps its eyes and ears open for other things and people. That is, it has a special interest in having its songs and stories heard and understood in the lands through which it passes on its trek. While it is only with difficulty aroused to invite the inhabitants into its pilgrim band—other travellers are better known for their evangelistic zeal—the UCC does seek to introduce itself to the strangers met, and learn their new language as it crosses a new border. It works very hard to translate its tale into the tongue of each new town, seeking to make it intelligible to new times and places. Thereby, it often discovers that in the crossing of these boundaries and in the enlarging of its language, it also enriches the tale itself. John Robinson's words continue to express the confessional horizons of the UCC: "More truth and light shall yet break forth from his holy word." Behind this affirmation is a commitment to the Spirit whose way is a journey and whose home is the Future. As such, the Story told in *via* will be given ever fresh expression. "Where the spirit of the Lord is, there is liberty."

The perception of adjacencies along the way takes another form in the heightened sensitivity to other Christian wayfarers. Thus, the ecumenical commitment that brought this very community into existence marks its mode of travel. There is a looking outward as well as a looking forward, yes even a yearning to walk together with those who just might have the same kind of map, sing similar tunes and tell like tales.

It must be said that each of these three manifestations of wide peripheral vision carry with them potential hazards. Looking around constantly can lend itself to losing the way. The very strengths of the UCC, its moral passion, open into intellectual horizons, and ecumenical breadth can degenerate (and have degenerated) into a self-righteous activism, chameleon-like accommodation to cultural or counter-cultural trends, and an uncritical togetherness. It is only when these movements are part of a total directionality, orienting the travelers beyond themselves to the One out ahead that they contribute to faithful wayfaring.

It must also be added that for all the pride with which we take note of these and the earlier mentioned features of UCC identity, we are in short supply of other resources for the journey. Thus, the sense that Christ is out ahead of us ever beckoning the church forward along the difficult trail sometimes does not allow for a perception of the *present*

Christ, whether it be the mystical Presence in the sacramental life, or the passionate personal Presence of the evangelical life. Again, the very strength of our way of confessing Christ in freedom, figurative imagination, and narrative idiom may predispose us to ignore the claims of other communions which give higher priority to doctrine because "ideas have consequences," and thus, cause us to neglect the forms of confession. And again, we have something to learn from those with the love and gift of liturgy, the sensibility to mystery, the appreciation for catholicity and more. We have provinder to share on this journey, but also much to receive.

Is it our provinder, our journey? No it is not. There is a Power and Presence in our midst that makes for whatever resources, movement and direction we have. Our songs and stories say that this is so: God bestows on us the *Holy Spirit*, "creating and renewing the Church of Jesus Christ." It is, finally, God the Holy Spirit who nurtures and empowers this pilgrim community, granting it whatever shared vision it has, and giving it the unity of one Great Story amidst the rich diversity of its tellings and translations, not rending, but "*binding* in covenant a faithful people of all ages, tongues and races."

## NOTES

1. Soren Kierkegaard, *Concluding Unscientific Postscript,* tr. by David Swenson and completed by Walter Lowrie (Princeton: Princeton University Press, 1994), passim.

2. John Bunyan, *The Pilgrim's Progress* in vol. 15, The Harvard Classics (New York: P.F. Collier & Sons), pp. 7–8.

3. Service of Word and Sacrament No. 1, United Church of Christ, *Services of the Church* (Philadelphia: United Church Press), 1969, p. 13.

4. *The Construction and Bylaws*, United Church of Christ, 1977 Edition. Published by the Executive Council for the United Church of Christ, New York, 1977, p. 4.

5. For commentary on this general posture of the UCC express in these various ways see Douglass Horton, *The United Church of Christ* (New York: Thomas Nelson & Sons, 1962); Louis Gunnemann, *The Shaping of the United Church of Christ* (New York: United Church Press, 1977); Loring Chase, *Words of Faith* (Philadelphia: United Church Press, 1968); Gabriel Fackre, *Conversation in Faith* (Philadelphia: United Church Press, 1968); *My Confirmation* (Philadelphia: United Church Press, 1963); Elmer Arndt, ed., *The Frontier Series* [Walter Brueggemann,

*The Renewing Word*; Roger Hazelton, *The Ways of Creativity*, Harland Hogue, *Prayer: The Vital Center*, Loring Chase, *The Church: Community of Response and Mission*] (Philadelphia: United Church Press, 1969); *United Church of Christ: History and Program*, produced by the Division of Publication, United Church Board for Homeland Ministries, (2nd rev. ed., Boston: United Church Press, 1974); Office of Church Life and Leadership, *A Manual on the Ministry* Perspectives and Procedures for Authorizing Ministry in the United Church of Christ, OCCL, 1977; Roger L. Shinn, *Unity and Diversity in the United Church of Christ* (Royal Oak, Michigan: Cathedral Publishers, 1972); United Church Board for Homeland Ministries, *Membership in the United Church of Christ* (UCBHM, 1978); Dorsie E. Ivy, *UCC Spirit* (Clear Lake, Iowa: Center for Growth, 1977).

    6. Robert Moss, "Evangelism and the United Church of Christ in the 1970s." *Evangelism for a New Day*, vol. 4, no. 1 (New York: United Church Board for Homeland Ministries, 1978), pp. 1–2.

    7. "A Statement of Commitment," (Revised) *Evangelism Training Manual* (New York: United Church Board for Homeland Ministries, 1974), pp. 72–73.

    8. Roger Lincoln Shinn and Daniel Day Williams, *We Believe: An Interpretation of the United Church Statement of Faith* (Philadelphia: United Church Press, 1966), p. 16.

    9. Harold Lindsell, *The Battle for the Bible* (Grand Rapids, Michigan: Zondervan Publishing House), p. 152.

    10. *The Heidelberg Catechism*, Philadelphia: Board of Christian Education of the Reformed Church of the United States, 1902, p. 67. See the contemporary translation and commentary on the 400th anniversary of the catechism: *The Heidelberg Catechism with Commentary* (Philadelphia: United Church Press, 1962), 1963, and Bard Thompson *et al.*, *Essays on Heidelberg Catechism* (Philadelphia: United Church Press, 1963).

    11. "Preamble," *The Constitution and Bylaws, op. cit.* p. 2.

    12. *The Evangelical Catechism* (rev. ed., St. Louis: Eden Publishing House, 1961).

    13. See William Walker, *The Creeds and Platforms of Congregationalism* (Boston: The Pilgrim Press, 1960).

    14. *The Heidelberg Catechism*, op. cit., p. 67.

Theology and Forms of Confession in the United Church of Christ. *Andover Newton Quarterly* Vol. 19, No. 3 (January 1979), 176–189. Used by permission.

## CHAPTER 3

# Listening for the Word

L ISTEN FOR THE WORD OF GOD . . . "intones the lesson reader in the Service of Word and Sacrament." (*Book of Worship*, p. 40). This widely used liturgical formula has a history.

In the midst of the Confessing Church's struggle against the racist teachings of the "German Christians" came the ringing words of the Barmen Declaration:

> Jesus Christ, as he is attested for us in Holy Scripture, is the one Word of God which we have to hear and which we have to trust and obey in life and in death. We reject the false doctrine, as though the Church could and would have to acknowledge as a source of its proclamation apart from and beside this one Word of God, still other events and powers, figures and truths, God's revelation.[1]

Listening for—being "attentive to"—and hearing the Word of God is no Sunday pleasantry. It is a matter of "life and . . . death."

As with Barmen, so with the UCC liturgy, "the Word" is *Jesus Christ*. A popular Christianity often treats the Word and the leather-bound pulpit Book as one and the same. So too do more sophisticated theories of "inerrancy" that view the "autographs" as protected from error in all about which they speak. No, there is dynamism in the Word, something that is heard through the Scripture, and, therefore, must be *listened for.*

Why so? Because the Word is Jesus Christ, incarnate then and living now. He will speak when he will speak, not on our say-so. Here again Barmen and the United Church of Christ are of one mind. In the for-

mer, *Jesus Christ* "is the one Word. . . . " In the latter, again from its
eucharistic rite, the worshiper praises "Christ the Word, in flesh born
low. . . . " (*Book of Worship*, p. 43). And in our official texts of the UCC,
Christ is the "sole," "the *one*" Word:

> The United Church of Christ acknowledges as its sole Head, Jesus
> Christ, Son of God and Saviour.[2]

The linkage here of "Word" and "Head" is traceable to one of the earliest of Reformed declarations of faith, the Berne theses of 1528:

> The holy Christian Church, whose only head is Christ, is born from
> God's Word, stays with it, and does not listen to any alien voice.[3]

Or again, in the matter of accountability of a local congregation, our
UCC Constitution speaks in similar fashion of "Jesus Christ as Lord and
Saviour. . . . Jesus Christ as Lord and Saviour. . . . Jesus Christ, the Head
of the Church."

It's no accident that forebears, midwifing our own Body of Christ in
the wake of struggles against ideologies that demanded fealty to other
gods, fixed upon the name United Church of *Christ*. We belong only to
*this* Lord, to this *Word,* not to other "events and powers, figures and
truths."

In making these crucial distinctions between Word and words,
between Christ and the pages of Scripture, we can, of course, err on the
other side—*separating* one from the other. "Distinctions" are not dissoci-
ations. The Word, Jesus Christ, is distinguishable but inseparable from
Scripture. The one Word is, as Barmen has it, "attested for us in Holy
Scripture." More about this later.

## TEXTS AND THEIR INTERPRETATION

The foregoing comments assume that our *charters,* preeminently the
Constitution of the United Church of Christ, shed basic light on what
it means to be "attentive to the Word." They

- brought us to be as a Church;

- stipulated the theological common ground for the uniting traditions (still the only United Church in this land);
- represent the unity to which we to this day give assent;
- make us a Church and not only 6000—plus congregations;
- are written into the ordaining and commissioning rites of our Church.

When representing our Church in ecumenical relationships (the Consultation on Church Union, the World Council of Churches, the Lutheran-Reformed Conversation), I quickly learned that it is corporate texts that constitute a primary means of identification, especially so when negotiations are under way for forms of greater unity. Within any denomination, the wide range of opinion on matters theological is a fact of life in these pluralistic days. However, the quest for unity to which we are resolutely committed goes forward among churches through attention to foundational and perduring charters that have defined who we are, and not just our sundry opinions about who we are. Surely, those opinions must and will enter into the *interpretation* of the charters, but the texts themselves must be our reference points.

Interpretation requires *conversation.* We all come at things from our own perspective and "social location." A corrective to a narrow reading of classical texts is a collegial inquiry; hence the value of a journal like *New Conversations.* Indeed, the promise of truth is greater when engaged by the diversity of the *whole people of God.* Our Church is uniquely positioned to honor this inclusivity, this "catholicity," formed as it is from a variety of Christian traditions which both enrich and share a unity, as the *United* Church of Christ. The understanding of the basics of corporate UCC faith should, therefore, grow out of a I Cor. 12–13 commitment in which "the eye cannot say to the hand, 'I have no need of you. . . .'" (I Cor. 12:21).

Within this interactive Corinthian catholicity, there are "privileged" places of knowing. The *oppressed* teach us the gospel truth about justice; the *lonely* bring their special grasp of the Word of divine friendship; the *sick* and the *dying* know depths unreached by the well; *sinners* who have faced the reality of "the Fall" can hear better the Word of forgiveness. We need all the help we can get from one another to discern the fullness of the Gospel, refusing to claim that our angle of vision is the only access to truth. Each *counts* in the conversation, but no one *controls* it.

*Note well:* this is not the same as the pop slogan of *theological* "pluralism." Pluralism, in the wider sense, is an important concept applicable to the needed variety of ethnic, racial, cultural, age and sex differences, and communities that enrich our society and churches. When carried into the theological arena, the slogan is bad business. There, what sounds radical is, in a fact, a justification of the status quo. The message is: "different strokes for different folks"; "you do your thing and I'll do mine." That means I do not have to look self-critically at my own views, and you can rest comfortably with yours. With these reactionary assumptions, no serious, transformative conversation can take place.

Theological *diversity* is different from and much more demanding than theological pluralism. A Corinthian encounter means that you cannot just "do *your own* thing." You have to move out of your comfortable corner and: a) engage those with different perspectives on the assumption that you might be changed; and b) "listen for Word" *with* them in the hope that the Spirit will illumine each with a larger understanding of the Gospel.

The Lutheran-Reformed Conversation is a telling example of how honest exchange among those of different perspective can make a difference. For years in this dialogue representatives paraded before each other the virtues of their own traditions. After a while, it began to dawn upon each partisan that the other side may just have a point. Could it be that we were *right* in what we affirmed, but *wrong* in what we denied? Could it be that the two separated Reformation streams were not contradictory but complementary? Lutherans keep stressing the *solidarity* of Christ with us (Christ is alive and well in the Church, "in, with and under" the bread and wine, etc.), while the Reformed tradition, wary of idolatry, stresses the *sovereignty* of God over us (always reforming the Church, calling us always to be accountable to the Lordship of Christ over society, etc.). Both have a grasp on a genuine truth. Born out of that realization was the formula, "mutual affirmation and admonition." We *affirm* what we find in the other and *admonish* the other not to neglect what they have to learn from us. "Do unto others. . . ."[5]

With this commitment to mutuality, let's take a more concentrated look at a key UCC text (with cross-references to other foundational documents) basic to anything we say in our Church about being "attentive to the Word": the theological Preamble to the UCC Constitution.

## THE PREAMBLE

Being "attentive to the Word" has to do with theological "prolegomena": the question of authority, or what authorizes the things we later say about God, Christ, salvation, mission, "life, death, destiny." Everyone has a conviction about this, even those who object to "authorities." Authority is not "authoritarianism," but the question of the place or places we go to find out what is so about ultimate matters.

Of course, Christians will all say, *God* is our final authority! But the question remains: where does God disclose what is so? That is the issue of *theological authority*.

In the history of Christian thought, three large-scale answers have come to the fore: 1) the *Bible* is the final authority 2) the *church and its traditions* are the final authority 3) the *world* of human experience in one or another of its dimensions or expressions—thinking, doing, or feeling—is our final authority. There are many variations on each of these. In fact, the bitterest disputes have often been among those who share the same over-all view! (For example, hard-line "inerrantists" battling "infallibists"—the former holding the Bible to be authoritative on matters of science and history as well as in theology and morals versus the latter who accept only scriptural trustworthiness on theology and morality.) So, we have only gone half-way into the real issues when we land on one or the other of the three major "types"—Bible, Church, World.

The controversies are often traceable to different notions about *how* we approach the *where*—and thus the matter of *interpretation* ("hermeneutics"). We've already begun to talk about that.

The Preamble to the UCC Constitution has a view of both the *where* and the *how*. It entails modest but crucial assumptions about theological authority and interpretation. These assumptions are much like those discernible in the ecumenical movement out of which our Church was born. (They are at work in such key documents of the WCC as its Faith and Order statements on baptism, eucharist, and ministry and the authority of the Bible;[7] in the *COCU Consensus*;[8] and the statements and study documents of the Lutheran-Reformed dialogues, international and national.⁹) And they look a lot like the working assumptions of many pastors and teachers in the UCC.

Characteristic of both ecumenical theology and the UCC spirit, the Preamble's authority structure is inclusive/catholic/irenic. *All* three of the major types appear in it: Bible, Church, and World. But there are priorities and special interrelationships within them. Preamblic assumptions are already at work in the previous section of this essay. We identify them now with greater specificity.

## THE CHRIST OF SCRIPTURE

The Constitution declares that Jesus Christ is the sole *head* of the Body of Christ, and in the same "breath" it speaks in comparable Johannine metaphor of "the *Word* of God in the Scriptures. . . . " Thus the Preamble echoes here Barmen's declaration that "Jesus Christ, as he is attested to us in Scripture is the one Word of God which we have to hear. . . . " As affirmed earlier, our fundamental standard for deciding theological matters in the United Church of Christ is "Christ."

The where of knowledge of Christ does not hang in the air. Nor does it come from what we think or feel—our philosophical systems, political commitments, economic theories, our prized or privileged experiences. Nor does it derive from our most hallowed church traditions. The knowledge of Jesus Christ, the Word, derives from "the Scriptures." To be attentive to the Word, Jesus Christ, is to be attentive to the Bible. This belief is reaffirmed every Sunday in our churches as the Word is preached from a Bible that is read. With the dramatic increase in recent years of the use of the lectionary—for preaching, church school curriculum, desk calendar, etc.—even the same biblical texts become focal.

The Bible, yes, but the Bible as the place where the *Word,* Jesus Christ, is heard. That means Scripture as it speaks in accord with its Lord, its head, its Center is the *how* of the matter. In the UCC we interpret the Bible, "christologically." What bears witness to Christ is the authoritative Word. We read Scripture through the lens of Christ. For example, our struggle against the oppression of women today and slavery yesterday is informed by a christological reading of Scripture: In Christ "there is neither slave nor free . . . male nor female" (Gal. 3:28). Thus the Scriptures are the *source* of authority and Christ is the *norm* of the Scriptures.

Why we go where we do, and interpret it how we do, is a companion question. The answer, historically, has been a teaching about "revelation" that warrants what we say about "authority." If the biblical Word is authoritative, then a revelatory presence and power must have something to do with it. While the Preamble does not go into detail, it does link attention to "the Word of God in the Scriptures" in the very next phrase with "the presence and power of the Holy Spirit." And it does so in a very UCC fashion—refusing to separate "the Word" from the "the world." We'll return to this latter point. But the historic warrant for the primacy of Scripture—the in-Spiriting, the "inspiration," of Scripture—here appears also in our UCC charter, albeit conceived dynamically not statically.

## CHRIST AND THE COMMUNITY

Is it just the individual reader—attentive to the Word of Scripture spoken by the presence and power of the Spirit—that constitutes authority in the UCC? The Constitution has something else in mind, indeed, also *someone* else:

> It claims as its own the faith of the historic Church expressed in the ancient creeds and reclaimed in the insights of the Protestant Reformers.

In these constitutional words, the community enters the arena of authority. Not just our own UCC, but the length and breadth of the Christian community. Herein lies our UCC commitment to "catholicity" understood ecumenically. The *Basis of Union*, another text without which there would be no UCC, laid the groundwork for this catholicity and helps us interpret the Preamble. It speaks of the "ecumenical creeds" and declares that "We acknowledge one holy catholic Church, the innumerable company of those who in every age and nation are united by the Holy Spirit to God in Christ. . . ."[10]

Of course there is more to the larger Christian community than the "ancient" of ages; we are a Church of the Now as well as the Then. But the struggles and the hard-won agreements of our forebears are not excluded from our conversation. We honor our ecumenical fathers and mothers, especially so in this ecumenical Church that defines itself as "united and uniting."

We have a *particular* ancestry as well as a universal one. Again, the *Basis of Union* sheds light on the Preamble. "The faith of the historic Church . . . reclaimed in the basic of insights of the Protestant Reformers" (Constitution) is given "utterance in the evangelical confessions of the Reformation" (*Basis of Union*). We stand squarely in the Reformation tradition. To be clear about what "the basic insights of the Protestant Reformers" are, we need to attend, as the Basis says, to the official texts of our uniting Reformation traditions: "the creeds and platforms of Congregationalism,"[11] the three "symbols" of the Evangelical and Reformed Church (The *Heidelberg Catechism,* Luther's *Small Catechism,* the *Augsburg Confession*), and the christological confession of the Christian Churches. The Constitution is very clear that these traditions—both the ecumenical and Reformation ones—are integral to who we are and what we believe in the UCC, declaring that the denominations that came together "unite in the United Church of Christ without break in their respective continuities and traditions." [12]

"Please! Don't tie us down to the past! We believe in the living Word!" *Amen.* In fact, that is a refrain heard constantly in this very lore. The creeds, confessions and covenants are always accountable to the living biblical Word. They are subject to change, corrigible, not cast in stone. This conviction characterizes the Reformed stream in which we stand: *semper reformanda!* is the watchword. That's why we are always about the task of making new statements of faith *(viz.* The United Church of Christ Statement of Faith). And it's true of our Evangelical roots as well. [13] Our treasured inheritance is not the source of faith but a valued resource to faith.

To be a "resource," however, means that in hearing the Word and in interpreting Scripture we do really listen to this voice of "the other." We are not captive to the present moment, any more than we are chained to the past. We invite into our councils even the voices of the dead, as Chesterton reminded us. [14] As resource, not source, the tradition of the Church is *ministerial,* not magisterial. It serves the Christian community and does not dominate it.

## THE COMMUNITY IN CONTEXT

*The United Church of Christ affirms:*

The responsibility of the Church in each generation to make this faith its own in reality of worship, in honesty of thought and expression, and in purity of heart before God.

—Preamble, 2

Two things leap out from this sequel to the previous assertions of christological centrality, biblical authority, and the resource role of tradition: 1) The *present* Church is integral to "the Community," and 2) the dynamisms, issues, and idiom of the times in which that Church lives and witnesses are the context in which "the faith" is to be interpreted.

To make the historic faith "its own" requires a grasp of the particular challenges of the present context and a communication of that faith in contemporary terms. To affirm this task as constitutive of our UCC understanding of authority is to distinguish our point of view from two other proposals with high visibility in the churches today. We are different from: a) those who would see theological work and witness as the *repristination*—the simple repetition—of the inherited faith in new contexts; and b) from those who would see theological work and witness as the *replacement* of the inherited faith by premises derived from new contexts. The Preamble's alternative to both of these is the *reinterpretation* of the inherited faith. The way of "reinterpretation" is an extremely difficult row to hoe. The evidence of that are current tendencies in both the UCC and the wider Church to drift toward the other two simplistic alternatives.

The thirty-five years of our existence as a new Church have been marked by the commanding presence of a *new* historical context in this country and beyond—especially so for a Church like ours, with strong Reformed roots in "world-transformative" theological soil.[15] A fundamental aspect of that new setting, one having to do with our world-transformative heritage, is almost exactly coterminous with our beginnings: the struggles for justice and peace in the 1960s. The deep participation of national and regional leaders, our agencies, and our congregations in the civil rights and peace movements epitomized by

Martin Luther King, Jr., significantly shaped the ethos of the UCC. It is no accident, therefore, that the description of the UCC as "Just Peace Church" took its place alongside our earlier self-identification as a "Church United and Uniting." Making the faith "its own" has meant for us relating the gospel to the justice and peace issues of our time.

The contextual dimension of our UCC authority structure, however, entails more than concern for social ethical issues. It has to do also with broad cultural and intellectual currents. Once again, our lineage, this time that of a "learned ministry," has been influential. We sometimes speak (too proudly!) of ourselves as a "thinking person's church." Thus loving God "with the mind" is our heritage and will be our horizon. One evidence is the number of educational institutions we have founded. All this makes us sensitive to the intellectual and cultural challenges of our day, open to learnings there-from, and insistent upon the use of critical faculties in our approach to faith.

The present Community, therefore, as it is faced with the social, cultural, and intellectual context of its time and place, rightly strives to makes the faith "its own," to let new light and truth break forth from God's holy Word, as our forebear John Robinson put it so memorably.

*Who* this present Community is that contextualizes its faith must also be made clear. It is, as the Preamble says, a *praying* as well as a *doing* community, making the faith its own in "the reality of worship." Thus "purity of heart before God" is central to life in the UCC, as is the previously noted need for "honesty of thought and expression." And again, as a *covenantal* people, and further as a "united and uniting Church" that holds kindred all who share its "confession," the present Community is wide-ranging one. While its "base community"—the local congregation—is focal in its polity, it takes into account the *whole people of God*, "faithful people of all ages, tongues and races."

## THE STATEMENT OF FAITH

An important convergence of all these factors—contemporary meaningfulness, action-orientation, doxological sensibility,[16] and faithfulness to christologically-read Scripture and tradition—takes place in the United Church of Christ Statement of Faith, one of our important, though derivative, UCC charters that help us to be attentive to the Word. Indeed, its content and character is a model of the working of the Preamble's principles of theological interpretation. The Statement, built itself on the themes identified in the "Faith" section of the *Basis of Union,* is in the words of Roger Shinn, its early drafter, Scripture's "Great Story."[17] The Statement recognizes that Christ, the "Word" of Scripture, is at the same time Christ the central "Chapter" of the biblical story.

The Statement is therefore really a *narrative,* and thus an early anticipation of the movement of "narrative theology." As such, it is a powerful way of communicating faith in the drama-drenched world in which we today live. In this genre it manages to set forth many of the basic themes of classical Christian faith found in the ecumenical creeds and the evangelical confessions:

*The triune God (in three "missions")*—call(s) the worlds into being. . . . In Jesus Christ . . . you have come to us . . . You bestow upon us your Spirit . . .

*The humanity and deity of Christ*—We believe in you, O God. . . . In Jesus Christ, the man of Nazareth. . . . you have come to us and shared our common lot . . .

*The saving Work of Christ*—In Jesus Christ, the man of Nazareth, our crucified and risen Lord, you have come to us . . . conquering sin and death and reconciling the world to yourself . . .

*Justification by grace through faith*—You promise to all who trust you forgiveness of sins and fullness of grace . . .

*The means of grace as Word and Sacrament*—You call us into your church. . . . to proclaim the gospel . . . to share in Christ's baptism and eat at his table . . .

*The fruit of grace as works of love and justice*—You call us into your church to accept the cost and joy of discipleship, to be servants in the service of others . . . and resist the powers of evil . . .

*The fruit of grace in the mission of word as well as deed*—You call us into the church . . . to proclaim the gospel to all the world...

*The life of faith and love made firm in hope*—You promise . . . courage in the struggle for justice and peace, your presence in trial and rejoicing, and eternal life in the realm which has no end.

And all this "doctrine" is in the genre of doxological narrative! Blessing and honor, glory and power be unto you!

## PUTTING IT TOGETHER

In light of the above considerations, being "attentive to the Word" in the United Church of Christ means:

- At every level of our Church, when witness is made to the gospel in word or in deed, our guiding star, our standard, our norm is our "sole Head," our "one Word," Jesus Christ.

- Jesus Christ is not a figure or idea of our making, controlled by our notions, current or ancient, but the biblical Word, the Word listened for and heard as we attend to the words of Scripture. And those words, in turn, are read through the lens of Christ.

- Listening for that one Word requires *readiness* to learn with all the assistances available. As Christ is the head of the Body of Christ, and as the Bible is the Church's Book, Scripture is to be read in the Christian Community from deep within its life, worship, and witness, past and present. Both the fathers and mothers and the sisters and brothers—the heritage of the Church and its horizon—are crucial resources in listening for the Word.

- The world at large, as well as the church, belongs to Jesus Christ. Readiness to hear the Word requires the biblical people of God to be deeply immersed in its streams, especially those in which Christ himself points in Scripture. If Christ meets us wherever there is hunger, hurt, sorrow, oppression, sickness, sin, death, then we are called to read his Book from deep within those places. If we are to love God with all our minds, as well as our heart and soul, then the disciplines of the mind as well as the piety of heart are necessary to the reading of Scripture.

- The who that does the listening for Christ, the biblical Word is the "whole people of God,"—the hard-working Bible study group in First Church as well as the seminary scholar, those who cry for justice and those who cry in beds of pain, the bearers of ancient wisdom and the stewards of current insight—each bringing their special gifts to the task and joy of hearing the biblical Word.

- At the end of the day, the biblical Word will be spoken when Christ chooses so to speak. We can pursue for it, position ourselves in the circle of conversation for it, draw on all the resources, ancient and current, but the Bible only comes alive, the words become the Word, only by the power of the Holy Spirit. We wait for it, listen for it, but it is by the grace of God, that sovereign and free God that the Word is spoken. That Word may, indeed, by against all coveted experiences, notions and traditions. So, ever and again, we pray for the Holy Spirit to open our ears, to make us "attentive to the Word."

## THE UCC ATTENTIVE

How do we practice what we preach? What does all of the above really mean in the day-to-day life of the United Church of Christ? Here is some personal testimony about UCC attentiveness to the Word.

## THE WORD IN THE WORLD

Exactly thirty years ago—Spring, 1964—came a call from our Council for Christian Social Action to go to Mississippi to aid in the voter registration campaign for and with disenfranchised black citizens. This was on the heels of the earlier call for UCC participation in the 1963 March on Washington, one that resulted in a large UCC contingent at the historic March led by Martin Luther King, Jr., A. Philip Randolph and others. The burning of numerous black churches in Mississippi, the killing of three civil rights workers a few months after our own trips to Mississippi, and the siege conditions of our UCC college (Tougaloo) made for hair-raising days. These things, along with the leadership of

African-American clergy in the UCC and numerous struggles in local communities for justice in housing, public accommodations, education and jobs (we spent years in Lancaster, Pennsylvania, in a church-led effort to desegregate the junior high schools and introduce black history into the textbooks), left a deep mark on the soul of our Church. It was the major shaping force, I believe, of our present multifaceted commitment to justice for oppressed peoples—African American, Hispanic, American Indian and other ethnic minorities, women, people of different ages, classes, and conditions.

"All you are doing is adopting the political agenda of the Left!" our critics charged. Nonsense. It had to do with being "attentive to the Word." Why so?

As the United Church of *Christ,* like Jesus Christ as attested by Scripture we face the claims of our present context in company with our ancient fathers and mothers and living sisters and brothers. Brothers and sisters who are experiencing first-hand the pain of this present world, and refusing to accept this tribulation passively, call for solidarity with them in their struggle. Our fathers and mothers underscore these claims, for the Reformed heritage bequeathed to us—from Calvin's Geneva to Puritan Boston—with all its shortcomings, holds the civil order responsible to the Lordship of Jesus Christ, making us thereby responsive to demands to right social wrongs. In their company, and in this context, the rest of us—folk in ordinary congregations of the UCC—read our Book and hear a Word that speaks of the God who "brought down the powerful from their thrones and lifted up the lowly . . . [and] has filled the hungry with good things" (Luke 1:52–53); of "the Spirit of the Lord who anointed Christ to proclaim release to the captives and recovery of sight to the blind [and] to let the oppressed go free . . . " (Luke 4:18); of the Christ who is present wherever the prisoner is visited, the hungry fed, the naked clothed (Matt. 25:31–46), and for whom there is "neither slave nor free, male nor female, Greek nor Jew" (Gal. 3:28).

Because of these biblical convictions, throughout the UCC, in congregations and assemblies, in prayer, preaching, study, a Word begins to be heard: "Go into all the world . . ." "God so loved the world . . . ," the world criss-crossed by Jericho roads in which the people of Christ must share in the sufferings of Christ with all the consequent "cost and joy of discipleship." This time—thirty years ago—was an historic moment that taught many of us something of what it means to be "attentive to the Word" in the *world*.

## THE WORD IN THE CHURCH

The world in which the Word is at work is not as it should be. "The powers of evil" are much with us. We are able to "resist" them with "courage" because Christians know these powers have met their match in Jesus Christ. This Good News is given to the Christian community to "proclaim . . . to all the world"! (all from the *Statement of Faith*) Without the Word of proclamation the world would not know of the Lord that reigns over it (the cross and crown symbol of the United Church of Christ). Indeed, the Easter confidence that Christ has already liberated the world from the powers of evil in his incarnation, life, death, and resurrection is the power that sustains us in the "struggle for justice and peace."

Just about ten years ago, a *second* movement began to take shape that represents another kind of attentiveness to the Word. It had to with the "Word in the church," as partner to "the Word in the world." This "theological ferment," as it came to be described, came to higher visibility in the 1983–84 season: the Executive Council issued a statement citing evidence of a "*theological* renewal" in our Church; thirty-nine UCC seminary faculty members signed a document, "A Most Difficult and Urgent Time," warning that judgments on worship resources, language practices, life-styles, and modes of accountability in the Church" appeared to be made on the grounds of "pragmatism . . . liberalism . . . conservatism . . . pluralism" which are inappropriate to the church of Jesus Christ . . . postures [arrived at] happenstance, without the discipline and guidance offered to us in our theological tradition. . . ."

OCLL launched a church-wide Thank Offering theological project to discern how theology might be done in the UCC; the subject of a "theological centerline" came to the fore at a joint meeting of Conference Ministers, instrumentality heads, and denominational officers; the first of many Craigville Colloquies was launched to recognize the fiftieth anniversary of the Barmen Declaration, bringing together theologically concerned pastors and laity from around the country who declared, in a Witness Statement aired by the wire services, that the UCC needed to reassert clearly its christological, biblical, and confessional foundations. All this and much more.[18]

The momentum of theological renewal continues to this day, expressing itself in both of its earlier forms: more official ways, as in current General Synod call for "seasons of theological reflection," and grassroots endeavors, as in the "Confessing Christ" movement to establish regional centers of theological study and affirmation.

In the soul of our Church has appeared a determination not to lose sight of the "Word in the *church,*" the Gospel proclaimed as well as the Gospel practiced. If the worldly Christ of Matt. 25 was the premise of the secular mission rediscovered in the sixties, the known Christ of Luke 24 became the presupposition of the theological renewal of the eighties. Yes, our hearts burned within us when the incognito Christ spoke to us on *the road* in the struggles for justice and peace, but he disclosed who he was in the Word spoken in *the room* and in the "breaking of bread" there. Indeed, it soon became apparent that without the sustaining Word of faith and hope to be heard in the church's life of worship, prayer, preaching and belief, those committed to deeds of love in the world risked burn-out.

The recovery of worship, preaching, spirituality, and theology that marked the eighties, in fact, was anticipated by a grassroots UCC movement in evangelism in the previous decade, an effort to join personal transformation with systemic change. The byword of the movement that trained one-hundred evangelism facilitators for work throughout the denomination was "Word in deed," the word of testimony spoken in the context of deeds of mercy and justice.[19]

The efforts in theological recovery turned for resources to the theological lore of the UCC. The "ancient creeds" and the Reformation confessions and covenants were earlier attempts to clarify the identity of the Christian faith in times when "the world," in the negative sense, was too much with the church. Cultural trends in the first five hundred years and in the sixteenth and seventeenth centuries pressed our forebears to underscore the essentials in danger of erosion—the Trinity, the Person of

Christ, justification by faith, the sovereignty of God. Attention to this and subsequent theological ancestry now takes a dramatic step forward in our Church in the seven volume series of formative UCC theological texts, *The Living Theological Heritage of the United Church of Christ.* As with the Word/World commitments, so in the Word/Church accents, being attentive means attention to the Community's tradition and the world's conditions as the Church listens for the Word in Scripture.

## THE PARTNERSHIP OF WORLD AND CHURCH

Recurring UCC controversies demonstrate how difficult attentiveness to the Word in both spheres, in fact, is. Word/World advocates are sometimes tempted to interpret determined efforts to affirm Word/Church as a retreat from their own concerns. Word/Church partisans sometimes treat Word/World actions as a defection from Word/Church premises. Indeed, the polemics of and tendency within each camp may produce points of view in which the Word does get reduced to either the world's issues and ideologies, values and agendas, or to the church's inward-looking preoccupations. When this kind of reductionism happens, the Word-in-the-world or the Word-in-the-church may have to become bold and the other bashful, as indeed happened in the foreground emphases of 1964 and 1984.

The challenge to our Church continues to be that of living up to its name, the *United* Church of Christ, an ecumenical exemplar that strives to embody the wholeness of the gospel. To that end, the unifying framework of the Preamble to our Constitution has served us well in the past. And it can prepare us in our own time to be attentive to the one Word which we must trust and obey in life and in death.

## NOTES

1. "The Theological Declaration of Barmen," in Arthur Cochrane, *The Church's Confession Under Hitler* (Philadelphia: Westminster Press, 1962), pp. 237–242.

2. Preamble, UCC Constitution.

3. "Theses Bernenses. AD I" in Philip Schaff, *The Creeds of Christendom,* Vol. III (Grand Rapids: Baker Book House, 1966), p. 208.

4. Constitution, IV, 8, 9;VI, 14.

5. For a summary of these last four years of dialogue and proposal for "church fellowship" among the Evangelical Lutheran Church in America, the Reformed Church in America, the Presbyterian Church (U.S.A), and the UCC see *A Common Calling: the Witness of Reformation Churches in North America Today,* K.F. Nickle and T. Lull, eds. (Minneapolis: Augsburg Fortress, 1993).

6. For a survey of the range of subtypes in each major category see the writer's *The Christian Story, Authority: Scripture in the Church for the World.* (Grand Rapids: Eerdmans, 1987), pp. 60–156.

7. As in *Baptism, Eucharist and Ministry,* Faith and Order Paper no. 111 (Geneva: WCC, 1982) and behind it *The Bible: Its Authority and Interpretation in Ecumenical Movement,* Ellen Flesseman-van Leer, ed. Faith and Order Paper no. 99 (Geneva: WCC, 1980).

8. *The COCU Consensus: In Quest of a Church of Christ Uniting,* edited by G.F. Moede (Princeton: The Consultation on Church Unity, 1984), especially pp. 15–21, 29–33.

9. For example, James E. Andrews and Joseph A. Burgess, editors, *An Invitation to Action* (Philadelphia: Fortress Press, 1984), pp. 1–7; *A Common Calling, op. cit., passim.*

10. "II. Faith," *Basis of Union of the Congregational Christian Churches and the Evangelical and Reformed Church with the Interpretations.*

11. Williston Walker, *The Creeds and Platforms of Congregationalism,* new Introduction by Beth Nordbeck (New York: The Pilgrim Press, 1992).

12. Constitution, Article IV, 11.

13. See Frederick R. Trost, "'If Thou But Suffer God to Guide Thee': Reflections on the Evangelical Synod of the Northwest," 125th Annual Meeting of the Evangelical and Reformed Historical Society, St. Paul's Church, Oct. 16, 1993. Mimeograph, especially pp. 9–11.

14. Are the ecumenical texts and Reformation confessions only the products of "Dead White Males"? Ethnic and feminist scholars have found much "hidden history" in the Scripture written by men. We are beginning to discover the same in the historic traditions of Christianity. If classical Christian teaching is, as historians claim, "theology from below" or *consensus fidelium*—the consensus of faithful women and men at prayer, work and witness *later* cast into official formulas—then the judgment of early church councils and later Reformation synods is much more than the opinions of those present. The Holy Spirit has a way of using "the weak things of this world" (I Cor. 1:28) for larger ends.

15. See Nicholas Wolterstorff's description of this tradition that has from Genevan beginnings held that Christ is Lord of the secular as well as the ecclesial realm and calls the Church to bear witness therein. *When Justice and Peace Embrace,* (Grand Rapids: Eerdmans, 1983).

16. Our Statement of Faith is itself a form of doxology. See the writer's "Theology and Forms of Confession," in *Encounter,* Vol. 4, No. 1, (Winter, 1980), pp. 37–52, chapter 2 in this book and "Christian Doctrine in the United Church of Christ," *Theology and Identity,* D.L. Johnson and C. Hambrick-Stowe, eds. (New York: The Pilgrim Press, 1990), pp. 139–151.

17. See Roger Shinn's excellent *Confessing Our Faith: An Interpretation of the Statement of Faith of the United Church of Christ,* (New York: The Pilgrim Press, 1990), p. 3–32 and *passim.*

18. For more details, see the writer's "Theological Soul-Searching in the United Church of Christ," *Midstream,* Vol. XXIV, No. 2 (April, 1985), pp. 155–164, also as chapter 18 of this book.

19. For a period in the early 1970s, the UCC had no evangelism secretary. At a 1972 BHM Deering conference, a group of pastors and missioners issued a "word-in-deed" evangelism manifesto that shaped the subsequent grassroots effort and laid the groundwork for reestablishing a department of evangelism. See E.E. Powers, *Signs of Shalom* (Philadelphia: United Church Press, 1973), pp. 56–57.

"Listening for the Word," *New Conversations,* Vol. 16, No. 2 (Summer 1994), 5–15. Used by permission.

CHAPTER 4

# The Confessional Heritage of the United Church of Christ

WHICH DENOMINATION PUBLISHED a seven volume series on its "confessional heritage"? The only one attempting such an ambitious project? The United Church of Christ. There is an irony here. The UCC is regularly accused of having no theology, and not paying attention to its heritage! Isn't it "the social justice Church," all "doing" and no "doctrine"? Of course, there is enough truth in the indictment to prompt a Lancaster meeting of the Confessing Christ movement on this subject for which this paper was written. The charge may also explain the industrious seven volume series, *The Living Theological Heritage of the United Church of Christ.*

*Why* is it important for the UCC to know its confessional heritage? *What* is a confessional heritage? *What* is the UCC confessional heritage? *How* can we honor and use it? We turn to these key questions.

## WHY IS IT IMPORTANT FOR THE UCC TO KNOW ITS CONFESSIONAL HERITAGE?

Amnesia is loss of memory about personal identity. A person so afflicted does not know who he or she is. Theological amnesia is a comparable loss of memory and identity. Churches sometimes forget who they are. Absent such self-identity, they are prey to all the forces current in their culture, "blown about by every wind of doctrine." To change the figure, they become chameleon-like, taking on the coloration of their environment.

We have a dramatic example of how this happens in the Germany of the 1930s. Establishment churches began to succumb to the blood and soil philosophy of Adolf Hitler. "*German* Christianity" became the byword, making its way into preaching, teaching, worship and confirmation training, with self-identified "German Christians" taking leadership positions. But then a counter-movement was born, the "Confessing Church," holding a synod in the city of Barmen in 1934 and issuing the famous Barmen Declaration. Consider a few of its sentences:

> The inviolable foundation of the German Evangelical Church is the gospel of Jesus Christ as it is attested for us in Holy Scripture and brought to light again in the Confessions of the Reformation. . . . This Confession is grievously imperiled . . . by the teaching methods and actions of the ruling party of the "German Christians". . .(II, para 1,3). . . . Jesus Christ…is the one Word which we have to hear and which we have to trust and obey in life and in death (II, para 7). . . . The Confessional Synod calls upon the congregations to range themselves behind it in prayer, and to steadfastly gather around those pastors and teachers who are loyal to the Confessions (I, para 2) and "reject [the temptation] to abandon . . . its message . . . to prevailing ideological and political convictions" (II, para 14).

Here was Barmen medicine, administered for the sickness of confessional amnesia. Remember who you are! And so resist the powers of evil! We do not face such a Hitler-scale peril in our own time and place. However, Barmen reminds us how easy it is for the church to become chameleon-like in any time and place when it forgets its defining "confession." Know who you are so you will not be seduced by the "prevailing ideological and political convictions."

There are other reasons for retrieving that corporate memory. One of them is the influx today of new people into UCC churches. Do they know who we are? I am thinking not only of the folk transferring from other denominations, or coming from no Christian tradition, but the upcoming generation—the children who gather each Sunday in the chancel to hear the children's sermon, the confirmands, the church school students. Do they hear about the heritage that makes us who we are?

And another reason: do we in the UCC know enough about our own distinctive lineage—the things that make us different from the Lutherans down the block, the Methodists around the corner, the "Bible church" on the edge of town—so that we can share with them the special charism given to us ... and also receive from them what we might have to learn from *their* charism? 1 Cor. 12 tells us that we need one another to make the full Body of Christ, knowing that the eye cannot say to the hand "I have no need of you."

Yet again, whether we recognize it or not, UCC congregations have a heritage right there in front of their noses—in the hymns we sing, the ways we pray, the church architecture and stained glass windows that surrounds us, the decisions we make, the deeds we do, the very "church air" we breathe. We should know why it is there and what it means.

And most of all, we should know that confessional heritage simply because, by our presence in the midst of it, we have declared that it is true.

## WHAT IS A CONFESSIONAL HERITAGE?

What is it, this "confessional heritage"? What is a "confession of faith"? According to the dictionary: "the avowal of belief in the doctrines of a particular faith."[1] For Christians, such a confession of faith is *corporate*. The community that makes it is usually a larger body of believers.[2] The Reformed confessions of the sixteenth century were made by Reformed bodies in Germany, Switzerland, France, and Scotland. Lutheran Churches made their own about the same time. Even presumed nonconfessional groups have developed their confessions. The Anabaptists of the same century have their Schleithheim Confession. The Congregationalists in the 17th century put forward in England their Savoy Declaration, a *"Confession of the Faith. . . . the substance of the same common salvation, or unity of their faith...joyned in the same minde, and in the same judgement,"*[3] based largely on the Westminster Confession of Faith.

While the term "confession" in Protestantism has been associated with polemics vis a vis Roman Catholics or other Protestants, a corporate statement can be a church-wide, *ecumenical* declaration. The ecumenical creeds of Christendom are such, notably the Apostles and the Nicene. Another cross-denominational confession is the earlier-cited Barmen Declaration made by Reformed, Lutheran and United

Churches in Germany. Its significance has made it a treasure for the wider Christian community, and a model for *status confessionis,* the time when the very gospel is threatened by the church's cultural captivity and a defining stand must be taken.

While confessions can grow out of polemics, they also come to be as pedagogy, nurturing members of the church in the essentials of the faith. In that sense a catechism is a vital part of a confessional heritage. So, too, is a "statement of faith," as in the UCC Statement of Faith which reminds us ever and again of our central convictions.

Confessions of one sort or another, especially brief ones, are often lodged in the act of worship. In that location, Christians remind themselves before God, ever and again, who they are, offering up their fundamental identity in praise to God, especially so in "the innermost sanctuary of the whole Christian worship," the Eucharist.

What is the weight of a confession, its authority? Here traditions differ. In tightly connectional Churches, confessions are considered unalterable and binding on all constituents. "This is who we are, take it or leave it. Say it and you are in, don't subscribe and you are out." Often they are part of the Constitution of a Church to which pastors, seminary professors, and new church members swear allegiance. Sanctions are deployed when people step out of line.

There is another way to treat them. Consider what Karl Barth had to say about our Reformed confessional heritage:

> There are documentary statements of [our] beliefs . . . but . . . our fathers had good reason for leaving us *no* Augsburg Confession authentically interpreting the word of God, *no* Formula of Concord, *no* "Symbolic Books" which might later, like the Lutheran, come to possess the odor of sanctity. . . . It *may* be our doctrinal task to make a careful revision of the theology of Geneva or the Heidelberg Catechism or of the Synod of Dort or . . . it may be our task to draw up a new creed. . . .[4]

Barth was profoundly respectful of the Heidelberg Catechism, the Reformed confessions, the ancient creeds, citing them throughout his writings and insisting that subsequent theology should build on them. And it was Barth who drafted the Barmen confession, contextually new but appealing to its forebears. The difference in the way he treated the confessional heritage was a reflection of his tradition. Reformed folk stress that God is sovereign over all our puny attempts to witness to the truth. We accent the divine majesty, acknowledging that our confessions are all short of perfection, in need of restatement and reinterpretation in the light of fresh challenges to the faith. *Semper reformanda,* always re-forming, is the watchword of a tradition that calls itself "reformed."

The temptation of this kind of tradition is to so stress this note of re-form and change that the baby gets thrown out with the bathwater. We become mesmerized by the new and different. Here we have things to learn from the Lutherans, as acknowledged in the language of "mutual affirmation and mutual admonition" in the 1997 Formula of Agreement. Lutherans have great respect for the past. Don't tamper with that 1530 Augsburg Confession as in the slightly altered version of 1540! And they have things to learn from us who bring a witness to the importance of restating the faith for the ears of the present.[5] Taking both into account, we need to retrieve what our forebears had to say about our identity so we can live out of that memory as we confront new times.

Contributing to the difference between a rigid confessional*ism* and the honoring of a confessional heritage under the divine sovereignty is the matter of polity, church governance. For example, in a congregation-al polity, or in the UCC's mixed presbyteral-congregational polity "—covenantal congregationalism" as it is sometimes called—final doctrinal decisions *for* congregations are vested *in* congregations (Article V, para-graph 18 of the newly revised UCC Constitution continuing the much commented-on Article IV, paragraph 15 of the earlier version), with larger corporate Church decisions to be "held in highest regard" and taken under advisement (Article V, paragraphs 17 and 19 surrounding 16, as 14 and 16 did the former 15). The Church-wide corporate confes-sions are, therefore, "testimonies, not tests" in the venerable language of the *Basis of Union* of the E&R and CC Churches, a phrase much quot-ed but not always understood. The confessional heritage of the UCC found, for example, in such corporate resources cited in the UCC *Book of Worship* (Apostles and Nicene Creeds, UCC Statement of Faith, the Kansas City Statement of Faith) are testimonies of the UCC-at-large to the world beyond of the pattern of belief to be found among us. They are also testimonies to its congregations about their heritage. Each congregation is counseled to attend to that lore in setting up its own standards for membership. Such confessional testimony, while not binding on its members in the same way as a confessional "test" is in more centrally organized Churches, is very serious business.

A testimonial view of confessions is serious business in ecumenical affairs. The Lutherans, Presbyterians, and Reformed Church in America take us at our word when we point to our Constitution, Statement of Faith and other corporate theological declarations as definitive of who we are. So we said in the negotiations with them, as in the section on the confessional tradition of the UCC in the document on which the 1997 Formula of Agreement is based.[6]

One of the ironies of our time is that the creeds, confessions and statements of faith of other Christian communions that hold them to be authoritatively binding—Roman Catholic, Lutheran, Episcopal, Methodist—often *function* today as testimonies rather than tests, much to the consternation of their hierarchies. Thus, Cardinal Ratzinger is dismayed by trends of independence in his own Church that he sees as a kind of neo-congregationalism.[7] And as disputes current in other top-down denominations reveal, presumably binding creeds, confessions and denominational rules are often contested or ignored by members. What a chance for the UCC to show how to honor a confessional heritage in a covenantal congregational polity without that heritage falling prey to rigidity or to the "odor of sanctity"! But we have to *know* that confessional heritage if we are going to make a case for how it can be creatively deployed.

## WHAT IS THE UCC CONFESSIONAL HERITAGE?

An interesting agreement was reached between the CC and E&R Churches when the UCC was born. It appeared in the "Interpretations of the Basis of Union":

> In consummating this union [the Churches] are uniting without break in their historic continuities.[8]

This agreement is carried over into the present UCC Constitution:

> Congregational Christian Churches and the Evangelical and Reformed Churches unite in the United Church of Christ without break in their respective historic continuities and traditions[9]

As applied to the subject at hand, this means that the confessional heritage of the two uniting Churches is expected to continue. Up North where I live, the Congregational lineage is very much in evidence. "Down South," in Pennsylvania, the E&R heritage lives on. Both are authorized to do so out of UCC respect for "historic continuities."

It would be illuminating to know how that plays out in Pennsylvania. My guess is that the Heidelberg Catechism is still alive and well in many places. One evidence of that is my 1980 copy of the 1962 United Church Press translation of the Heidelberg Catechism. It was in its 11th printing back then, and must have had many reprints in the years since. The *Heidelberg Catechism* is a *present* gift to the UCC from the E&R wing of the Church. It is recognized as such in a variety of ways: reproduced on the UCC Web site; active as background to a Pennsylvania Confessing Christ catechetical project, "Pass Along the Faith"; cited from time to time, authoritatively, in Confessing Christ events, in annual Craigville Colloquies and in Mercersburg Society meetings and publications; quoted by heart by UCC president John Thomas when he appeared as our then ecumenical officer before the ELCA assembly in 1997 about to vote on the Formula of Agreement (the first question and answer); printed in full in Volume 2 of *The Living Theological Heritage* series, with a Preface to the English edition appearing in Volume 3; used as a continuing resource in confirmation training in many UCC congregations. The *Heidelberg Catechism* is in the memory bank of the UCC, reminding us of who we are.

There is more from that historic continuity with E&R roots, reflected in the statement of the committee that produced *The Faith We Proclaim,* a book articulating in 1960 what the E&R confessional heritage brought to the UCC:

> Its doctrines are those expressed in the ancient creeds—the Apostles', the Nicene, the Chalcedonian, the Athanasian, together with the

Augsburg Confession, Luther's Catechism and the Heidelberg Catechism. These creeds are revered as conformable to the biblical teaching and historic expressions of Christian faith. The creeds and confessional books are not substitutes for the Bible; their authority is dependent on the Bible. They are understood as the response of a faithful and devout church to God's revelation. [10]

The E&R authors have listed with specificity what the Preamble to the UCC Constitution speaks of in more general terms when it says that the UCC

claims as its own the faith of the historic Church expressed in the ancient creeds and reclaimed in the basic insights of the Protestant Reformers.[11]

And the Basis of Union refers to as

The faith . . . expressed in the ecumenical creeds [and] the evangelical confessions of the Reformation. [12]

The authors of *The Faith We Proclaim* had in mind in the latter part of that quotation the three confessions stipulated in the old E&R Constitution —the *Heidelberg Catechism,* the Augsburg Confession, and Luther's Small Catechism, asserting that where disagreement might occur, let Scripture decide. In the former part, they mix together the two ecumenical creeds which the *Preamble* and the *Basis of Union* presuppose, Apostles' and Nicene, and the more technical theological statements that are part of our history but not given the same kind of confessional status, the Definition of Chalcedon and the Athanasian Creed. Interestingly, the ELCA includes the Athanasian Creed in its doctrinal corpus, and in the 1980s re-ordained an Orthodox priest and a UCC pastor entering that denomination because their previous clergy status had not included subscription to it. This was before the adoption of the 1997 Formula of Agreement (FOA). Of course, even after it, a UCC pastor seeking ministry in the ELCA still has to subscribe to the Athanasian Creed, but would not be required to be re-ordained. Incidentally, the Athanasian

Creed is included in Volume 1 of the UCC's *Living Theological Heritage*.[13]

What about the *other* historic wing of the UCC, the Congregational-Christian Churches and their confessional heritage? All in the UCC, former E&Rs included, are called to know, to honor, to engage, and to reinterpret it in this time and place. Some of it has already been referenced, as the CC side of the Church historically also affirmed the ecumenical symbols, the *Pilgrim Hymnal* including the Apostles' and Nicene Creeds.[14] For a full-scale account of "the creeds and platform of Congregationalism," we have Williston Walker to thank, with Douglas Horton introducing them, and more recently Beth Nordbeck with a new introduction to the same important volume. This work includes such formative statements as The First Confession of the London-Amsterdam Church of 1589, the Salem Covenant of 1633, the Cambridge Platform of 1648 (presupposing the Westminster Confession), the already-mentioned Savoy Declaration (again building on the Westminster Confession), the Burial Hill Declaration of 1865, and the Creed of 1883. Not included there, but also a piece of Congregational heritage is the 1913 Kansas City Statement, identified by its contemporaries as a "confession," and important enough to be included in the UCC *Book of Worship*.[15]

When it comes to catechisms, the Congregational heritage of the UCC brims with them: the Salem catechisms that came out from 1641 to 1648, the Boston catechisms from 1642 to 1669, the Ipswich Catechism of 1648, the New Haven Catechism of 1659, the Andover Catechism of 1738, the Indian Catechisms 1654 to 1795, the famous New England Primer with its Apostles' Creed and Catechism, the Teachers Catechism "in accordance with the Congregational Creed of 1883)," and on and on. Who said Congregationalism is not a creedal, catechetical, or confessional tradition?

Well, where does the "Christian connection" and its heritage come in? Isn't this an anti-confessional lineage in our UCC? Not exactly. In fact, the high Christology it espoused, along with that of Barmen, may well account for the leading sentences in the Preamble of the UCC Constitution:

> The United Church of Christ acknowledges as its sole Head, Jesus Christ, Son of God and Savior. It acknowledges as kindred in Christ all who share in this confession.[16]

Note, the word "confession" associated with Christ, "the sole Head" and one Word we have to trust and obey in life and in death. Hence, the very name of this communion, the United Church of *Christ*. Is all this connected to the "no creed but Christ" of the Christian tradition? If you read the sentence in question in light of the rest of the paragraph of the Preamble, it is clear that an either-or is not intended, for "the ancient creeds . . . and the insights of the Protestant reformers" flesh out the meaning of confessing "Christ," as does the secondary clause, "Son of God and Savior" that has reference in technical terms to the Person of Christ and the Work of Christ. All four of our confessional heritages must be kept together in a Church that prides itself on being "united and uniting."

In detailing the confessions that are part of the UCC heritage I've said little about their actual content. One way to summarize such is to turn to their encapsulation in the more recent official documents of our confessional heritage, the *Basis of Union,* the UCC Statement of Faith and the theological Preamble of the UCC Constitution.

When the Church that brought together four streams of the Reformation was launched, its *Basis of Union* set out what it called a "confession . . . embodying those things most surely believed and taught among us"[17] which laid out the key themes to be formulated in an "ampler statement." That "ampler statement" came to be as the 1959 United Church of Christ Statement of Faith. Following the confessional language of the Basis, Roger Shinn, its principal drafter, gives an account of its origins and meaning in *Confessing Our Faith.*[18] In that important work, he speaks of "our faith" in the language of narrative, "the Great Story . . . the story of God, creation . . . history . . . hope."[19] The Statement of Faith is the telling of the Great Story, from creation to consummation. Shinn notes that the Statement "follows the lead of the biblical declarations, rather than the typical creeds of later Christian history. It abandons the triadic form (although keeping the testimony to Father, Son, and Holy Spirit)[20] and returns to the kerygmatic account of the deeds of God."[21] While it is true that the form of the Statement, as narrative, is different than the creeds, it is also the case that the creeds themselves have a narrative-like quality, the form being the drama of the theater rather than story of literature. Thus the three paragraphs of the Apostles' and Nicene creeds can be understood as acts in a trinitarian drama, each with its different scenes. In technical terms, the creeds are explicitly the economic Trinity, the three great missions of God, and implicitly, the ontological Trinity, a declaration of who God is in the inner triune being of Father, Son, and Spirit.

Our contemporary Statement of Faith takes up the content of the ancient creeds and also the doctrinal loci of the Reformation confessions and covenants: creation, fall, covenant, the Person and Work of Christ, the church and its mission, salvation and consummation. Of course, we need the specifics of the confessional heritage to fill out the picture, and that it is why it is important to steep ourselves in this background in order better to understand the Story we tell today.

The Preamble of the UCC Constitution plays a vital role in summing up aspects of our confessional heritage, not so much in the specifics of doctrine, although it makes its strong christological point in the affirmation of Christ as "Son of God and Savior." The Preamble is the formulation of the UCC concept of theological authority. It states what authorizes UCC teaching, where it goes to discern what is so about God, Christ, the church, salvation and consummation. The preamblic concept of authority can be portrayed by a series of concentric circles. At the center of authority is Jesus Christ, "the sole Head" language reflecting the background Barmen image of the one Word of God which we have to hear, and which we have to trust and obey in life and in death." Where do we find the one Word? The Preamble says the UCC "looks to the Word of God in the Scriptures…" again echoing Barmen's reference to Christ "as he is attested for us in Holy Scripture." Christ stands at the *center* of the biblical *source,* the inner ring of authority. But Scripture, read christologically, is held in the hands of the church. The church and its tradition are the second ring out, a *resource* for the hearing the Word and interpreting the Scripture. Here is the place of the confessional heritage of the UCC that sets forth "the faith of the historic Church expressed in the ancient creeds and reclaimed in the basic insights of the Protestant Reformers." The third circle of authority is referenced in the Preamble as "the responsibility of the Church in each generation to make this faith its own in reality of worship, in honesty of thought and expression and in purity of heart before God." Thus the contemporary setting must be taken into account for the contemporizing of the heritage. Here is the UCC's commitment to restating and reinterpreting the received texts in ever-new contexts. *Semper reformanda* is the watchword of the Reformed tradition, always reforming the church and its inheritance in the light of new occasions and new duties. Note: the Preamble is very clear that it is "this faith," the "faith of the historic Church," that is the guide for all attempts at contemporary relevance, not something we make up from the fashions and ideologies of the hour. The UCC Statement of Faith is a model for how this is done, translating into narrative terms with ecumenical and justice import the historic faith of the church.

## HOW DO WE HONOR AND MAKE USE OF OUR CONFESSIONAL HERITAGE

Not to steep a congregation in both the story and its confessional background is to impoverish it, and to let it fall prey to amnesia. How do we help it sharpen its memory so it can be what it is? Here are some suggestions.

From the beginnings of Christian history, worship was the bearer of the gospel for the Christian community, as it was for its Jewish forebears. So it can still be. As a pastor in Pittsburgh for ten years, never a Sunday went by without the Apostles' Creed, or a Eucharist without the Nicene Creed. That was before the Statement of Faith and in the E&R ethos. But it is still true if we "go by the book," for the UCC *Book of Worship* prescribes an "Affirmation of Faith" for those services, with choices suggested among our Statement of Faith and the historic creeds. And why not the same in daily worship? The Confessing Christ movement in the UCC has a daily prayer discipline which suggests the daily use of an affirmation of faith in its liturgy.

Of course, Sunday worship, as such, especially so the Eucharist is a teaching moment for the UCC confessional heritage. The hymns carry it forward; the prayers do also; so does the confession of sin and assurance of pardon; every sermon is a chance to tell the Story, or parts thereof. As Mercersburg testifies, the Eucharist is the high moment of living into the faith. The eucharistic prayer *is* immersion in the sacred Story, and all parts of that service point to one or another classical teaching.

Baptism, as well, is the time for confessing the faith, and its liturgy lives out of the Great Narrative.

Naturally, the ancient and present church communicates its confessional lore in teaching as well as in worship. UCC forebears in Pennsylvania made the *Heidelberg Catechism* an integral part of confirmation. Mid-western counterparts in the E tradition had Luther's Small Catechism or their own Evangelical Catechism. Congregational churches in New England had a rich assortment of catechisms and covenants into which its young were introduced. While we have different ways of doing it today, why not at the very least acquaint youth with their confessional heritage? Maybe memorize the first question and answer of Heidelberg as counterpoint to heads filled with the latest rock lyrics? Of course, adults need to be familiarized with their confessional memory bank as well, in church school classes and other educational venues, and of course in preaching. There is no better resource for all this than *The Living Theological Heritage* in one's church library.

The heritage, as we have noted, is also carried on by the reinterpretation of it in our own time and place, the church "making this faith its own ... in each generation." It can happen in a variety of venues. In congregations, for one. The Congregational tradition in the UCC does it this way, with its local church covenants. The Salem Covenant is an early example, appearing in the UCC *Book of Worship*. We should keep in mind that Congregational local church covenants always presupposed the larger corporate ones, the ancient creeds, the Cambridge Platform, the Savoy Declaration. And now in many congregations they often refer back to the Statement of Faith and other confessions of the Church-at-large. Congregations of E&R lineage that state their faith tend to make specific reference to these larger confessions. St. Andrew, Lancaster has given us a model of that in its new "A Book of Confessions," compiled under the leadership of Pastor Robert Hunsicker.[23] It includes, among other things, the Apostles' and Nicene Creeds, parts of the Barmen Declaration, key questions and answers from the Heidelberg Catechism, the 1997 Declaration of Debrecen from the World Alliance of Reformed Churches, the UCC Statement of Faith, a UCC Statement of Mission, and its own congregational Mission Statement that incorporates the Preamble to the UCC Constitution.

Restatement and reinterpretation can happen at the supra-local level. Recent efforts include the new Presbyterian Catechism in three forms, for children, confirmands and adults, an excellent resource for UCC congregations. In the UCC tradition itself, we have the "Pass Along the Faith" project just completed by the Pennsylvania centers of Confessing Christ, Deborah Rahn Clemens, key facilitator along with a hard-working committee. Then too, there are ecumenical resources. The *COCU Consensus* is a confession of sorts, developed by the nine denominations soon to declare themselves in a new covenantal relationship after over 30 years of dialogue, the UCC a key member of the same. The 1997 Formula of Agreement that brings the Evangelical Lutheran Church in America, the Presbyterian Church, USA, the Reformed Church in America and the United Church of Christ into full communion cites the theological agreements set forth in *Invitation to Action* as foundational to the signing.[24]

When you add all this up . . . when you *pile* all this up [heavy volumes of the *Living Theological Heritage,* the venerable creeds of classical faith and the formative texts of both the E&R and the CC traditions, the narrative testimonies the Statement of Faith and Basis of Union, the covenants and confessions of local congregations past and present, the Preamble to the Constitution], what a marvelous confessional heritage! To forget it is to lose our memory, and with it, our identity. To remember it is to be the body of Christ we are called to be, complete with the theological "mind of Christ" that knows who we are and what we must do.

## NOTES

1. "Confession," meaning 6, *The American Heritage Dictionary of the English Language* (New York: American Publishing Co., 1973), 279.

2. It can be the local church, as well, as in congregational polity.

3. Williston Walker, editor, *Creeds and Platforms of Congregationalism* (Boston: Pilgrim Press, 1960, 1969), 354.

4. Karl Barth, *The Word of God and the Word of Man,* trans. Douglas Horton (Boston: The Pilgrim Press, 1928), 229, 230.

5. This is the point of the volume by Michael Root and Gabriel Fackre, *Affirmations and Admonitions: Lutheran Decisions and Dialogue with Reformed Episcopal and Roman Catholic Churches* (Grand Rapids: Eerdmans Pub. Co., 1998).

6. See "Reformed Heritage and Lutheran Connections in the Life of the UCC," *A Common Calling: The Witness of Our Reformation Churches in North America Today,* Keith F. Nickle and Timothy F. Lull, eds. (Minneapolis: Augsburg Fortress, 1993), 75–80.

7. See Joseph Cardinal Ratzinger and Vittorrio Messori, *The Ratzinger Report,* trans. Salvator Attanasio and Graham Harrison (San Francisco: Ignatius Press, 1986), 155–158.

8. "The Basis of Union of the Congregational Christian Churches and the Evangelical and Reformed Church with the Interpretations," in Louis H. Gunnemann, *The Shaping of the United Church of Christ: An Essay in the History of American Christianity* (New York: United Church Press, 1977), 224.

9. Article V, paragraph 13.

10. Elmer F. J. Arndt, *The Faith We Proclaim: The Doctrinal Viewpoint Generally Prevailing in the Evangelical and Reformed Church* (Philadelphia: Christian Education Press, 1960), 6.

11. "Preamble, Para 2, The Constitution of the United Church of Christ.

12. "The Faith," Basis of Union in The Shaping of the United Church of Christ *op. cit.,* 208.

13. "The Athanasian Creed," The Living Theological Heritage· Of the United Church of Christ Vol. 1, Reinhard Ulrich, editor (Cleveland: The Pilgrim Press), 242–245. Editor Ulrich notes that "Puritan Richard Baxter deemed it the best thing ever written on the Trinity."

14. "Affirmations of Faith," Pilgrim Hymnal (Boston: Pilgrim Press, 1968), 511–512.

15. See Gabriel Fackre, "The Kansas City Statement as a Confession of Faith," Bulletin of the Congregational Library Vol. 34, No. 3 (Spring/Summer, 1988), 5–12.

16. Preamble, 2.

17. of Union, in *The Shaping of the United Church of Christ op cit.,* 208.

18. Roger Shinn, *Confessing Our Faith: An Interpretation of the Statement of Faith of the United Church of Christ* (New York: The Pilgrim Press, 1990).

19. Ibid, 3.

20. Note this trinitarian reference in the UCC Constitution, Article V, paragraph 10: "A Local Church is composed of persons who, believing in God as Heavenly Father, and accepting Jesus Christ as Lord and Savior, and depending on the guidance of the Holy Spirit, are organized for Christian worship, for the furtherance of Christian fellowship, and for the ongoing work of Christian witness."

21. Ibid, 17.

22. For a review of the specific doctrinal refrains that run through the Statement of Faith, the Faith section of the Basis of Union and the Preamble to the UCC Constitution, in the light of current issues, see the writer's "UCC Theological Basics: An Interpretation," in *How Shall We Sing the Lord's Song?* Richard

Christensen, ed. (Pittsburgh: Pickwick Press, 1997), 5–18. In more detail the narrative theme is developed in Gabriel Fackre, *The Christian Story: A Narrative Interpretation of Christian Doctrine,* Vol. 1, Third Edition (Grand Rapids: Wm. B. Eerdmans Pub. Co., 1996).

23. *A Book of Confessions,* St Andrew Church of the United Church of Christ, Lancaster, Pennsylvania, January, 2001.

24. See James E. Andrews and Joseph A. Burgess, eds., *An Invitation to Action: The Lutheran-Reformed Dialogue,* Series III, 1981–1983 (Philadelphia: Fortress Press, 1984), 2–3. Fourteen points are cited, among which are included: "both Lutheran and Reformed traditions . . . affirm themselves a living part of the church catholic; confess the Apostles' and Nicene Creeds; affirm the doctrine of justification by faith as fundamental; affirm the unique and final authority of Holy Scriptures in the church; affirm the real presence of Christ in the Lord's Supper . . . [to] affirm the church must be open to further growth and reformation." The General Synod of the UCC adopted the proposals of *An Invitation to Action* in 1989, and reaffirmed them in the FOA at the General Synod of 1997.

This is the substance of a presentation given at a Confessing Christ meeting in the Church of the Apostles, Lancaster, Pennsylvania, March 23, 2001. "The Confessional Heritage of the United Church of Christ," New Mercersburg Review, No. XXVIII (Spring 2001), 4–19. Used by permission.

## CHAPTER 5

# The UCC's Living Theological Heritage

In 1989, The United Church of Christ launched a seven volume series of documents from its doctrinal lineage. Growing out of the theological ferment in the United Church of Christ of that time, it was conceived by church leaders Frederick Trost and Barbara Brown Zikmund (co-editors of volume seven) and funded by the United Church Board for Homeland Ministries. This monumental venture of 5500 pages includes not only a heritage of creeds, confessions, catechisms, and covenants, but also the hymns, prayers, liturgies, tracts, letters, diary entries, journal articles, court case papers, protest declarations and other documents of a denomination that traces its ancestry to both European and English Reformations. These are the creedal sources and medieval pieties still at work in its present *Book of Worship* and hymnody. And additionally through the modern missionary, ecumenical, and activist eras that shape its present life. Passing reference will also be made here to volume seven.

An editorial board met yearly giving input and reviewing the work of the editors of each volume, historians and theologians who provide introductory essays to their volumes and prefatory comments to each entry. The result of their work and the endeavor itself bespeak an irony that should not be lost on this Church's critics. Sometimes portrayed as without theological interest or substance, the UCC is the only denomination in the country to have laid out in such detail the theological heritage that makes it what it is, warts and all.

The very name of the denomination is a clue to the dominant accent of the volumes, a Church committed to "united and uniting," its

Kampfbegriff and the title of its concluding volume. Not by chance, therefore, is the "Mercersburg theology" of John Williamson Nevin and Phillip Schaff of the German Reformed Church threaded through three of the volumes with sections from their key writings and those of their heirs, a movement that helped to plant the seeds of ecumenism in North America. Their "evangelical Catholicism" envisioned the church of Peter (Rome/"hope") and the church of Paul (the Reformation/"faith") moving someday to the Church of John (a united church catholic/" love"). A small portent of such is the confluence in 1957 of four diverse traditions within "the church of Paul," constituting the present UCC. Hence the formative documents of the German Reformed Church, the Evangelical Synod of North America (then united as the Evangelical and Reformed Church), the Congregational and "Christian" Churches (then also united) that appear in volumes three to six, with their antecedents in volume one that houses major writings and creeds of the Great Tradition ("the church of Peter" and the Fathers of the East) and volume two with the key confessions and catechisms of the magisterial Reformation and also their subsequent reinterpretation in the Puritan tradition formative of the Congregational stream of the UCC, a lineage also documented in volume three.

Mercersburg's influence in all this yes, but striking parallels are to be found in the three other streams. The irenicism of the Lutheran/ Reformed Evangelical Synod of North America is a natural counterpart. Congregationalism, especially in the nineteenth century, had its own history of outreach to other communions, from Episcopalian to Presbyterian. The "Christian Churches" were in their own way in quest for unity, as indicated by the name they chose, one that sought to transcend denominationalism. The centrality of the struggle toward unity is marked in this series by devotion of an entire volume to the subject, volume six's 784 pages edited by Elsabeth Hilke, with a cascade of texts from all four traditions, both national and international, up through key statements of the founders of the UCC, including Douglas Horton, George Richards, Truman Douglass and James Wagner, and also documents of dissent.

For Nevin and Schaff, the ultimate rationale for the unity of the Body of Christ lies in the Person of Christ, an accent that continues in the

Church's name and the christological hermeneutic of the theological Preamble to its Constitution (influenced also by the Barmen Declaration's "one Word, Jesus Christ" wrought out in the years that led up to the UCC's birth in 1957). Volume three, edited by Charles Hambrick-Stowe has key writings from both theologians (excerpts from Schaff's *Principle of Protestantism*, Nevin's *Catholicism,* and *Vindication of Revised Liturgy*) but also includes documents from their opponents such as John H.A. Bomberger, no less committed to the Incarnation, but also accenting the atonement and with it nonliturgical worship. Whatever its dimension, the christological norm is part and parcel of the heritage of the other three uniting traditions as well, as discernible in the *Evangelical Catechism* of the Evangelical Synod of North America, Congregationalism's stress on the divine Person in its separation from Unitarianism in the nineteenth century, and the Christian Church's "No creed but Christ" declaration (one that the documents show presupposed much more doctrine than the slogan suggests). These affirmations scattered through volumes two to six appear in official texts from each tradition and in commentary on them in articles, sections from books, letters, hymns and sermons. Their christological antecedents appear in volume one, "Ancient and Medieval Legacies" edited by Reinhard Ulrich, beginning with the "ancient creeds" cited in the UCC Constitution, Apostles and Nicene, through Theodore of Mopsuestia on the Incarnation, the Chalcedonian formula, Anselm's *Cur Deus Homo?* Julian of Norwich's *God in Christ, Our True Mother* and extracts from similar writings.

The Trinity is another doctrine central to the UCC's historic roots. It appears in volume one in the Rule of Faith in the writings of Irenaeus and Tertullian, the aforementioned ecumenical creeds and trinitarian commentary from Eusebius and Gregory of Nyssa to Augustine and Aquinas, hymns in praise of the triune God and the narrative of the economic Trinity in the Great Eucharistic Prayer from the early church. Also found in this initial volume is a broad range of texts on classical faith from liturgical and sacramental writings by Chrysostom, Paschausius Radbertus, Ratramnus and John Wycliffe, to "praise and prayer" documents from Bernard of Clairvaux, Benedict, Hildegaard of Bingen and Francis of Assisi.

The Trinity continues as part of the core doctrine of the UCC heritage in volume two devoted to the Church's sixteenth century Reformation roots in Germany, Switzerland and the Netherlands, and in the English Reformation. It is joined by characteristic teachings on justification, sanctification, and biblical authority in this work, edited by John Payne. These affirmations appear in confessional documents that include Luther's *Small Catechism,* the *Augsburg Confession* (1530), and the *Heidelberg Catechism* (the three symbols of the Evangelical and Reformed Church), the *Geneva Confession* and the *Schleitheim Confession,* alongside doctrinal statements in the Congregational tradition such as the first 21 chapters of the *Westminster Confession* (assumes in its Cambridge Platform and Savoy Declaration) and the *Principles and Foundations of the Christian Religion* (Henry Jacob). Included also are representative writings from Luther *(The Freedom of a Christian),* Calvin ( "The Law" from the *Institutes of the Christian Religion*), Zwingli's *Sixty-Seven Articles* and William Ames' *The Marrow of Theology.* In this volume, also, a place is given to sacramental and liturgical texts and representative hymnody of the Reformation, such as the Palatinate and Strasbourg liturgies, Luther's hymn, "Out of the depth, I cry to Thee," Calvin's hymn, "For Us Our God is Firm Support," and his Church Prayers and Hymns, sections from the *Book of Common Prayer* in the Puritan stream, John Knox's *The Form of Prayers* and Katherine Schutz Zell's hymnbook *Foreword.* Controversy in the past is not avoided, hence the inclusion of The Marburg Colloquy, separatist Robert Browne's "A Treatise of Reformation without Tarrying for Anie," and Hans Sach's "a Conversation Between an Evangelical Christian and a Lutheran in Which the Offensive Behavior of Some Who Call Themselves Lutherans is Exposed and Admonished in a Brotherly Spirit." Diary entries and letters are also found here reflecting the doctrinal debates of the day.

Trinitarianism became a focal issue in the UCC heritage on the Congregational side in the early nineteenth century with the Unitarian secession marked by a representative document in both volume three, *Colonial and National Beginnings,* edited by Charles Hambrick-Stowe, and volume four, *Consolidation and Expansion,* edited by Elizabeth C. Nordbeck and Lowell H. Zuck, with counterpoint documents as Congregationalism asserted its continuity with classical Christianity in the 1807 to 1808 "Andover Creed" of the first free-standing seminary in the country, separating itself from Unitarian developments at Harvard, the 1865 *Burial Hill Declaration* and its *Creed of 1883*. Both of the latter, however, reflected modifications of an earlier hard-line Puritan Calvinism.

A mix of the reaffirmation, softening and reinterpretation of Calvinism are taken up in volume three, with excerpts from the seventeenth century *Bay Psalm Book* to eighteenth century Great Awakening texts (Jonathan Edwards) and Samuel Hopkins essay on the "New Divinity," on to nineteenth century commentary on the "New Haven Theology" by Nathaniel William Taylor and Horace Bushnell's *Christian Nurture* with accents throughout on the ethical import of doctrine that marks the UCC forebears and its present posture.

Volume four also treats the other three UCC streams in their formative years. The European origins of "The German Evangelicals" are laid out in "the Luther-Reformed merger" of 1817, Pietism's "Six Proposals," the Basel Mission Society's "Announcement," the German Evangelicals' nineteenth century US-based confessional statements and their kin, right up to twentieth century theological ruminations including two early pieces from the UCC's best-known theologian, Reinhold Niebuhr. The "Christian" linkage, now virtually extinct in the present UCC except for African-American congregations in the South, gets 200 pages here, probably because it is so little known to its heirs. Its Methodist and Presbyterian roots are cited, texts showing its distinction from the other like-minded followers of Alexander Campbell, with its key documents on teaching, on the one hand a fervent Biblicism and Pietism, and on the other, a passionate anti-creedalism.

The German Reformed tradition is represented in this volume, as well as in volume three, this time with Philip Schaff's 1863 introduction to the three hundredth anniversary of the *Heidelberg Catechism* and as counterpoint, a 1708 "frontier revival sermon" by Philip Otterbein. A similar tension in its history is marked by two Nevin documents and pieces by Henry Harbaugh and Emmanuel Gerhart representing the incarnational cum sacramental/liturgical themes of Mercersburg theology, and "old Reformed" statements objecting to the former's "Revised Liturgy," and criticizing Mercersburg's "catholicising" tendencies.

In the same volume "newer challenges" begin to be noted, as in the increasing role of women in all four traditions, mission movements in the German Reformed Church and Evangelical Synod of North America, the Congregational-Presbyterian joint efforts in mission, but also their later "abrogation," emerging social justice theologies as in the Congregational *Kansas City Statement of Faith* (1913), and an Evangelical Synod piece by Elmer Arndt on "Industrial Ethics." As in other volumes, hymnody and poetry find their place as expressions of theology as in the Congregational hymns of Timothy Dwight, Washington Gladden and others, and the Hungarian Martyrs moving "Lift Up Your Head, O Ye Martyrs" as part of the Reformed Church in the U.S. legacy.

A prominent feature of the present UCC is its commitment to "mission" as outreach in its double meaning: the ecclesial hand extended to the hurt and forgotten in both social action and social service, as well as the word proclaimed to the unreached. Its antecedents occur in texts found in every volume. Volume one has Pope Gregory's *Mission Work in England,* volume two includes sections from the fifteenth century *The Book of the Craft of Dying* and Thomas A. Kempis' *The Imitation of Christ,* volume three has Jonathan Edwards' on the *Great Awakening* and *Village Hymns* of revivalism by Asahel Nettleton, on the one hand, and Samuel West's sermon on revolution, on the other. Volume four takes up nineteenth century writings on "global mission" and attacks on slavery, as well as the mission to immigrants. The entire volume five edited by Margaret Lambert Bendroth, Lawrence N. Jones, and Robert A. Schneider is devoted to mission as *Outreach and Diversity* including a series of sermons, speeches, and extracts from books on evangelization vis-a-vis global Christianity related to its historic 1812 American Board of Commissioners for Foreign Missions together with "home missions" writings including Congregational texts from its Hawaii mission, China mission, native American and Magyar outreach, the formative documents of the American Missionary Society with its establishment of hundreds of "Freedman's Schools" in the South and five African-American colleges thriving today; the famous Amistad story, Lemuel Hayes' eighteenth century black perspective "Liberty Further Extended," the protest of the "Cherokee removal," and "child labor," Henry Ward Beecher's, "Prayer for a Grieving Nation," up through early twentieth century essays on social justice by such as Washington Gladden, Charles Sheldon and Reinhold and H. Richard Niebuhr. Volume six also includes the outreach dimension, often a catalyst for the ecumenical efforts there detailed.

At every step along the way, documents on the role of women in UCC heritage appear, establishing a trajectory toward its present emphasis: from the narratives of martyrdom of Perpetua and Felicitas, the writings of Julian of Norwich and Catherine of Siena, through sixteenth century diary entries (Lady Margaret Hoby), the seventeenth century meditative poetry of Anne Bradstreet, to nineteenth century essays on "Women's Rights" including "Women's Right to preach the Gospel," the first expression of such being in 1812 in the Christian Connection, followed by Congregational preacher Antoinette Brown's 1849 "Exegesis," the role of women in deaconess movements and overseas and home missions in the German Reformed and the German Evangelical streams, to social service, social action and education involvements in all branches, with notable letters from such as Sarah H. Grimke and Sarah Stanley, and an essay by Hulda Niebuhr.

Running through all these accents in the UCC tradition are two interlocking problematics: the relation of continuity to change and unity to diversity, issues to the fore in the UCC to this day.

The first has to do with the battle-cry of its largely Reformed tradition, *semper reformanda!* . . . the church always called forward and out of captivity to the givens by the sovereign God. The UCC heritage set out in these volumes is a study in responsiveness to the new contexts in which its forebears found themselves. Yet, how to relate to new times and settings and not capitulate to their trends? How does one have a "heritage" that is at the same time "living," holding the two together, as in the title of the series? The volumes are a study in how such was done, and not done, in the past, and thus wisdom for the present and future.

The second poses the question of how this Church and its antecedents embody and espouse unity around core convictions, while at the same time allowing for, and encouraging, a wide-ranging diversity of ecclesial traditions, theological perspectives, racial, ethnic, class, cultural and geographic constituencies. The variety manifest in these volumes made for tension in the past, and continues to do so in the present, as in volume seven, now in the works, will show. However, the UCC is still the only Church in the United States that has brought together in official union four different ecclesial traditions (along with their "hidden histories" of yet further diversity), has managed to avoid schism, and has shown enough commitment to core ecumenical faith to be joined with other mainstream Protestant Churches in multilateral and bilateral "full communion" agreements both here and overseas. The series itself is a demonstration that theology, both unitive and diverse, is a vital part of UCC identity. Is it a model of the "reconciled diversity" and "mutual affirmation and admonition" much talked about these days in ecumenical circles?

These volumes are invaluable for local UCC congregations and pastors, putting at their fingertips the theological heritage of their Church. But the significance of the series is much wider. The general reader and libraries, theological and secular, will find in one or more of the volumes key documents of western church history not otherwise easily accessible. And the church catholic, struggling with the same issues of continuity and change, unity and diversity, can learn from this case study about both their possibilities and pitfalls.

## NOTES

A review by Barbara Brown Zikmund, Series Editor, *The Living Theological Heritage of the United Church of Christ*, Vols. 1–6 (Cleveland: Pilgrim Press, 1995, 1997, 1998, 1999, 2000, 2001) in Pro Ecclesia, Vol. XII, No. 3 (summer, 2003), 368–372. Used by permission.

## CHAPTER 6

# The Kansas City Statement as a Confession of Faith

A Congregational Statement of Faith
*Adopted by the National Council of
Congregational Churches
at Kansas City, Missouri, October 25, 1913*

*Preamble to the New Constitution*

THE CONGREGATIONAL CHURCHES of the United States, by delegates in National Council assembled, reserving all the rights and cherished memories belonging to this organization under its former constitution, and declaring the steadfast allegiance of the churches composing the Council to the faith which our fathers confessed, which from age to age has found its expression in the historic creeds of the Church universal and of this communion, and affirming our loyalty to the basic principles of our representative democracy, hereby set forth the things most surely believed among us concerning faith, polity, and fellowship:

*Faith.* We believe in God the Father, infinite in wisdom, goodness, and love; and in Jesus Christ, his Son, our Lord and Saviour, who for us and our salvation lived and died and rose again and liveth evermore; and in the Holy Spirit, who taketh the things of Christ and revealeth them to us, renewing, comforting, and inspiring the souls of men.

We are united in striving to know the will of God as taught in the Holy Scriptures, and in our purpose to walk in the ways of the Lord, made known or to be made known to us.

We hold it to be the mission of the Church of Christ to proclaim the gospel to all mankind, exalting the worship of the one true God, and laboring for the progress of knowledge, the promotion of justice, the reign of peace, and the realization of human brotherhood.

Depending, as did our fathers, upon the continued guidance of the Holy Spirit to lead us into all truth, we work and pray for the transformation of the world into the kingdom of God; and we look with faith for the triumph of righteousness and the life everlasting.

*Polity.* We believe in the freedom and responsibility of the individual soul, and the right of private judgment. We hold to the autonomy of the local church and its independence of all ecclesiastical control. We cherish the fellowship of the churches, united in district, state, and national bodies, for counsel and cooperation in matters of common concern.

*The Wider Fellowship.* While affirming the liberty of our churches, and the validity of our ministry, we hold to the unity and catholicity of the Church of Christ, and will unite with all its branches in hearty cooperation; and will earnestly seek, so far as in us lies, that the prayer of our Lord for his disciples may be answered, that they all may be one.

Congregationalists have always been concerned about "theology." They have covenanted together not only because of common doings or feelings, but because of common faith. Loving God with the mind— faith as belief of the mind as well as trust of the heart—produces a tradition of learned ministry and great theologians, one that has established schools of the caliber of Yale and Harvard, and created the first graduate school of theology, Andover Seminary, with its founding chair in systematic theology. It is very fitting for the Congregational Christian Historical Society to honor the 75th anniversary of a theological confession. (We might note in passing that this is also the 105th anniversary of the "Congregational Creed of 1883," the one that preceded the Kansas City Statement and which sheds light on the latter's meaning.)

But Congregationalism does not have creeds and confessions! So it is said by some who do not know their history. Congregationalists do have them, but they construe them differently. Denomination-wide confessions in Congregationalism are "testimonies, not tests," as it is often expressed. The reason is that the local congregation is the basic unit of ecclesial life, or, borrowing some contemporary terminology, the "base community." As such, the local church is the final locus of doctrinal self-expression. For all that, the transcongregational testimonies of faith made in historic Congregationalism, though nonbinding on congregations, do attempt to capture what is believed throughout the churches, and thus they function much as confessions do in other church bodies, as articulations of shared theological identity.

All this is true of the key "faith" section of the Kansas City Statement. Hear the lead editorial of *The Congregationalist and Christian World* on the subject, entitled "The New Confession of Faith":

> The putting forth of a new confession of faith by representative Congregationalists is an act of no small moment. It is exactly thirty years since the last declaration that might be construed as embodying the faith of American Congregationalism was issued in what is known as the Creed of 1883. Only once before that time has the common faith of the churches from Atlantic to Pacific found expression, in the Burial Hill declaration of 1865, approved by the first national assemblage of Congregationalists in Boston in the same year. . . . As the years go on, it (The Kansas City Statement) may be adopted as the creedal basis of many churches. It should also help to revive interest in doctrinal matters which have been pushed to one side by the wave of enthusiasm for social reforms and readjustments. In every congregation are men and women who have not ceased to think on the great themes of God and Christ and salvation. They crave light and leadership.
>
> This new statement may crystallize their thinking and give them a satisfactory, intellectual basis for their convictions. . . . It does not include all the beliefs which all Congregationalists hold. But it lays strong emphasis on what they hold in common. Its positive, comprehensive, evangelical, catholic note accords with our best traditions. . . . If every one of our 700,000 members could utter this confession from the heart, and feel in every fiber of their being the great truths which it declares we should have a body of Christian men and women against whom the gates of hell could not prevail.[1]

And from the commentary surrounding its adoption, hear the venerable Washington Gladden: "What a large and noble Confession of Faith! It's all there. There is no needless word; there is no word wanting; we can write that on our banner and go forth . . . to conquer." The Kansas City drafters were at pains to connect their confession to the creedal stream of Christianity, and managed to say just that in the preamble section of the Statement "declaring the steadfast allegiance of the churches composing the Council to the faith which our fathers confessed, which from age to age has found its expression in the historic creeds of the Church universal and of this communion. . . ." The floor debate is instructive. Hear the ringing words of Dr. Newman Smyth:

> I hope that this preamble and declaration of faith may stand. It means the Congregational churches have a faith which they are not ashamed to confess before the world. It means that they are not to lapse into a state of childish creedlessness. We are not about to disown our forefathers. The preamble affirms our line of descent, and the historic continuity of faith from the apostolic days, through the ancient creed and the confessions and declarations of our own fathers, as the mind of Christ has thus varied from age to age in the mind of the church. . . . May the day never come that the Congregational churches of our country shall cease to declare their right, their share, their fellowship in the apostolic succession of the faith of the holy Catholic Church throughout the world.

The editorial writer of *The Congregationalist and Christian World* was prescient about the influence of the Kansas City confession on local churches for it became widely used in congregations, appearing in the worship aids section of various editions of the *Pilgrim Hymnal,* and in the *Book of Worship* of the United Church of Christ.

The evidence of the confessional nature of historic Congregationalism has, as noted, to be placed in the context of its polity. So it is specifically said in the Kansas City Statement itself in its section on polity: "We hold to the autonomy of the local church and its independence of all ecclesiastical control." But right on the heels of this sentence appears the assertion: "We cherish the fellowship of the churches, united in district, state, and national bodies, for counsel and co-operation in matters of common concern." The Kansas City meeting (and its Statement) was a significant strengthening of that latter affirmation. Nehemiah Boynton, one of the moving spirits of Kansas City, expressed this duality in Congregationalism as an ellipse with two foci, the church local and the church universal, the church congregational and the church catholic. (He made the same point also in the characteristically militant imagery of that day: "March separately, but strike together!") The base of the ellipse for Congregationalism is the base community, the church congregational. Because that is so, the local church covenant, including its theological commitments, is binding upon those who are members of that community. When a national church theological covenant is made—a confession of faith like the Burial Hill Declaration, the Creed of 1883, or the Kansas City confession—corporate testimony is given therein to the basic belief of its basic communities. While non-binding on those local congregations as individual units, it is nevertheless a witness to the wider world as to what is commonly held to be true in these congregations, and, therefore, what constitutes the working assumptions of their corporate life. And in turn, the confession is a witness to individual congregations as to the common mind of the wider faith community. As Congregationalists have entered the ecumenical age and have had to relate to other bodies of Christian belief, these corporate confessions of faith take on added significance. This is true, for example, in such arenas as the Lutheran-Reformed and the Catholic-Reformed bilaterals, the Consultation on Church Union, and the World Council of Churches theological projects, notably the BEM document and now the next dramatic step, "Toward a Common Expression of the Apostolic Faith."[4] How the United Church of Christ got temporarily sidetracked by its conversation partners from the Lutheran-Reformed dialogue because of misunderstandings of these partners about both our confessional identity and our polity makes an interesting story.

The attempt to remind others that Congregationalism is covenantal, confessional, and catholic is underscored in the last paragraph of the Kansas City Statement under the caption, "The Wider Fellowship": "While affirming the liberty of our churches, . . . we hold to the unity and catholicity of the Church of Christ . . .; and will earnestly seek, so far as in us lies, that the prayer of our Lord for his disciples may be answered, that they all may be one."

## Faith

Well, what does the Confession really say? What is "the faith" according to these forebears of 1913? Let's do a theological exegesis of the Statement.

The first thing to note is its trinitarian theme and structure. One hundred years after the Unitarian split, this matter was still on the minds of our theological ancestors. And rightly so, for the choices made by these respective constituencies—Congregational and Unitarian—had their fateful consequences. (1) In world ecumenism, and in interdenominational affairs, Unitarianism considered itself, and was regarded by others increasingly, as a body apart from the Christian community. (2) In matters theological, the rejection of the Trinity (and with it, the assertion that Jesus is only an inspired human figure) was succeeded by the gradual disappearance of many other key Christian beliefs, including the rejection of theism itself in some parts of what is now the Unitarian Universalist Association. Concern about the erosion of Christian identity has, indeed, produced a sharp reaction in other quarters of the U.U.A., eventuating in the creation of a U.U.A. Christian caucus. With this history, and its associated desire to stay in continuity with "the historic creeds of the Church universal" (as it is stated in the preamble to the Confession), the trinitarian accents of the Kansas City confession could have been expected. So it is declared: "We believe in God the Father, infinite in wisdom, goodness and love, and in Jesus Christ, his Son, our Lord and Saviour, who for us and our salvation lived and died and rose again and liveth evermore; and in the Holy Spirit, who taketh the things of Christ and revealeth them to us, renewing, comforting, and inspiring . . . "

There is here a direct lineage from earlier Congregational confessions. So the Burial Hill Declaration of 1865: " . . . we confess our faith in God, the Father, the Son, and the Holy Ghost, the only living and true God; in Jesus Christ, the incarnate Word, who is exalted to be our Redeemer and King; and in the Holy Comforter, who is present in the Church to regenerate and sanctify the soul." So also in the Creed of 1883: "We believe in one God, the Father Almighty, Maker of heaven and earth, and of all things visible and invisible; And in Jesus Christ, His only Son, our Lord, who is of one substance with the Father; by whom all things were made; And in the Holy Spirit, the Lord and Giver of life, who is sent from the Father and Son, and who together with the Father and Son is worshipped and glorified."

For a body of Christians to declare that God is triune means, essentially, two things. First, it is to affirm that life is a great drama in three acts: God the Creator brings the world to be and providentially parents it through all its ups and downs, covenanting with creation, and again in the rainbow sign of the Noachic covenant, and again in a very special way with Abraham and Moses to watch in stubborn, long-suffering love over what has been wrought. Then, act two: God mysteriously enters creation itself in the body of a child, born from the womb-compassion of deity. And this God-in-the-flesh grows up in our midst, suffers from our hates and hurts, dies under our hand, and rises again. And the third act: the power of God is released among the people of God bringing to be the Body of Christ which points in word and deed, worship and witness to the One with whom we have to do, and so moves in a world newly graced toward the close of the drama, when the prayer of Christ is answered, the Kingdom comes and God is all in all.

In the technical language of theology, this drama is the "economic Trinity," the outworking of the purposes of God, in the divine economy of three missions—God as Creator, Reconciler and Sanctifier. Today we sometimes talk about this epic as "the Christian story" and identify its chapters as creation, fall, covenant, Christ (Person and Work), church (nature and mission), salvation and consummation.[5]

The second aspect of the Trinity is called the immanent Trinity. It has to do not with what God does in the drama, but who God is—the inner life of God, the mysterious inner-trinitarian community. That means God as three "Persons," each of whom is described in our story book, the Bible, as agent of action. Yet how could they be persons in our sense? That would be polytheism, three gods—God as a "club" rather than the one God of Christian monotheism. The teaching on the Trinity says that these three Persons are so together in loving unity that the three are really one. They are coinherent, permeable to one another. Or putting it more simply, as in the first letter of John: "God is love." (The importance of the "social Trinity" is being increasingly stressed in ethics today, for as God is a perfect co-equal life together, so we are to show our commitment to partnership and co-equality.)

While an affirmation of the immanent Trinity is implicit in the Kansas City Statement, the words put more of a stress on the doing than the being of God, and thus upon the economic Trinity. Why? The answer is obvious when the social context of American Christianity in 1913, especially Congregationalism, is considered. Once again quoting Boynton, speaking on the "social question":

> If the Church has no ministry for suffering humanity under new conditions; no clarion message of rugged honesty; no ethical demand for straight righteousness between man and man; no condemnation direct and unapologizing for pious hypocrites, no summons of the practice of the law of love in the gainful occupations of the world; no sense of the indignity of city slums; no appreciation of the value of the personality of every last one of the submerged tenth; no commendation for the rehabilitation of human society, through laws and through the endeavors which represent the intelligent, the humanitarian, and the scientific advances of the age; if the Church has no sympathy to extend and no services to offer in these comparatively new fields of human necessity and want, then the Church is moribund. . . . [6]

Congregationalism in this epoch of growing sensitivity to social injustice, and apprehension about the gathering clouds of war, increasingly put its emphasis on the social mission of the church. And the Kansas City leaders did it in a familiar framework: the American "can do" optimism of the age. Thus we hear both the sense of urgency and the sanguine hopes for the future in the Statement: the mission of the church being a "laboring for the progress of knowledge, the promotion of justice, the reign of peace, and the realization of human brotherhood, . . . we work and pray for the transformation of the world into the kingdom of God. . . . " The anticipation of our human effort building the Kingdom of God had yet to be confronted with the horrors of World Wars I and II, the Holocaust, and the threat of a nuclear winter, realities that would drive another generation of Congregationalists to rediscover the biblical realism that must go with prophetic commitments and hopes.

For the Kansas City signatories the mission of the church was not only horizontal, seeking to change this world by works of mercy and justice. The vertical dimension is cited as well in the Statement's witness to the Good News of God's forgiveness and the call to personal faith; "We hold it to be the mission of the Church of Christ to proclaim the gospel to all, . . . exalting the worship of the one true God. . . ."

The general structure of the confession in making these various points follows the storyline mentioned earlier, as does its predecessor Creed of 1883 and its successor in the United Church of Christ, the Statement of Faith, beginning with the trinitarian Source of the narrative, centering in the deed of God in Christ, moving to the church's life and mission and culminating in "the life everlasting."

There is an interesting sentence in the confession which in theological lingo is often called the concept of authority, or sometimes the issue of hermeneutics. It has to do with Scripture: "We are united in striving to know the will of God as taught in the Holy Scriptures, and in our purpose to walk in the ways of the Lord, made known or to be made known to us." Clearly Scripture is the source of authority for these forebears. However, it is authoritative with respect to the "will" and "walk" of God. That means normativity in "faith and morals" as it is expressed in today's hermeneutical debates, rather than "inerrant" in all matters including science and history. And the leading theme of the Statement as a whole lets us know what the heart of that faith and those morals are. Further, there is a growth in our understanding of Scripture implied, and thus a concept of "the development of doctrine," a belief with a long history in Congregationalism going back to the much-quoted declaration of John Robinson that "ever-new light and truth shall break from God's holy Word."

## Limitations

It's tempting on such an anniversary as this to settle for all the good things to be found in the Statement. But our tradition views confessions as a *resource* of faith, not the *source* of faith, and thus assumes their frailties and fallibilities. So the limitations of Kansas City have to be frankly faced.

The first thing many of us will notice, sensitized as we are to inclusivity in language, is the exclusivity of it here. I am not referring to language about God, still an inflamed and unresolved issue (from the elimination or balancing of gender pronouns, the exclusion of Father and Son language in trinitarian discourse including the baptismal formula with its ecumenical implications, the proposal to alternate "goddess" with the male-rooted "God" language, etc.). I am talking about the patriarchal references to "the souls of men," proclaiming the Gospel to "mankind," depending as did "our fathers," realizing "human brotherhood," etc. Yes, these formularies and their formulators were children of their time. As such, they contributed linguistically to the second-class status of women. Indeed the official photograph of the delegates makes it very clear that Kansas City was a male assembly. The consciousness of Congregationalism had yet to be raised about the partnership of women and men, and that limitation is reflected theologically.

And there are other deficiencies: (1) The work of the Holy Spirit is found only in "the souls" of humans, not in the systems of the world—social, economic, and political. As such, the proper call to justice and peace is not undergirded by a theology of the Spirit's work among the "principalities and powers," and thus the need to "resist the powers of evil." (2) As mentioned earlier, there is a naïveté about the possibilities of historical advance, an escalator theory of progress that was the conventional wisdom of that period, soon to be refuted by the tragedies of subsequent decades which prompted a return to the Christian doctrine of sin and with it a fresh grasp of the meaning of grace. (3) While the Statement refers to the call to "proclaim the gospel," it is a muted theme not enjoying full partnership with the dominating emphasis on doing the social deed. This tendency to horizontalize the mission of the church contributed to the cultural captivity that marked some later expressions of Congregationalism. (4) And there is an absence of some key beliefs of historic Congregationalism that could have been included,—the sacraments, justification by faith, the immanent Trinity, and eschatology.

Limitations acknowledged, the 1913 confession at Kansas City clearly expressed the commitment of Congregationalism to essential points in the classic Christian faith, points shared by the universal Christian church. It sought to say these things in the idiom and according to the issues of that historical context. Simply put, the Statement tells the Christian story—what God did, is doing and will do, as Creator, Reconciler and Redeemer. And at the center of this macro-story, the great drama, there is the micro-story, the little drama on which it all turns: Jesus Christ, Lord and Saviour, who for our salvation lived, died, rose again, and lives forevermore. This is the faith delivered to those Kansas City saints, expressed in their way in their place and time, and passed on to us, so we can confess it, and live it, in our way, in our place and time.

## NOTES

1. "The New Confession of Faith," *The Congregationalist and Christian World,* Vol. XCVIII, No. 42 (October 16, 1913), 525.

2. Washington Gladden, "Deepen the Religious Life," *The Congregationalist and Christian World,* Vol. XCVIII, No. 41 (October 9, 1913), 502.

3. [Howard A. Bridgman], "A Great Day for Congregationalism," *The Congregationalist and Christian World,* Vol. XCVIII, No. 45 (November 6, 1913), 654. For other commentary on the confession as well as the Kansas City meeting in general, see: Raymond Calkins, *A New Era in Congregationalism; Being a Report of the Commission of Nineteen* (Boston: Congregational Christian Historical Society, 1962); Frederick L. Fagley, *The Congregational Churches* (Boston: The Pilgrim Press, 1925), 59–60; Gaius Glenn Atkins and Frederick L. Fagley, History of American Congregationalism (Boston: The Pilgrim Press, 1942), 215–216, 258, 260, 316–320, 331, 337, 404–405; *The National Council of Congregational Churches of the United States: Addresses, Reports, . . . Etc. of the Fifteenth Triennial Session, Kansas City, Mo., October 22–30, 1913* (Boston: Office of Secretary of National Council, 1913).

4. Commission on Faith and Order, *Confessing One Faith: Towards an Ecumenical Explication of the Apostolic Faith as Expressed in the Nicene-Constantinopolitan Creed (331)* (Geneva: World Council of Churches, 1987).

5. For expansion on this narrative theme, see Gabriel Fackre, *The Christian Story,* Revised Edition (Grand Rapids: William B. Eerdmans Publishing Co. 1984).

6. Nehemiah Boynton, "Moderator's Address," *The National Council of Congregational Churches of the United States: Addresses, Reports, . . . Etc. of the Fifteenth Triennial Session, Kansas City, Mo., October 22–30, 1913,* 21.

"The Kansas City Statement as a Confession of Faith," *The Bulletin of the Congregational Library,* Vol. 39, No. 3 (Summer 1988), 5–12. Used by permission.

# PART TWO

# Caring

## ECUMENICAL CARING

CHAPTER 7

# What the Lutherans and the Reformed Can Learn from One Another

ECUMENICAL DECISIONS WILL BE MADE in North America this summer that could "begin a dramatic new chapter in the near five-century history of the Reformation." So says Günther Gassmann, former director of the World Council of Churches' Faith and Order Commission. Gassmann was contemplating the proposals before the Evangelical Lutheran Church in America (ELCA) which call for establishing "full communion" with the Episcopal Church and with three Reformed churches—the Presbyterian Church (U.S.A.), the Reformed Church in America (RCA) and the United Church of Christ (UCC)—and which would mutually lift the Lutheran-Roman Catholic condemnations of the sixteenth century.

The Lutheran-Reformed Formula of Agreement requires approval from the four churches involved, all of which will meet in assembly this summer—the RCA and PC USA in June, the UCC in July, and the ELCA in August. If any one of the church bodies votes the proposal down, the agreement will be scuttled.

Why, from this Reformed participant's viewpoint, is the Lutheran-Reformed agreement so important? The document spelling out the Lutheran-Reformed discussions, *A Common Calling,* speaks of "mutual affirmation *and* mutual admonition." Mutual affirmation means the two parties have enough in common to take the stipulated steps forward. Mutual admonition means they acknowledge the positive import of historic differences.

Can the differences which heretofore have been the cause of separation be viewed in a new ecumenical context as legitimate varying perspectives on the commonalities, and, thus not church-dividing? More than that, are the differences needed emphases, charisms in the church catholic, brought to the fore by historical differences be regarded as complementary to, and even corrective of, one another?

Mutual affirmation is a standard theme in ecumenical negotiations, and is integral also to the Lutheran-Reformed proposal: "If you hold to these essentials, we can take a step toward you." Mutual admonition goes further, requiring the partners to affirm the differences as well as the similarities, thus forswearing inordinate claims that have said to the other, "I have no need of you" (1 Cor. 12:21). While we may be right in what we affirm, we may be wrong in what we deny or ignore. Thus, if one's own Corinthian charism does not, in principle, preclude the other, the time has come to cease denying or ignoring it.

By the same token, admonition is the warning to the other that the exclusion of one's own gift is a wound in the Body of Christ and an impoverishment of the gospel. The tough-mindedness in this proposal prompts ecumenist Harding Myer to say that "there is definitely something new about it. This 'new' element is that now a clearly *positive function* is being attributed to the differences, the function of mutual admonition, or mutual correction, of being 'no-trespassing signs'" (*Ecumenical Trends,* September 1994).

Lutheran-Reformed diversity is manifest in matters that run from sacramental theology, worship practice, confessional subscription and understandings of grace to concepts of social witness and personal piety. One way to sum up the differences is by utilizing some historic fighting words: the Lutheran *finitum capax infiniti* (the finite is capable of receiving the infinite) vs. the Reformed *finitum non capax infiniti* (the finite is not capable of receiving the infinite). Put otherwise, Lutherans have accented Christ's continuing *solidarity with us* in ecclesial tangibilities. The Reformed stress Christ's continuing *sovereignty over us* in both church and world.

Some early remarks by Dietrich Bonhoeffer and Karl Barth develop just this distinction. Identifying his own Lutheran perspective, Bonhoeffer contrasts Barth's stress on God's "freedom on the far side of us" with his own view of God in Christ as "haveable, graspable within his Word within the Church" *(Act and Being).* Barth, on the other hand, in a discussion of confessions, asserts the Reformed *non capax,* contending that historic texts, while a resource for interpreting scripture, are accountable to sovereignty beyond them and thus reformable. For Barth, therefore, there is "no Augsburg Confession . . . *no* Formula of Concord . . . which might later, like the Lutheran, come to process the odor of sanctity" *(The Word of God and the Word of Man).*

The difference between the Lutheran emphasis on Christ's solidarity with us and the Reformed emphasis on divine sovereignty over us can be tracked in several key issues:

- Debates on the Eucharist: Lutherans insist on the ubiquity of Christ's human nature, which means that Christ's body and blood are present "in, with and under" the elements. In contrast, the Reformed insist that believers participate in the body and blood by an ascent through the power of the Spirit to the divine-human person who sits at the right hand of God, "above" the elements. Mutual admonition means that Lutherans have a right to worry that the Reformed stress on sovereignty will lead to the dissolution of the eucharistic Presence. The Reformed have a right to be concerned that the Lutheran stress on Christ's "haveability" will domesticate the Presence. The differences are real. They are necessary testimonies to an aspect of eucharistic teaching and are warnings about the other's reductionist temptations.

- The function of confessions: Lutherans adhere to an unalterable 16th century corpus of confessional writings, collected in the Book of Concord. The Reformed are committed to updating and revising their doctrinal tradition. Lutherans steward the Reformation doctrinal landmarks, regarding them as signs of the divine faithfulness with and in the historic church, and they are rightly wary of the temptation to accommodate the gospel to every new cultural twist and turn. The Reformed steward the message of *semper reformanda,* believing the divine sovereignty calls for the recontextualization of the ancient faith, and they are rightly wary of allowing the gospel to be captive to past formulations.

- The social mission of the church: The Lutheran tradition has emphasized the doctrine of vocation. Christ's solidarity with the church expresses itself in the laity being "Christ to the neighbor" *within* the structures of society. The Reformed tradition has emphasized Christ's sovereignty over both church and society, calling the church, as church, to shape society to the glory of God in obedience to Christ's regency in the secular realm. Lutherans remind the Reformed churches that their approach invites theocracy and tempts them to reduce mission to social action or to accede to current ideologies of the political left or right. The Reformed remind Lutherans of the temptations of quietism, of an uncritical acceptance of the status quo as "orders of creation" and of a retreat from the church's vocation to seek systemic social change.

There are many other points of Lutheran-Reformed disagreement that reflect the solidarity/sovereignty distinction. Consider the historic Reformed stress on the doctrine of election in contrast to the Lutheran accent on the appropriation of salvation in personal faith and its communication through the sacramental means of grace; or, in the area of Christology, the Reformed temptation to separate the divine and human natures of Christ (Nestorianism) and the Lutheran temptation to affirm that Christ had only one nature (Monophysitism); or, in worship patterns, the respective emphases on pulpit and altar.

Mutual corrigibility and complementarity could also address another longstanding Lutheran-Reformed difference—the difference between the Lutheran theme of *simul iustus et peccator* (the Christian is simultaneously righteous and sinner) and the Reformed theme of *sanctificatio* (the Christian is not only declared righteous but is to become holy). Lutherans stress the persistence of sin in the life of the redeemed; the Reformed accent growth in grace and the call to obedience through the "third use of the law." Lutherans, while also speaking of sanctification, are wary of being so preoccupied with it that one has pretensions to perfection or falls prey to works-righteousness. Reformed, also sober about the persistence of sin, are concerned that a one-note stress on it obscures a grace that both makes for and calls for holiness in the Christian life and society.

An illustration of how Lutheran and Reformed perspectives can come together in a mutually fructifying way is the theology of Reinhold

Niebuhr, shaped as it was by both traditions in his early years in the Evangelical Synod of North America. Niebuhr evidences both Lutheran "simultaneity" and Reformed "sanctification." In his Gifford Lectures he speaks of the conjunction of a justifying grace that is "mercy towards us" and a sanctifying grace that is "power in us." Niebuhr appropriates the Reformed mandate to strive for change and the Reformed hope for genuine moral advance. The work of sanctification is translated into the social struggle and the "infinite possibilities" of history, an activity he finds most clearly evident in later Calvinism. Yet at the same time he expresses a Lutheran sobriety about the corruptibility of every historical advance.

Allied with this partnership of vision and realism is Niebuhr's version of the Lutheran two-kingdoms doctrine which distinguishes between achievable goals in a fallen world and the eschatological norm of agape. Yet he also insists that the modest possibilities of the kingdom of the left hand are accountable to the regnant Christ—invoking the Reformed standard of a radical love that never lets us rest comfortable with the given state of society.

In terms of sovereignty and solidarity, Niebuhr's doctrine of the church has little of the Lutheran sense of sacramentality; and Reformed sovereignty functions actively in his ethics. Yet his most noted prayer captures something of the dialectic between the two: "the courage to change" reflects the Reformed imperatives; "the serenity to accept" reminds us of Lutheran assurances about grace given in the midst of history. Niebuhr's own example of ecumenical convergence can goad us toward what he called elsewhere and "impossible possibility."

Whatever the commendations of ecumenical observers or the attractiveness of this model complementarity, sharp questions have been raised about the Lutheran-Reformed proposal. Three issues recur:

1. Are the affirmations of common belief in the texts and traditions of all the partners *in fact* espoused by the congregations and clergy of the participating churches? My own denomination, the United Church of Christ, is regularly charged (usually anecdotal evidence is cited) with being theologically incoherent.

   The question is a fair one. Full communion in bilateral ecumenics—or the comparable "covenant communion" in multilaterals, like the nine-denomination Consultation on Church Union—requires a theological consensus on certain basics. In bilaterals and multilaterals of this sort, official "texts and traditions" are the criteria, and these are indeed in place in both cases. The Lutheran-Reformed Coordinating Committee for the current proposal further clarified the consensus in its Formula of Agreement this year, using references to common Christian teaching cited in an earlier North American Lutheran-Reformed document, *Invitation to Action,* approved in the 1980s by the national assemblies of all the participating Reformed churches and most of the Lutheran bodies that formed the ELCA.

The critics are right, however, to point to the disparity between what is declared officially and what is held functionally. But the charge must go much deeper than anecdotal reports that single out one denomination (and which do not take account of the current vigorous movements of theological renewal in the UCC). The Search Institute's recent careful study of Christian teaching in six denominations does rate the UCC next to lowest in "Faith Maturity" and lowest in "Growth in Faith Maturity." At the same time, the ELCA is rated the very lowest in "Faith Maturity" and next to lowest in "Growth in Faith Maturity." We are all in the same boat and there is no safe ecclesiastical harbor.

What this dissonance between proclamation and practice means in negotiations on full communion is the need to attend carefully to the second stage of the proposed agreement—variously called "actualization," "reception" or "realization." The proposed process of reception recognizes today's theological diversity and new localisms. Actualization of this bilateral will be appropriate only when and where congregations and judicatories do, in fact, affirm the unity that is professed to be the case in the official agreement. To ascertain such, or grow toward such, can be a sobering recognition of reality, and more important, a teaching moment in Christian basics for the congregations and clergy of all the partner churches.

2. Are the participating churches really open to admonition about the limitations of their own tradition? Disagreement on the Eucharist is

a case in point, and along with it the related diversity in patterns of worship and piety.

Commitment to mutual learning means that the Reformed must understand that another member of the Reformation family has had to remind it of the inseparability of Christ and his Body, a Presence pervading its life, focal in the visibilities of a symbol-laden worship and definitive in the tangibilities of bread and wine. And that witness to the "haveable" entails legitimate Lutheran concerns about dissolution of the promise of Christ to be among us, as in the case of the Reformed flirtation with a "memorialism" that reduces the Eucharist to the recollection of a past event, or patterns of worship awash in religious subjectivities.

In turn, Lutherans must understand that mature Reformed teaching on the Lord's Supper (in its confessions, catechisms, statements of faith and sacramental liturgies) affirms unambiguously the real Presence but does so in its characteristic idiom of sovereignty. The Reformed language of "spiritual Presence" refers to the work of the Spirit in bringing the believer, in eating and drinking, into communion with the glorified humanity of Christ. The Reformed witness to the divine sovereignty shows itself in comparable restraint in the use of symbols of the "haveable," along with the historic prominence of the pulpit and the sermon through which we are reminded of the divine freedom *over* us.

3. How can there be "interchange of clergy," given our different standards for the ordination and calling of clergy? Often the neuralgic point here is the issue of openly gay and lesbian pastors. The ELCA faces this question in its discussions with both the Episcopal and Reformed churches. After the recent church judgment in the case of Bishop Walter Righter that this issue is not prescribed by the "common core" of Episcopal doctrine, it is evident that the Episcopal circumstances are not unlike those in the UCC—namely, regional or local bodies exercise their own option and a sharp division of opinion makes for diversity of practice. Whatever national resolutions are passed in each church, Episcopal and UCC congregations will have latitude in decision-making.

Two things are germane in responding to this question. One of them is the premise written into the Formula of Agreement that whatever clergy interchange might take place (there is little evidence in any church of a move toward such) must be done "in orderly exchange," according to the norms of ordained ministry observed in the participating churches—standards that will not be set aside. The agreement does not require a congregation or judicatory in one church to accept a pastor if that pastor does not meet that church's standards for doctrine and behavior.

A second has to do with the gift and admonition brought by the respective Lutheran and Reformed traditions. In three of the bodies with which the ELCA is contemplating full communion (all shaped by the Reformed tradition)—the Episcopal Church, the United Church of Christ and the Presbyterian Church (U.S.A.)—the issue of ordaining gays and lesbians is a newly disputed question. While the Presbyterian Church (U.S.A.) has just passed a measure designed to exclude openly gay and lesbians persons from leadership positions, the closeness of the presbytery vote, the complexity of enforcement procedures, and the announcement of planned noncompliance by a significant number of congregations and clergy assure that it will continue to be a controverted issue in that church. The debate over this question, on which devout Christians disagree, can be understood as an expression of the *semper reformanda* of the Reformed churches, which requires the scrutiny, ever and again, of tradition, accountable as it is to the sovereign Word, Jesus Christ.

What would "mutual admonition" mean here? Would it entail a Lutheran acknowledgment that somewhere in the church catholic a critic-in-residence is needed, one that presses us to re-examine inherited positions, albeit always under the Word? Would it also require a Reformed acknowledgment that this matter is still a disputed question for which there is yet no "mind of the church," one needing continuing conversation within the whole Body, including the stewards of a long moral tradition (with the Lutheran *capax* making the church the custodian of that tradition on just this subject)? Mutual admonition is risky business for all concerned—particularly so for those on either side of the question who would make opinion on this matter the litmus test of faithfulness, and thus, ironically, allow a culture-war issue rather than a doctrinal basic to define the church's identity.

Some say the traditional ecumenical moves of mainline churches, such as the Lutheran-Reformed proposal, are obsolete and even boring, that the pioneering movement toward Christian unity is now outside the present ecumenical structures. But is this an either-or? The intense cyberspace debates and lively journalistic attention to the bilaterals and the volatility of the issue in most of the participating churches tell another story.

Further, in Europe and elsewhere significant advances have been made following the 1973 Leuenberg Agreement that brought into full communion 80 Lutheran and Reformed national churches. Related to the apparent durability of such bilaterals is the fact that all serious ecumenism will someday have to venture structural and governance decisions of the kind being risked in the Formula of Agreement, in the Episcopal-Lutheran Concordat and in multilaterals like COCU.

Beyond these facts and forecasts, an important opportunity in pedagogy is at stake. In-depth study of basic issues such as those demanded by the Formula of Agreement could press laity and clergy to a level of theological struggle about Christian doctrine that is desperately needed in these pluralist days. Such mind-stretching and soul-searching, done in an admonitory framework, would surely make for a catholicity of faith commensurate with the fullness of the Body of Christ, and with it a thirst for a wider ecumenism with its own waiting charisms.

## TOWARD "FULL COMMUNIONS"

It is recommended that four churches of Reformation heritage declare that they are in full communion with one another. The term "full communion" is understood specifically to mean that the four churches:

- recognize each other as churches in which the gospel is rightly preached and the sacraments rightly administered according to the Word of God;

- withdraw any historic condemnation by one side or the other as inappropriate for the life and faith of our churches today;

- continue to recognize each other's baptism and encourage the sharing of the Lord's Supper among their members;

- recognize each other's various ministries and make provision for the orderly exchange of ordained ministers of Word and sacrament;

- establish appropriate channels of consultation and decision-making within the existing structures of the churches;

- commit themselves to an ongoing process of theological dialogue in order to clarify further the common understanding of the faith and foster its common expression evangelism, witness and service;

- pledge themselves to living together under the gospel in such a way that the principle of mutual affirmation and admonition becomes the basis of a trusting relationship in which respect and love for the other will have a chance to grow.

—From the proposed Formula of Agreement among the Evangelical Lutheran Church in America, the Presbyterian Church (U.S.A.), the Reformed Church in America, and the United Church of Christ

What the Lutherans and the Reformed Can Learn from One Another, *The Christian Century,* Vol. 114, No. 18 (June 4–11, 1997), 558–561. Used by permission.

## CHAPTER 8

# The Ecumenical Import of the Joint Declaration:

## A REFORMED PERSPECTIVE

MIGHT OTHER ECCLESIAL BODIES sign the Lutheran-Catholic Joint Declaration? The question was put to Walter Kasper at a recent Yale consultation on the document."[1] The Columbus consultation, of course, is an answer to the question posed, as are the essays in this issue. Probably not, he replied, because of some specific Catholic-Lutheran issues, ones worked on over a long period of preliminary studies and statements. However, he saw no reason why parallel agreements with Rome could not be developed, with the *Joint Declaration* as a model. Bishop (now Cardinal) Kasper's comment suggests that whatever formal actions of this sort might be taken, the Augsburg accord provides a fruitful occasion for wider ecumenical inquiry.

Here is a Reformed response to that question based on the "mutual affirmation and mutual admonition" formula developed in the 1997 North American Lutheran-Reformed agreement.[2] In that dialogue, "mutual affirmation" referred to the recognition of enough consensus on a core of Christian teaching to go forward toward full communion. "Mutual admonition" was proposed as a way of dealing with continuing differences. Rather than construing them as insuperable barriers, they are reconceived as having a salutary role in these senses: 1) Each partner admonishes the other not to caricature its position, attributing to it views it does not espouse; 2) Each partner admonishes the other that what it accents does not, as such, exclude what the other emphasizes; 3) Each partner admonishes the other to avoid reducing the meaning of the doctrine to its particular emphases; 4) Each partner admonishes the other to receive its own perspective as a charism necessary for a fuller understanding of the doctrine. Ecumenist Harding Meyer commended the formula as something of an ecumenical breakthrough. That is, "a clearly positive function is being attributed to the differences, the function of mutual admonition, or mutual correction, of being "no trespassing signs."[3]

I want to show how this formula illumines the Augsburg agreement, suggesting an ecumenical way ahead for this doctrine and for other controverted questions;[4] and how the Reformed tradition can make use of it in engaging the *Joint Declaration*.

## MUTUAL AFFIRMATION IN THE JOINT DECLARATION

A crucial section of the Joint Declaration describes "justification" in these words:

> In faith we together hold the conviction that justification is the work of the triune God. The Father sent his Son into the world to save sinners. The foundation and presupposition of justification is the incarnation, death and resurrection of Christ. Justification thus means that Christ himself is our righteousness, in which we share through the Holy Spirit in accord with the will of the Father. Together we confess: by grace alone, in faith in Christ's saving work and not because of any merit on our part, we are accepted by God and receive the Holy Spirit, who renews our hearts while equipping and calling us to good works.[5]

Intrinsic to its meaning, therefore, is its christological "foundation and presupposition," the justifying work of the incarnate Son. Indeed, such is the very "heart" of the Gospel:

> We also share the conviction that the message of justification directs us in a special way toward the heart of the New Testament witness to God's saving action in Christ: it tells us that because we are sinners our new life is solely due to the forgiving and renewing mercy that God imparts as a gift and we receive in faith, and never can merit in any way.[6]

The description of justification that grounds it in the deed of God done in Jesus Christ reflects a key theme in the documents on which the *Joint Declaration* draws. Such is the case in the U.S. dialogue, italicized there for emphasis:

> *Our hope of justification and salvation rests in Christ Jesus and on the gospel whereby the good news of God's merciful action in Christ is made known; we do not place our ultimate trust in anything other than God's promise and saving work in Christ.*[7]

The European dialogue takes note approvingly of this accent in its U.S. counterpart:

> . . . the barricades can be torn down only if we remain unswervingly on the Christological foundation expressed—with particular reference to the doctrine of justification—in the Lutheran-Catholic dialogue that took place in the United States: "Christ and his gospel are the source, center, and norm of Christian life, individual and corporate, in church and world. Christians have no other basis for eternal life and hope of final salvation than God's free gift in Jesus Christ, extended to them in the Holy Spirit."[8]

George Tavard, a participant in the dialogue, echoes the importance of christocentricity in his "ecumenical study" of the doctrine of justification declaring it the determinative "focus" of Roman Catholic-Reformation convergences.[9] The *Joint Declaration* puts it in just those terms as the basis for the agreement:

Lutherans and Catholics share the goal of confessing Christ in all things, who alone is to be trusted as the one Mediator (1 Tim. 2:5) through whom God in the Holy Spirit gives himself and pours out his renewing gifts.[10]

What is identified as a "Christological foundation" is, as can be seen in the last citation as well as the earlier ones, a *trinitarian-christological* one. The Person and Work to which allusion is made are about "the Father" who "sent his Son into the world to save sinners," and thus "justification is the work of the triune God."(3/15)

The "foundation" has as its superstructure justification *pro nobis* and *pro me*. To change the figure, justification "writ large" runs down toward justification "writ small." Or again, the drama moves to the next act when what is wrought by the Father through the Son in the Spirit in "the incarnation, death and resurrection of Christ" comes to us in the church by faith. At this ecclesial cum personal end of justification, "Christ himself is our righteousness, in which we share through the Holy Spirit in accord with the will of the Father." (3/15) Justification "achieved" in Christ as "applied" to us by a grace received in faith is a veritable participation in the Person and his trinitarian relations. To "share in Christ" (4.2/22) is by the "will of the Father" through the power of the Holy Spirit. Thus, whatever the metaphor, up from the foundation, down from large to small, or along the path of the drama, it is trinitarian-christological all the way.

By locating the standard discussion of justification—"subjective soteriology"—entailing questions about the relation of faith to works, faith to love and hope, forensic to infused grace—in the larger trinitarian-christological framework, the *Joint Declaration* and its predecessor documents have set forth an encompassing understanding of the doctrine. This *focus* had its effect, I believe, on the way long-standing disputed questions were treated. Indeed, it made for a fresh *method* of discussing them to be explored below. The agreement on the trinitarian christological focus constituted a "mutual affirmation" on commonalities that enabled the partners to judge the continuing differences as no longer church-dividing. In a time in which Jesus Christ, the Mediator, this "one Word of God which we have to hear and which we have to trust and obey in life and in death" (Barmen Declaration) must be boldly declared, divided Christians find each other so they might speak it with one voice and live it out together."[11]

This foregoing mutuality has vast ecumenical import. Other Christian traditions *also* share this focus. If agreement can be reached here based on this trinitarian-christological framework, it is possible elsewhere. I will illustrate that contention by briefly examining the parallels in the Reformed tradition. But first, another significant contribution of the *Joint Declaration,* one that employs a creative method of dealing with the different construals of how in justification "writ small" the saving grace of God in Christ is received. Thus a generosity made possible by mutual affirmation is played out in a tough-minded *mutual admonition*. This, too, has an ecumenical import that I will attempt to illustrate subsequently by a Reformed admonitory exchange with Lutheran and Catholic perspectives on justification.

## MUTUAL ADMONITION

The *Joint Declaration* and its predecessor texts, while not using the language of mutuality, strike just these notes, speaking of the "concerns" and "emphases" of each partner and the "salutary warnings" rightfully given to one another.[12] This recognition of difference as an occasion for co-learning reflects the aforementioned ecumenical method. Its four-fold mutuality of admonition can be seen throughout the *Joint Declaration,* as in this representative section on "Justification as Forgiveness of Sins and Making Righteous."[13]

The commonality asserted in the first paragraph incorporates the historic accents of each tradition, ones recognized as either caricatured by an opponent or deployed in a reductionist fashion by an advocate.

> We confess together that God forgives sin by grace and at the same time frees human beings from sin's enslaving power and imparts the gift of new life in Christ. When persons come by faith to share in Christ, God no longer imputes to them their sin and through the Holy Spirit effects in them an active love. The two aspects of God's gracious action are not to be separated, for persons are by faith united with Christ, who in his person is our righteousness (1 Cor. 1:30): both forgiveness of sin and the saving presence of God himself. . . .[14]

Thus, each is tacitly admonished that the other does not hold to the partial and reductionist view attributed to it, given what "we can confess together," each acknowledging that a full understanding of justification entails "two aspects" that are not reducible to the single theme historically associated with each tradition. What is implicit regarding the particularity of each is rendered explicit in the paragraphs that follow:

When Lutherans emphasize that the righteousness of Christ is our righteousness, their intention is above all to insist that the sinner is granted righteousness before God in Christ in the declaration of forgiveness and that only in union with Christ is one's life renewed. When they stress that God's grace is forgiving love ("the favor of God"), they do not thereby deny the renewal of the Christian life. They intend rather to express that justification remains free from human cooperation and is not dependent on the life-renewing effects of grace in human beings.[15]

This concept of "emphasis" applies to the other partner:

When Catholics emphasize the renewal of the interior person through the reception of grace imparted as a gift to the believer, they wish to insist that God's forgiving grace always brings with it a gift of new life, which in the Holy Spirit becomes effective in active love. They do not thereby deny that God's gift of grace in justification remains independent of human cooperation. [16]

What we have here are admonitions to remember that the historic emphasis of a partner does not preclude that brought by the other, and to consider the emphasis of each as a gift brought to the other making for a fuller understanding of justification.

What the *Joint Declaration* has succeeded in doing is to reconstrue the meaning of long-standing theological differences on the doctrine of justification that have been Church-dividing since the Reformation. It has done so by attempting to see the "positive function" of difference. But there surely are precedents for this and even a charter for it, in Paul's counsel to the parties in the Corinthian congregation. In 1 Cor. 12 we have comparable admonitions; 1) not to reduce the body of Christ to one or another of its parts; 2) to remember the partiality of one's own organ; 3) to see that one's own particularity does not preclude the particularity of another; 4) to give your own gift to the others, and receive from them the charisms needed for the fullness of the body. In short, "the eye cannot say to the hand, 'I have no need of you.'"(1 Cor. 12:21).

Where does this counsel on the unity-in-diversity of the church come from? It rises out of a christological foundation. Paul asks a splintered Corinthian congregation "Has Christ been divided?"(1 Cor, 1:13) If Christ is one—one Person in two natures as the Chalcedonian formula later expressed it—how can the Body of Christ be otherwise? And the second Person in turn reflects the triune God's own differentiated oneness.

How was it possible for the *Joint Declaration* to conceive of the historic Catholic-Lutheran differences on justification as no longer churchdividing? And to reconsider them in terms of mutually fructifying admonitions? Allusion is made in the document to the "insights of recent biblical studies," to "modern investigations of the history of theology and dogma," and to the many years of "post-Vatican II dialogue."[17] Surely these are factors. But they do not exclude what appears to be a more fundamental one. Indeed, the "studies," "investigations" and "dialogue" could have been instrumental to its emergence. That decisive factor is the trinitarian-christological focus for interpreting justification. The mutual affirmation made on this basis opened the way for viewing the differences on "justification writ small" in terms of mutual admonition. Not only did the focus bring the agreements on the doctrine to the fore, but the model of mutuality from this trinitarian-christological foundation led as naturally to the sharing of charisms as did Paul's comparable counsel to the Corinthians.

If such mutualities on this doctrine can happen between Catholics and Lutherans, are they possible for others in the wider Christian community? I believe they are, but each tradition will have to speak for itself.[18] The ecumenical import of the *Joint Declaration* lies in its provision of a trinitarian-christological focus in understanding justification and a related method for dealing with differences. The former invites "mutual affirmation" and the latter "mutual admonition."

## MUTUAL AFFIRMATION AND ADMONITION

### Affirmation

With John Calvin's view of justification in the *Institutes of the Christian Religion* as exemplar of a Reformed perspective, and formative of its confessional tradition, we turn to a key passage and some corollaries. Interestingly, Calvin's John 3:16 citation and framework here is the same text that heads the section on scriptural citations in the Joint Declaration. Describing the doctrine from "the beginning of justification" in the causal categories of his time, he says:

> The efficient cause of our eternal salvation the Scripture uniformly proclaims to be the mercy and free love of the heavenly Father towards us; the material cause to be Christ, with the obedience by which he purchased righteousness for us; and what can the formal or instrumental cause be but faith? John includes the three in one sentence when he says, "God so loved the world, that he gave his only begotten Son, that whosoever believeth in him should not perish, but have everlasting life." (John 3: 16)[19]

He returns later to this conception with specific reference to all three Persons.

> The efficient cause of our salvation is placed in the love of the Father; the material cause in the obedience of the Son; the instrumental cause in the illumination of the Spirit, that is in faith. . . ."[20]

And elsewhere he cites Paul's allusions to this threesome in Romans and Galatians.[21]

What Calvin does in delineating his view is to lodge justification in its appropriative sense—subjective soteriology—in the more encompassing trinitarian-christological framework. This is the same narrative cum trinitarian-christological understanding of the doctrine found in the *Joint Declaration* including its Johannine warrant.

The writ large/writ small journey is echoed in the Reformed confessional tradition as in 1559 French Confession of Faith which locates the foundation and presupposition "on the cross we are reconciled to God and justified before him," moving them to the application of those benefits when we "are made partakers of this justification by faith alone."[22] While a Reformed scholasticism took this overarching view of justification in decretal and supralapsarian directions, it was Karl Barth who re-appropriated the christological-trinitarian impulse, turning it in a fresh direction, seeing on the cross:

> . . . the verdict in Jesus Christ by which man is justified. The justifying sentence of God is His decision in which man's being as the subject of that act [of human pride] is repudiated, his responsibility for that act, his guilt, is pardoned, canceled and removed. . . . Justification definitely means the sentence executed and revealed in Jesus Christ and His death and resurrection, the No and Yes with which God vindicates Himself in relation to covenant-breaking man. . . [23]

This same grounding of subjective soteriology in the Father's justifying purposes and the Son's Person and Work took ecumenical shape in the Lutheran-Reformed Leuenberg Agreement:

> The true understanding of the gospel was expressed by the fathers of the Reformation in the doctrine of justification. In this message, Jesus Christ is acknowledged as the one whom God became man and bound himself to mankind; and in so doing demonstrated God's love to sinners. . . . Through his word, God by his Holy Spirit calls all...to repent and believe, and assures the believing sinner of his righteousness in Jesus Christ.[24]

Thus in classic and contemporary Reformed thought, the doctrine of justification is lodged in a trinitarian-christological framework, with its clear parallels to the *Joint Declaration*. Such a demonstration should invite a mutual affirmation at the core of the doctrine.

With confidence in commonality at the center, each partner must be ready to receive the four-fold admonitory counsel at the circumference of a dialogue. Brief suggestions follow.

### Admonition Given

Characteristic Reformed accents may be identified as "sovereignty" and "sanctification."[25] In the North American dialogue, they were regularly contrasted to the Lutheran accents on ecclesial and sacramental "solidarity" (Christ "in, with and under"), and "simultaneity" (sin persisting in the life of the redeemed, *simul iustus et peccator*).[26] We draw on these emphases in the following.

A fuller understanding of justification is possible when the *theocentric* aspect of the doctrine is given higher profile, rather than the tendency to focus on its anthropocentric aspects, as in the dominant concern to adjudicate our ways of receiving justification found in the *Joint Declaration* (faith alone or faith, hope and love, imputation or impartation?). A Reformed charism, its stress on the divine sovereignty, brings its challenge not to bend the doctrine to fit historic Lutheran-Catholic disputed questions. In the same vein, the Reformed emphasis on the freedom of God must warn of the dangers of domesticating deity in the unqualified linkage of baptism and justification in *The Joint Declaration*. Catholic and Lutheran consensus on the divine "haveability" *(finitum capax infiniti* vis a vis the sacraments) must be in dialogue with the Reformed *finitum non capax infiniti* regarding the same. Again, a fuller understanding is possible when more attention is given to the public import of justification than is evident in the *Joint Declaration*. A Reformed charism, its accent on sanctification, brings it challenge not to privatize and interiorize the doctrine. Thus Jürgen Moltmann, questioning the *Joint Declaration* on this point, says, "We need a common doctrine of righteousness-justice-justification for the 21st century."[28]

### Admonition Received

Admonitions from Catholics and Lutherans relate to these charisms that the Reformed tradition brings to the table. Our accents on sovereignty and sanctification too easily transmogrify into conceptions of justification that exclude the insights of our potential partners in the dialogue, and foreclose a fuller articulation of the doctrine.

A constant in the history of Reformed theology is the tendency to let the right grounding of justification in the divine sovereignty grow into speculation about the who and how of a double foreordination of elect believers and reprobate sinners. Even the attempt to correct this inordinate curiosity about the divine purposes, Barth's christological reading of predestination, betrays the Reformed exclusionary focus on the divine sovereignty with its structural universalism, however repudiated as the intention of the reconception.[30] The stress on divine sovereignty that rightly makes us wary of taking deity captive in human institutions and processes, however, also can be tempted to deny the promises of God to be unswerving with us as the Body of Christ and to be truly present in sacramental means of grace.

The conjunction of sovereignty and sanctification, while making the Reformed tradition a "world-formative" faith, aggressively seeking to change political, social, and economic institutions, has also produced a history of theocratic regimes; utopian social, political and economic hopes; and the reduction of mission to a justice agenda alone. It needs to hear a corrective word from the Lutheran sobriety about sin at every stage of historical advance, and be reminded ever and again about the place of the personal faith journey, given much attention by both Lutheran and Catholic traditions as in the *Joint Declaration*.

## CONCLUSION

The *Joint Declaration* is an exemplification of the promising ecumenical formula articulated in the recent North American Lutheran-Reformed Conversation. Its achievement is based on the affirmation of the trinitarian-christological core of the doctrine of justification common to the Catholic and Lutheran traditions and the fruitful exchange of mutual admonitions made possible by that agreement. The Reformed tradition shares those foundational assertions, can bring its own charisms to the dialogue and can learn from the correctives of its potential partners, making for a fuller grasp of the doctrine of justification for all concerned.

## NOTES

1. Bishop Kasper, secretary of the Pontifical Council for the Promotion of Christian Unity, represented the Vatican at the consultation on the *Joint Declaration* sponsored by Yale Divinity School and Berkeley Divinity School at Yale, Feb. 4–6, 2000. Responses included papers from representatives of the Anglican and Reformed traditions as well as Catholic and Lutheran, setting the stage for the question posed. The papers will be published in *Ecumenical Perspectives on the Joint*

*Declaration,* William Rusch, editor (Collegeville, MN: Liturgical Press), forthcoming, 2002. Several of the themes discussed here draw on research for my chapter in that work, "The Joint Declaration and the Reformed Tradition."

2. Keith F Nickle and Timothy F. Lull, eds., *A Common Calling: The Witness of Our Reformation Churches in North America Today* (Minneapolis: Augsburg Fortress, 1993), 8, 30, 39–40, 66, and *passim.*

3. Harding Meyer, *"A Common Calling* in Relation to International Agreements," *Ecumenical Trends,* Vol. 23, No. 8 (September 1994), 4/116–5/117.

4. I have attempted, with Lutheran co-author Michael Root, to show how these mutualities are at work in three Lutheran ecumenical advances. Gabriel Fackre and Michael Root, *Affirmations and Admonitions: Lutheran Decisions and Dialogue with Reformed, Episcopal, and Roman Catholic Churches* (Grand Rapids: Wm. B. Eerdmans Pub. Co., 1998), 1–62.

5. The Lutheran World Federation and the Roman Catholic Church, *Joint Declaration on the Doctrine of Justification* (Grand Rapids; Wm. B. Eerdmans Pub. Co., 2000), Section 3, No. 15, page 15.

6. *Ibid,*

7. "Common Statement, Introduction," *Justification by Faith: Lutherans and Catholics in Dialogue VII,* H. G. Anderson, T. Austin Murphy, Joseph A. Burgess, eds., (Minneapolis: Augsburg, 1985), 16.

8. "Justification" in Karl Lehmann and Wolfhart Pannenberg, eds., *The Condemnations of the Reformation Era: Do They Still Divide?* Margaret Kohl, trans., Minneapolis: Augsburg Fortress, 1990), 36. The quotation is from, "Common Statement," *Justification by Faith: Lutherans and Catholics in Dialogue, VII, op. cit.,* 71.

9. George Tavard, *Justification: An Ecumenical Study* (New York: Paulist Press, 1983), 62.

10. JD, 3/18.

11. "So Avery Dulles after expressing doubts about the degree of agreement in the Joint Declaration in "Two Languages of Salvation: The Lutheran-Catholic Joint Declaration," *First Things,* No. 98 (December 1999), 29–30.

12. See *The Condemnations of the Reformation Era: Do They Still Divide?,* op. cit., 38, 40, 52, 68–69. The JD cites approvingly the phrase from the foregoing—"salutary warnings"—as the continuing function of the 16th century condemnations (5/43). For an attack on the idea of differences as "emphases" and "concerns," see Gerhard Forde, "What Finally To Do About the (Counter-) Reformation Condemnations," *The Lutheran Quarterly,* Vol. XI (1997, 3–16).

13. JD, 4.2

14. JD, 4.2/22

15. JD, 4.2.23

16. JD, 4.2/24

17. Of course, critics of the document from both sides allege the convergence to be the result of doctrinal indifferentism. See George Lindbeck's account of the

indictment of the SD by Gottfried Martens, "Martens on the Condemnations," *Lutheran Quarterly*, Vol. X, No. 1 (Spring 1996), 59–66.

18. Geoffrey Wainwright has done just that from a Methodist perspective in "Rechtfertigung: lutherisch oder katholisch?" *Kerygma und Dogma,* 45 Jahrgang, Heft 3, Juli/September 1999. See also, Henry Chadwick, "The Implications of the Joint Declaration on Justification: The Anglican Perspective," in Rusch, ed., *Ecumenical Perspectives on the Joint Declaration, op. cit.,* forthcoming.

19. John Calvin, *Institutes of the Christian Religion,* Vol. II, Book III, Paragraph 17 (Wm. B. Eerdmans Pub. Co., 1957), 85.

20. *Ibid,* 86–87.

21. *Ibid.* 88. See also Vol. II, Book II, Chapter XVII on the exegesis of John 3:16.

22. "The French Confession of Faith," XVII, XX in Arthur Cochrane, ed., *Reformed Confessions of the 16 Century* (Philadelphia: Westminster Press, 1966), 150, 151. For the further development of this full-orbed view in the Reformed confessional tradition, albeit increasingly framed in terms of the distinction between "the decree of justification" and "justification . . . made in this life" see Heinrich Heppe, *Reformed Dogmatics,* G.T. Thompson, trans., (Grand Rapids: Baker Book House, 1978), 557 and passim.

23. Karl Barth, *Church Dogmatics* IV/1 Geoffrey Bromiley, trans. (Edinburgh: T & T Clark, 1956), 145, 96.

24. "The Message of Justification as the Message of the Free Grace of God," *Leuenberg Agreement,* II/6/1 in *Invitation to Action: The Lutheran-Reformed Dialogue, Series III, 1981–1983,* James Andrews and Joseph Burgess, eds. (Minneapolis: Fortress Press, 1984), 67.

25. *Affirmations and Admonitions, op. cit.,* 21-43. See also, Gabriel Fackre, "What the Lutherans and the Reformed Can Learn from One Another," *The Christian Century,* Vol. 114, No. 18 (June 4–11, 1997), 558–561.

26. *Affirmations and Admonitions, op. cit.,* 1–20.

27. *Ibid,* 7–10, 23–31.

28. Jürgen Moltmann, *Bemerkungen zur 'Gemeinsamen Erklarung zur Rechfertigungslehre' (GER) und zur 'Gemeinsamen offiziellen Festlung' (GOF),* 2.

29. See Paul K. Jewett, *Election and Predestination* (Grand Rapids: Wm. B. Eerdmans Pub. Co., 1985), 83–105 for an illuminating discussion of supralapsarian, infralapsarian and sublapsarian debates.

30. The repudiation as in Karl Barth, *Church Dogmatics* IV/3/1 G.W. Bromiley and T. F. Torrance, trans. (Edinburgh: T. & T. Clark), 477–478.

31. Nicholas Wolterstorff, Until Justice and Peace Embrace (Grand Rapids: Wm. B. Eerdmans Pub. Co., 1983), 3–22.

The Ecumenical Import of the Joint Declaration, *Reformed World,* Vol. 52, No. 1 (March 2002), 46–55. Used by permission.

## CHAPTER 9

# BEM on the Eucharist:

## A UNITED CHURCH OF CHRIST PERSPECTIVE

THE DOCUMENT *Baptism, Eucharist and Ministry (BEM)* and its reception constitute a "first" in twentieth-century ecumenism.[1] No ecumenical statement has had such widespread attention and official response as this proposal of commonalities in church teaching on baptism, Holy Communion, and Christian ministry.[2] The United Church of Christ, as pioneering experiment in the United States in organic union of diverse theological traditions and ecclesial histories, has a special stake in the outcome of such a move toward larger Christian unity.

While it fits our unitive agenda, *BEM* also challenges it. How committed are we to being a "united and uniting" church when asked to go beyond our settled opinions and accustomed routines? Can those in the United Church of Christ who pride themselves on their autonomy respond to the call for a common confession of faith or be open to the ministry of bishops? Can others who regularly use classical creeds and would welcome episcopacy, also honor the full ministry of the laity, and find a place for believer's as well as infant baptism? Can those who think that "theology" is an escape from action take seriously the debate on the Real Presence in the Eucharistic meal? The *BEM* document puts these issues squarely before us. In short, are we as ready as the Disciples to say "The text offers several areas for theological growth among Disciples of Christ as we seek to build our historic teachings related to the Lord's Supper?"[3] Can we be as self-critical as the Eastern Orthodox who acknowledge that the statement "bears several significant challenges for the Orthodox Church"—challenges to the dangers in their tradition of "passive worship . . . formalism . . . and an individualist approach to the Holy Communion?"[4]

The answer to all these questions by a church born in the travail of an organic ecumenism and committed to "ever new light and truth" breaking forth from God's Word, should obviously be, "Yes!" Certain tendencies among us, however, militate against it. One is the disdain for theological matters found in some quarters. Another is the easy accommodation to the trends and assumptions of our surrounding culture (counterculture) that too often accompanies our valued heritage of openness to new truth. Thus, if the new spirit of the age is secular and pluralist, we are tempted to baptize secularity and pluralism, and become timid about transcendent visions and christological claims, matters integral to the eucharist as well as to Christian faith itself.

A sign of hope that theological indifferentism and cultural accommodation will not be our fate is the official reception given to *BEM* by the 1985 General Synod. Working with a text developed by the Council for Ecumenism, the synod declared: "We affirm, with respect to the issues to which it speaks, that we recognize in *Baptism, Eucharist and Ministry* an expression of the faith of the Church through the ages."[5] In elaborating this stand, specific comments on the eucharist section are made. They begin to form a picture of what our long-term response might be. To work toward that larger and longer end, we begin here with the 1985 General Synod judgments and then move beyond them.

## INTERPRETING THE GENERAL SYNOD RESPONSE

Two themes pervade the official United Church of Christ reply to *BEM*. The first is the refrain of inclusiveness, the covenantal catholicity that brought the United Church of Christ to be, one that is sustained in its name and expressed in its defining text, "That they may all be one" (John 17:21). United Church of Christ inclusivity is a fresh appropriation of the covenant theme found in both the England/New England and continental backgrounds of our church as well as the evangelical catholicity" that marks our traditions. The commitment to both covenant and catholicity are grounded in the bonding of the persons of the Trinity in the dynamic unity of One who, in turn, wills *Shalom* for us in the Reign of God, gives us signs of this promise in the historical covenants of Noah, Abraham, and Moses; fulfills it in the reconciling deed done in Jesus Christ; and calls us to be agents of reconciliation in the church and the world.

The United Church of Christ response is informed by this invitation to relationship and will to consociate. Thus, the opening paragraph endorses the "comprehensive inclusion of diverse biblical images that inform our common understanding and practice of Holy Communion" (p. 161). The synod presses for a journey beyond the inherited partial perspectives that bred "polemical argumentation and division among the churches" (p. 161), and toward the "convergence" that *BEM* seeks. This note is sounded again in an approval (p. 161) of the "list of various acts that are appropriately included in a full eucharistic celebration" ("hymn of praise, act of repentance, declaration of pardon, confession of faith, intercession for the whole church and the whole world . . . thanksgiving to the Father for the marvels of creation, redemption and sanctification . . . words of Christ's institution, an anamnesis or memorial of the great acts of redemption, passion, death, resurrection, ascension, and Pentecost . . . invocation of the Spirit on the community and the elements of bread and wine, etc."). The synod notes that this inclusiveness "has already influenced liturgical reform currently in process in the Church" (p. 161). The same vision of wholeness appears in the endorsement of the "document's breadth of interpretation concerning 'the real living and active presence' (par. 13) of Christ in the sacrament" (p. 161), and its agreement that the mystical Presence is at the heart of the church's eucharistic faith, while the mode of it is subject to varied interpretation. The same kind of catholicity is expressed on the controverted question of the locale of the Presence—by affirming its relation to bread and wine, but also its "relation to the entire eucharistic action" (p. 161). Again, the United Church of Christ consideration of the participation of children, after preparation, reflects its commitment to inclusion, as does its openness to extending the celebration of the Eucharist to a weekly service of Word and Sacrament.

The same United Church of Christ passion for integrity, wholeness, *shalom,* can be found in the synod's criticism of *BEM* for its failure to pursue the World Council of Churches' own commitment to ecumenical fullness. Thus, the response questions the omission of "the offering of the gifts of the people" in its list of necessary elements, expressing concern "that this important participatory act [also] be included in the list" (p. 161). Again, while *BEM* faithfully includes the preaching of the Word within the Eucharist, thereby holding together Word and Sacrament, response from churches for whom preaching is crucial has pressed for more attention to this partnership. The United Church of Christ is one of them in its plea for a "more substantive treatment of the parity of the preaching of the Word with Holy Communion in the conjoining of the two in one full service" (p. 164).

Finally, the synod urges "greater care, throughout the document, for the use of language that is truly inclusive of all the people of God" (p. 163). This reflects not only the commitment to catholicity but also puts us on the way to the second refrain in the UCC commentary on the Eucharist: The Ethical Import of the Means of Grace. Inclusive language is rightly seen as a matter of justice, one that has found a place in the revised eucharistic liturgy of our church. This second motif of ethics is symbolized by the specific synod request for a "clearer statement of Holy Communion as a meal of the Reign of God, by which we are nourished for ethical obedience as servants of Jesus Christ, who is the source of peace with justice" (p. 164). Thus "our operational emphases on ethical considerations" are brought "into the heart of our liturgical practice where they belong" (p. 161). The Reign of God is a reference to the "Meal of the Kingdom" in *BEM* in which the eucharist is understood as a call to be "in solidarity with the outcast" (p. 161).[6] Specifically, the United Church of Christ Statement calls for a better balancing ("more biblically") of the theme of propitiation with that of the eucharist as foretaste of and participation in the coming Reign.

In these latter comments the Synod has shown the implications of who we are as the Just Peace Church in our understanding of the "sacrament of discipleship."[7] Rooted in the Reformed tradition of "world-formative" faith, the United Church of Christ is called to make this witness in the words and deeds of worship as well as in preaching and conduct.

Taken together, the two United Church of Christ accents discussed here represent twin features of our twenty-nine-year history, the special turn we have given to the long traditions from which we have come: a church "united and uniting," and a church of "justice and peace." We seek to be agents of *reconciliation* of the inherited divisions of Christendom, and agents of *liberation* from the structures of oppression. In this respect we are a microcosm of the ecumenical movement moved by the same commitment to a Gospel that "frees and unites."[8] As a laboratory for the goals of ecumenism, the United Church of Christ needs the World Council of Churches (WCC), just as the latter does the former.

## THE PATH AHEAD

As we live with the *BEM* proposal and prepare for the next challenge of the World Council of Churches, its upcoming document, "Toward a Common Expression of the Apostolic Faith Today," we will have some of the time needed to assimilate the doctrinal issues posed in both these ecumenical ventures. The following comments on *BEM* point in that direction, seeking to follow our trajectory beyond the 1985 synodical statement.[9]

In particular, we must confront the question: What is the United Church of Christ's response to *BEM*'s trinitarian view of the eucharist, a framework that continues in the Nicene centerpiece of the World Council's apostolic faith study? As one part of our tradition (Congregational Christian) rose out of a strong declaration of trinitarian faith vis-à-vis the Unitarian controversy, and the other stream (Evangelical and Reformed) had a strong trinitarian commitment reflected, for example, in the Solemn Declaration that opened its Sunday liturgies, a thoughtful rejoinder will be expected from us. The remarks that follow try to take these matters into account.

*BEM*'s eucharistic commentary is organized around the threefold structure of "Thanksgiving to the Father," "Memorial of Christ," and "Invocation of the Spirit," with its internal (Communion of the Faithful) and external (Meal of the Kingdom) implications. These trinitarian formulations raise questions about the name of God as well as the nature of God. With regard to naming, the United Church of Christ must press for inclusivity in denominating the Persons of the Trinity, but do it according to the state of the art of theistic nomenclature and with sensitivity to basic theological and ecumenical questions involved. We leave that issue to the needed debate and focus here on the question of the *nature* of the triune God in UCC tradition and perception.

"Thanksgiving to the Father" is understood in *BEM* as blessing God for the mighty acts of creation and redemption. This theme is related directly to the central act of thanksgiving in the service, the eucharistic prayer, and also to the characterization of the entire event as "eucharist." There are things touching this account of thanksgiving that are fundamental to UCC tradition and perspective.

The first is the *substance* of the thanksgiving, what we are grateful for as described in the eucharistic prayer: the acts of God from creation to consummation, with their turning point in the deed done in Jesus Christ. Here is "the trinitarian history" of God (p. 161) that the earliest Christians confessed in their baptismal rules of faith, the heart of Christian belief that continues in the Apostles' and Nicene Creeds and in our own United Church of Christ Statement of Faith. The narrative in this "central prayer of the church" is a high point in the Eucharist because it lifts up in doxological fashion our basic theological identity. The narrative of faith, the Christian story, is integral to who we are as the United Church of Christ. Thanksgiving for what God has done, is doing, and will do in the Eucharist, and as the Eucharist, is very congenial to our tradition. Learnings from *BEM* on ways to state it, and to locate it as a regular part of a Sunday service, are a natural extension of that tradition.

A second aspect is the inclusiveness of the thanksgiving offered. Thus, the eucharistic prayer rightly draws in creation as well as redemption, and takes account of the covenant people, Israel, as well as Christ and the Church. Both of these accents converge with the strong Reformed emphasis on God's presence in, and sovereignty over, all of creation, and the special place of Israel, and thus the Hebrew Scripture, in God's purposes. World-encompassing issues, ethical and ecological, Jewish-Christian relations, and dialogue with the religions of the world thereby come within our purview as elements in this inclusive narrative of faith. A third aspect that connects with our trajectory is the gratitude expressed in the naming of this rite as "the eucharist." The Reformed heritage has, at its best, always focused on the majesty and mystery of the divine working, rather than on human beings turned self-ward or inward; the accent is on what God does, not what we do. As such, thankfulness for the action of that prevenient Other is accented in our heritage, rather than introspective self-concern. Here is a eucharistic piety, a receiving of the divine initiative in grateful trust and obedience. *Grace* is to the fore and *gratitude* the fit response.

The "Memorial of Christ" (anamnesis) is a trinitarian assertion set squarely in the tradition of the United Church of Christ, and that in at least three important respects. The connection here, as with the thanksgiving motifs, expresses both a convergence with our historical commitments and a suggestive extension of them.

In the first instance, "Memorial of Christ" underscores the christological norm before which all our judgments must pass. We are the United Church *of Christ*. The eucharistic remembrance is of the turning point in the Christian drama, the life, death, and resurrection of Jesus Christ. In the Holy Communion we focus on the center of the center, recalling what took place on the cross in the breaking of this body and the shedding of this blood: the victory of vulnerable Love in the forgiveness of sin, liberation from evil, and defeat of death. How fundamental it is to recollect regularly this decisive person and definitive point when so many other claims of decisiveness and definitiveness today confront us. As in the Synod of Barmen in 1934, so too in our own time we must say to the isms and idols: "Jesus Christ as he is attested for us in Holy Scripture is the one Word which we have to hear and which we have to trust and obey in life and in death."[10] And as Barmen had to deal with ideologies that sought to pass as Christian belief, we too must judge all such claims by the same christological standard. The substance for which we are thankful in our narrative of eucharistic faith (the content of the Gospel) must always and everywhere be scrutinized in the light of Jesus Christ.[11]

In the second instance, under the impact of the liturgical movement, the *BEM* treatment of this memorial has in a fresh way integrated the "memorialist" tradition, with its strong voice in the Reformed community, with the "real presence" tradition in that same Reformed family and beyond, and also with the classical "sacrifice" theme.[12] The Reformed theologian Max Thurian and the Taizé community, together with modern biblical studies and the liturgical renewal movement, have been influential in viewing old issues in a new light.[13] Thus, the Eucharist is seen to stand in vital continuity with the Hebrew *berakah-tôdah,* the blessing of God and offering of thanksgiving to God by the people, a blessing and thanksgiving that remembers the deliverance wrought by God, recalling it before God. This sacrifice of praise and thanksgiving *recollects* the liberating event, Exodus, so that the people participate in it as a present reality. The Christian Eucharist is also a celebration of a present, as well as a past, reality. Here we recall with grateful hearts the deliverance won by God in Christ from sin, evil, and death. But this memorial of Christ is not only a remembering of the long-ago decisive deed done in a crucified body and shed blood. It is also a present re-*membering* of that body so that the sacrifice done "once and for all" is represented to us, and its benefits shared with us. The One who lived, died, and rose again comes to us here and now as a real Presence in his glorified humanity. As we are united with Christ, so our praise and thanksgiving are mystically joined to his sacrifice. This encounter happens in the actions and tokens of bread and wine offered to God by the priesthood of all believers as led by the designated "president" of the Eucharist. So, the oblation that memorializes the deed of God is an *ordinance* of the recollection of Christ's saving work, a *sacrifice* of praise and thanksgiving, and a *sacrament* of the mystical Presence. To continue along the uniting path we have charted as our own, we must be open to understanding and appropriating language and perception that at first appear to seem strange to us. We can do this with integrity only if it truly coheres with what we most fundamentally are. *BEM's* memorial themes are found on this path and invite us to venture further along it.

The third theme, "Invocation of the Spirit," reflects the influence of the Eastern Church for whom this entreaty to the third Person of the Trinity has been prominent in ways that have not been so in either Protestant or Roman Catholic eucharistic theory and practice. However, it finds a strong echo in John Calvin's interpretation of the Supper's dependence on the work of the Holy Spirit for actualizing of the presence of Christ. The role of the Spirit is also to the fore in the free churches' attentiveness to the surprising and upsetting present and future workings of God. In a tradition that accents the freedom and sovereignty of God beyond our routines and expectations, we should joyfully receive and ask for the work of the third Person of the Trinity in the sacramental act. And in this *BEM* accent we are invited to invoke the Spirit on both the action and the elements, trusting that we shall in turn be open to the surprises of the Spirit who leads us in new, ever-fresh ways toward the Reign of God.

The United Church of Christ can recognize its own faith in these overall eucharistic themes of thanksgiving, memorial, and invocation, consonant as they are with its heritage of grateful obedience, sacramentality, and openness to the surprises of the Spirit. The kinships are not only present in the common attention given by both *BEM* and the United Church of Christ to the missions of the "economic" Trinity, the historic deeds done by Creator, Christ, and Spirit remembered and appropriated in the eucharist, but also in a shared "immanent" Trinity, the eternal sociality of the divine Being. Thus there is a remarkable parallel between the fourth and fifth motifs in *BEM,* the Eucharist as Communion of the Faithful and Meal of the Kingdom, and the marks of the United Church of Christ as a united and uniting, and a just-peace church. The first in each of the pairs expresses the vision of ecclesial unity, and the second the hope of a world at one with itself. For both the World Council of Churches and the United Church of Christ the grounding of these commitments is in the reality of the triune God, the One who *is* Life Together. It is no accident that the World Council of Churches and the United Church of Christ each point regularly to the passage on the intratrinitarian life in John 17 as the warrant for both unity and mission: "that they may all be one; even as thou, Father, art in me, and I in thee, that they also may be in us, so that the world may believe. . . ." A recent UCC task force on the nature and mission of the church described this trinitarian indicative that gives rise to the church's imperatives:

> The three Persons dwell eternally in Shalom. To believe in the Trinity is to hold that ultimate reality is a dynamic life together. The ancient Church spoke of the Father, Son and Holy Spirit as coinhering related in such intimate intermission that they are totally present to and in one another. The three are one. God is love! (I John 4:16)[14]

## SOBER HOPE

This reflection on the United Church of Christ and *BEM* cannot end without the sober note struck earlier. To put it sharply, do we have the sense of theological identity in our church necessary to make judgments and commitments about the kind of doctrinal questions posed by *BEM*? Do we have enough theological coherence to respond thoughtfully to the World Council of Churches' next project, "Toward a Common Expression of the Apostolic Faith Today?" One ecumenical leader suggested recently that our interchurch relationships might better be with the Unitarian Universalists and the metropolitan Community Churches than with other Christian bodies because our operational interests appear to be essentially ethical concerns. Those within the United Church of Christ who say we are not a confessional church in any sense, or who stress diversity with no accompanying unity, who do not ground their ethics in theology, or who declare for personal experience and individual opinion over Scripture and tradition, seem to corroborate this judgment. Some with strong confessional leanings also, ironically, provide ammunition for the charge of theological promiscuity by withdrawing into enclaves with little investment in the quest for theological commonalities in the United Church of Christ at large. These are all matters of very serious concern.

The current revival of theological conversation in the United Church of Christ is a sign of hope in the midst of our unclarities and avoidances.[15] Within this movement, and beyond it, are those who will resist the slide into doctrinal indifferentism and individualism. They—we—believe that there is a theological tie that binds us—to one another in the United Church of Christ and ultimately to the church ecumenical. We welcome the *BEM* effort to strengthen that tie; are encouraged by the sign given by the General Synod's first positive engagement with it; and look forward to the time when all Christians can together confess and live out the apostolic faith.

## NOTES

1. *Baptism, Eucharist and Ministry (BEM)* is the unanimously adopted statement of the Faith and Order Commission of the World Council of Churches voted at

its meeting in Lima, Peru, in 1982 and circulated for response to all churches in the World Council of Churches, and to other bodies such as the Roman Catholic Church.

2. See reports in *Information: Faith and Order,* February 1986, pp. 1–5, and *National Council of Churches News,* April 4, 1986, pp. 1–4; and also two forthcoming volumes, *Churches Respond to BEM* (Geneva: WCC, 1986).

3. *Baptism, Eucharist and Ministries: The Response of the Christian Church (Disciples of Christ),* 10.

4. "A Report on *Baptism, Eucharist and Ministry:* The Orthodox Theological Society in America Paper," in *The Orthodox Theological Society in America,* 411–12.

5. "A United Church of Christ Response to *Baptism, Eucharist and Ministry,*" *Minutes,* General Synod 15, 1985, p. 163. Hereafter quotations from this document will be cited by page number within the text.

6. The substitution of the "Reign of God" for "Meal of the Kingdom" represents the quest for more inclusive eucharistic language. We must say "more" rather than inclusive language as such, because a purist critique would hold that "God" is itself a masculine term and should be either eliminated or balanced by "Goddess." That the word "God" is retained in "Reign of God," itself an effort to rid theological language of traces of masculine or hierarchical metaphors, is a reminder of the subtleties and ambiguity in linguistic questions, ones which should warn us against simplistic solutions and self-righteous denunciation.

Our UCC struggle against the exclusion of women speaks a firm "No" to *BEM*'s equivocation on the ordination of women. While this appears in the section on "Ministry" (par. 18 and commentary) not in "Eucharist," it has implications for the latter in terms of the celebrant. Again the WCC must be held accountable to its own standards of ecumenicity and catholicity.

7. On the eucharist as "Sacrament of Discipleship" see Louis Gunnemann's essay by that name in *On the Way: Occasional Papers of the Wisconsin Conference of the United Church of Christ,* vol. 3, no. 2 (Winter 1985–86), 20–27.

8. See *Jesus Christ Frees and Unites:* Preparatory material for the Fifth Assembly of the World Council of Churches, Jakarta, Indonesia, (New York: Friendship Press, 1975). In another ecumenical venture in which the UCC is involved, the Consultation on Church Union, this duality appears as "liberation and reconciliation." Here, and in larger Christian usage, liberation is not only from systemic oppression but also from the sin in each human heart that causes it and other misery, from our guilt before God, and from death. And reconciliation is overcoming not only the estrangement of the churches, but also alienation within the whole human race and between the world and God. See *The COCU Consensus: In Quest of a Church of Christ Uniting,* ed. Gerald F. Moede, (Princeton, N.J.: Consultation on Church Union, 1985), passim.

9. Documents in our short history which are part of this momentum include the two officially sponsored eucharistic texts—*The Lord's Day Service with*

*Explanatory Notes* (Philadelphia: United Church Press, 1964), with Services of Word and Sacrament I and II subsequently printed in the UCC *Hymnal, and Proposed Services of Word and Sacrament* (Office of Church Life and Leadership, UCC, 1982); the 1978 papers of the Biblical Theological Liturgical Group (mimeographed)—"The Lord's Supper in Puritanism from Calvin to Jonathan Edwards," "The Sacrament in the Mercersburg Theology," "New Testament Understandings of the Lord's Supper," and "The Supper and our Identity"; UCC perspectives on the eucharist in *An Invitation to Action: A Study of Ministry, Sacraments, and Recognition,* Lutheran-Reformed Dialogue, series 3, 1981–1983; Louis H. Gunnemann, "A Critical Look at Worship in the United Church of Christ," *On the Way: Occasional Papers of the Wisconsin Conference,* vol. 2, no. I (Summer 1984), 16–24; Gunnemann, "The Eucharist: Sacrament of Discipleship," ibid., vol. 3, no. 2 (Winter 1985–86); Bette Anne Crowell and Rosemary S. Turner, *Children and Communion: Suggestions for Congregational Discussions* (New York: United Church Press, 1984); Howard Paine, "An Interpretation of the Lord's Day Service," no date, mimeographed; Theodore L. Trost, Jr. "The Sacrament of the Lord's Supper in the United Church of Christ," no date, mimeographed; and the Occasional Papers of the Mercersburg Society on the eucharist, 1983–1986, mimeographed.

10. The Theological Declaration of Barmen. In our own time, accountability to the christological norm has played a critical role in the struggle for the dignity of women and their place in the church, as when the vision of Galatians 3:28 and the practice of Christ become the standard by which all theory and practice is judged. So, too, the South African struggle pressed the World Alliance of Reformed Churches to declare racism a heresy on christological grounds.

11. Joseph Williamson's juxtaposition of christological and pneumatological commitments and his polarization of creedal and covenantal traditions illustrate the resistance still present in the United Church of Christ to the inclusive vision of its founders. See his "Confessions, Creeds, and Covenants in the United Church of Christ," *Prism,* Introductory Issue (Fall 1985), 57–71. The classical teaching on the Trinity in Congregationalism as well as in the wider church never sundered the Person of the Spirit from the Person of the Logos, or the work of the Spirit from the work of Christ. Their unity is the ground of our teaching on the covenant. The covenant that is the life together of the triune God entails the coinherence of the Persons and its consequence that "the works of the Trinity are one" (Anselm). In the matter in question, the work of the Spirit is the work of Christ, not a spirit identified by some other norm.

The history of pneumatological advocacy is instructive. Spirit-drenched movements have been important critics-in-residence when they have called the church to account for its domestication of Christ in inherited patterns or lackluster practice. The vitalities of mission, church reform and renewal, a lively piety and spirituality, and the ministry of the laity have all been associated with appeals to the power of the Holy Spirit. On the other hand, the claim to "have the Spirit" or be "led by the Spirit" because our experience, personal or corporate, validates it has left a trail of spiritual hauteur, divisiveness, and disdain for the covenants of faith, one that runs from the early Montanists to today's political fundamentalists. The Christian community learned early that it had to 'test the spirits" and accordingly developed its christological standards to challenge sectarianism and subjectivism. Williamson is right that appeal to "Christ" as such is not conclusive since we all construe Christ perspectively, and, therefore, must deal with the hermeneutical question. Fundamental to the UCC hermeneutic is its inclusive vision. In our history as well as our charters (again, "operational" cannot be polarized with "official" in a united and uniting church) we declare that the fullness of Christ is known by the wideness of perspective on the biblical testimony to Christ. Thus, the covenantal catholicity of the church, vis-a-vis the scriptural standard of teaching, is the way to the authenticity of its doctrine. This, incidentally, is the intent of the Craigville Colloquies to which Williamson refers, in which the theological conversation is broadened to include diverse and often unheard voices in our church and also a highly participatory decision-making process its attendant trust in the Spirit.

12. The Constitution of the UCC identifies Holy Communion as one of the two sacraments of the church. The strong sacramental tradition in the two churches joining in 1957 to form the United Church of Christ has been observed by Roman Catholic scholar Michael Taylor in his research on Protestant denominations, described in *The Protestant Liturgical Renewal: A Catholic Viewpoint* (Westminster, Md.: Newman Press, 1963), 95. Seventy percent of the UCC clergy surveyed believed the sacraments to be "conveyors of grace" ("sacramentalist" in his classification), in contrast to thirty percent who viewed them as psychological stimulators of faith ("symbolist" in his terms). Sixty-five percent of the UCC-CC pastors were sacramentalists and 35 percent were symbolists. These figures are significantly higher than clergy of other Protestant churches like the Methodists (50 percent sacramentalist and 50 percent symbolist) and the Presbyterians (53 percent sacramentalist and 45 percent symbolist). Also 70 percent of the UCC-CC clergy believed that the Supper is in some sense a sacrifice, as did 60 percent of the UCC-E&R respondents. As liturgical renewal has made significant progress in all these Protestant communions since this survey, the degree of sacramentalist (and sacrificial) conviction could well be higher.

13. See Max Thurian, The Mystery of the Eucharist: An Ecumenical Approach, trans. Emily Chisolm (Grand Rapids, Mich.: Eerdmans, 1981).

14. Preamble to "The Mission and Nature of the Church," a 1986 working paper of the Task Force on the Nature and Mission of the Church, Family Thank Offering Project, UCC Office of Church Life and Leadership.

15. For glimpses of the current theological ferment in the UCC, see Gabriel Fackre, "Theological Soul-Searching in the United Church of Christ," *TSF*

*Bulletin,* vol. 8, no. 2, pp. 5–9, reprinted in *Mid-Stream,* vol. 24, no. 2 (April 1985); the Spring 1985 issue of *New Conversations* (vol. 8, no. 1); and Barbara Brown Zikmund, "Theology in the United Church of Christ: A Documentary Trail," *Prism,* Introductory Issue (Fall 1985), 7–25.

*BEM* on the Eucharist: A United Church of Christ Perspective, *Prism,* Vol. 1, No. 2 (Fall 1986), 47–58. Used by permission.

## CHAPTER 10

# Israel's Continuing Covenant and God's Deed in Christ

THE THEOLOGICAL COMMITTEE's "Message to the Churches" affirms the paradox of God's irrevocable covenant with Israel and the affirmation of the United Church of Christ Statement of Faith that God came to us in Jesus Christ, "conquering sin and death, and reconciling the world. . . ." Paradoxes cannot be explained. But they can be explored. Here we investigate aspects of the questions of "covenant," "Christology," "anti-Semitism," and "ethics," by going to Paul's own struggle with the paradox in Romans 9–11. As Scripture, interpreted christologically, is the standard of teaching in the United Church of Christ (Preamble, Constitution), exegesis is fundamental to our theological work. Here are some judgments that rise from reflection on the Romans passages as they are read in the context of the whole canon.

1. "The gifts and call of God are irrevocable . . . all Israel will be saved." (Romans 11:29, 26) These are two of 14 references in Romans 9–11 to the positive role and destiny of Israel in the purposes of God. (Other themes vis-a-vis Israel: the urging of Gentiles to value their engrafting (12), the hardening/disobedience of Israel (9), affirmation of a remnant in Israel who received Christ, among them Paul (4), etc.) As a major theme in these chapters, consonant with canonical accents, the irrevocability of the covenant, including the promise of salvation for "all Israel," is a fundamental New Testament teaching.

2. From the same chapters: "If you confess with your lips that Jesus is Lord and believe in your heart that God raised him from the dead, you will be saved.... How beautiful are the feet of those who preach the good news! (Romans 10:9, 14b, 15b) This "scandal of particularity," repeated hundreds of times through the New Testament, is also integral to Christian teaching. The affirmation of christological singularity (John 14:6), the new covenant/New Testament in Jesus Christ, is a Christian non-negotiable.

3. The partnership of new and old covenants is not an innovation. The covenant with Abraham does not eliminate the covenant with Noah. The covenant with Moses does not revoke the covenant with Abraham. Each new chapter in the Great Story incorporates the earlier ones. This is a canonical refrain. The difficult question is how the covenants with Abraham/Moses/David continue in the time of the new covenant in Christ. A minimalist view asserts the partnership but goes no further, as in the case of our message. But let us pursue the inquiry here a step beyond—exploring, not explaining.

4. How does Israel's covenant continue after the unique deed of God in Christ? Christians believe that in Christ's life, death, and resurrection, the powers of sin, evil, and death were finally defeated. Paul's effort to hold together both the continuing old and the new covenant, read canonically, can be understood this way:

   a. Israel plays a unique role in the salvation story. "To them belong the sonship, the glory, the covenants, the giving of the law, the worship, the promises. . . . And of their race is the Christ." (Rom. 9:4) Indeed, Abraham is "the father of faith," and those who are his true children in Israel before Christ are "saved"—albeit by the retroactive "application of the benefits of Christ," as the traditional teaching has it. Yet Paul extends this special claim forward, as well as backward. Thus the future tense: "All Israel will be saved." The "all," however, must be read in the light of Paul's statement that "not all who are descended from Israel belong to Israel." (Rom. 9:6b) Only those of true Abrahamic faith are heirs. By

implication, those in the future (after Christ) who stand in this
faithful line constitute "all Israel." Where there is Abrahamic faith,
then and now there is saving faith.

b. Yet how can Paul say this if a knowledge of Christ is the need
and goal of all humanity? And this entails a confession of Christ
in the "heart" and with the "lips?"

Some resources from patristic theology, and from Karl Barth, give
help here. The early theologians, interpreting the "descent of Christ" to
the place of the dead on Good Friday (see I Peter 3:18–20, 4:6, and the
Apostles' Creed) believed that the faithful in Israel before Christ were
confronted by him in his descent into death, evoking confession of
Christ as the fulfillment of their proleptic faith. Barth, in a complimen-
tary line of thought, held that all humanity died and rose again in Christ.
Christian mission tells the world what it does not yet know about its
already reconciled life in the New Age.

Pressing the early theologians' insight beyond Good Friday and limit-
ing Barth's neo-universalism to the Israel of Romans 11 point to an
eschatological encounter of Christ with all of Abrahamic faith. Those
redeemed in that faith then come to know the reconciler, Jesus Christ. In
this way both the christological centralities and the irrevocable covenant
with Israel are affirmed. (This eschatological disclosure is similar to the
view of believing Jews who hold that Christians are saved by their faithfulness to the "covenant of Noah," i.e., by living a life responsive to universal conscience or to the truth they know as Christians—but only learn
of the saving God of Abraham, Isaac, and Jacob in the world to come.)

c. Another consideration is closely related to Paul's own personal
journey. "I myself am an Israelite, a descendant of Abraham. . . ."
(Rom. 11:1b) Before the Damascus Road, Paul was no
Abrahamic believer, but a devotee of the law, one who "did not
pursue it though faith, but as if it were based on works." (Rom.
9:32a) Yet there was hope even for this "chiefest of sinners," who
was saved by grace through faith in Christ.

He puzzled over why only a "remnant" in Israel so responded, but
went on to urge the proclamation of faith to Jews as well as Gentiles.

With him, and with those few who then believed, faith is not only noetic, as in b., but also fiducial, a saving faith contingent on the knowledge of Christ. Might Paul's "all Israel" also include those zealous for the law who must also first meet Christ—in time or eternity—as Paul did on the Damascus Road, to learn of the kind of gracious faith that saves? Did Paul have a special place in his heart for others, like himself, whose ardor for God proved to be the first step on the path from works to faith? Anti-supersessionism does not forbid sharing the Gospel with Jewish people. Exclusion, in fact, is a subtle form of discrimination, denying to Jews what Christians believe to be their own most precious gift. How this nonexclusionary mission mandate is carried out, while honoring the continuing covenant of God with Israel, is not clear. What is clear is that targeting Jews for evangelism, on the grounds that they will not be saved without Christian ministrations, does conflict with Paul's judgments in Romans 11. Further, it seems to presuppose the will to extinguish a people with whom God has chosen to be in covenant until the End.

5. Paul struggles mightily with how the continuing covenant with Israel worked, collectively, as well as personally. He does so with an eye on symbiosis: what happens to Israel affects in a salutary way the church.

One sign of the symbiotic relation today is Israel's custodianship of basic codes of human life together. The heirs of Amos and Isaiah are regularly found in the front ranks of causes of justice and peace. As Reinhold Niebuhr observed, one soon learns that it is Jews in the community who can be counted on as allies in the struggles for humanization. Indeed, the witness of Israel reminds the church of its own historical commitments, and often saves it from Marcionite temptations to write off the Old Testament and over-spiritualize the Gospel. As a special community of conscience to both church and world, it reminds Christians, "It's not you that supports the root, but the root that supports you." (Rom. 11:18)

6. Does a continuing covenant entail the promise of land? For many Jews what Christians have to say on this subject is of more interest than the strictly theological questions addressed above.

Christian Zionism to the contrary not withstanding, there are no New Testament warrants for the reacquisition of the soil of ancient Israel. Nor can there be any straight-line theological endorsement of the modern state of Israel. The uncritical identification of the will of God with human institutions violates the divine sovereignty. In the Romans passage no linkage is made between the continuing covenant and a future nation-state. However, a too sharp disjunction between land and covenant is not in order, either. For the following reasons:

   a. The God of Abraham and Sarah, the same God incarnate in Jesus Christ, is One who lives and acts in human history, and thus is active in our political moil and toil.

   b. The hardships of the people of Israel over time are directly related to its stewardship of God's Torah. As conscience of the human community, this people evoke the hostility of a fallen creation. As such, space—geography with defensible borders—is needed to assure its continued witness. Especially so, in the face of the twentieth century record of hate toward the bearers of the prophetic tradition.

   c. Geographic stewardship is inseparable from the covenant mandate: a land flowing with the milk and honey of the law and the prophets. The most painful testing place for such a model of *shalom* in the late twentieth century is on the fertile crescent, where marching armies from North and South have ever again challenged this vision, and from whose womb three great religions, all proclaiming *shalom,* were born. Here is an opportunity for the state of Israel to be what it is: the world's community of conscience, demonstrating what life together can mean. No realization of this vision is possible without the partnership of the Palestinian people. What more dramatic witness could there be to a political life together in our time than such a "light to the nations?"

7. The rise of anti-Semitism and anti-Judaism demands solidarity of Christians with Jews. The historic complicity of Christians and churches in the infliction of suffering on Jews is cause for a repen-

tance that propels Christians to the front lines of the struggle today against this ethnic and religious hate and hurt.

8. Authentic Christian belief in the singular deed of the suffering God in Jesus Christ is the ground of Christian solidarity with Jews, and is an antidote to inauthentic teaching about Christ that has provided an ideological smokescreen for ethnic and religious hate and hurt. Hence, a rightly understood anti-supersessionism has profound ethical as well as theological consequences.

Israel's Continuing Covenant and God's Deed in Christ, *New Conversations,* Vol. 12, No. 3 (Summer 1990), 25–27. Used by permission.

# PART THREE

# Doing

## THE CHURCH IN ACTION

## CHAPTER 11

# Emphasis:

## THE LOCAL CHURCH IN GOD'S MISSION

*When your son asks you in time to come, "What is the meaning of the testi-*
*monies and the statutes and the ordinances which the Lord our God has com-*
*manded you?" then you shall say to your son, "We were Pharaoh's slaves in*
*Egypt; and the Lord brought us out of Egypt with a mighty hand . . . that he*
*might bring us in and give us the land which he swore to give to our fathers.*
*And the Lord commanded us to do all these statutes, to fear the Lord our God,*
*for our good always, that he might preserve us alive, as at this day."*

—Deuteronomy 6:20–25

WHEN AMNESIA AMPUTATES the past, it takes away our identity. Who
we *were* shapes who we *are.* Israel's remembered call to commitment is our commission today, and Abraham is the father of our family.

"The Lord said, 'Abraham, Go.' . . . So Abraham went." That's what
Israel's memory is all about. God called; Abraham did. Something happened.

"By you all the families of the earth will bless themselves." The Lord
has a vision of a new land flowing with milk and honey, a land of peace,
where the wolf and the lamb lie down together, where swords are beat-
en into plowshares. God needs someone to take the first steps toward
that new land.

Abraham was elected. He was chosen not for privilege but for hard
work and long hours—he was a man in mission.

Today is another time for remembering and renewing Abraham's mission. Today is 1967, 1968, 1969—the time of the church in mission, the
time of the local church in God's mission. We follow a new Abraham.

The one who sent Abraham has come into the world to make the journey—"In Jesus Christ, the man of Nazareth, our crucified and risen Lord . . . has come to us and shared our common lot."

As fellow pilgrims and disciples in his church we are called—according to our faith—*to accept the cost and joy of discipleship, to be his servants in the service of others, to proclaim the gospel to all the world and resist the powers of evil, to share in Christ's baptism and eat at his table, to join him in his passion and victory.*

Yet, it is St. John's-by-the-Gas-Station—that strange assortment of the humble and the haughty, the weak and the strong, the saint and the sinner, the wheat and the tare—to whom the invitation is extended to be the wayfaring people of God. It is over *our* heads that the claiming waters of baptism have flowed and into *our* mouths and lives that the bread and wine of passion and victory have passed.

To know who we are is the beginning of wisdom—and the beginning of pilgrimage. We seek to ground the years of emphasis renewal ahead in the remembering of the events that make us who we are and give us our identity.

We call upon the congregations of the United Church of Christ to go to their roots, to be radical, to examine the source from which they have come and the goal which gives them their reason for being.

We encourage them to use as one tool for digging the Statement of Faith. Light for the pilgrim's journey comes from the lamp of faith—a faith that knows its gift and claim, its election and mandate.

Donald Michael, author of *Cybernation,* says that every institution in the world of tomorrow ought to have a "critic-in-residence." The pace of change will be so rapid in the decades ahead that no business, government, school or hospital will survive if it does not have a built-in mechanism for keeping on its toes. In order not to go under, you must pay someone to think up devastating attacks on the way the organization is doing things. That person will keep it flexible, updated, and in step with the times.

The church is the Body of Christ. But it is a body of people as well as the Body of Christ, human as well as holy. Because the church has an earthy underside, because it has to pay its heat and light bills, empty the wastebaskets, and organize human beings like any other institution, it lives by the same rules as human institutions.

In short, the church must retool. And such updating—the Catholics now call *aggiornamento* should come natural to it, *just because* it has a pilgrim faith that was born in *a moving-out moment of history* under the banner of the God of Abraham.

It should come easy to us. But let's face it—it doesn't. Take a look at some of our hang-ups!

1. Our crisis in belief. Horst Symanowski summed it up by saying that men no longer launch crusades or lay awake at night worrying about the question that turned Luther on: "How can I find a gracious God?" Rather, what speeds the pulse today is the question, "How can I find a gracious neighbor?"—not page one of Paul's letters to the Romans but page one of the daily newspaper, with its struggles between black and white, rich and poor, East and West, male and female, young and old. And the real rub comes when we who are immersed in this world begin to find this world's answers for this worldly problem without benefit of clergy, church, or Godtalk.

Crisis and puzzlement come in answer to those questions when the church gets in a frenzy over this process of secularization. When, fearful of the new time of freedom into which God is leading us, Her church wants to repeat the old formulas uncritically—wants to keep thinking of God as a cosmic bellhop.

Just the opposite can result from this puzzlement too, of course, when caught up in the new secularism and the new freedom we want to write God out of the picture!

Yet could not the true and living God be behind the new urge to solve our problems? Could crisis be opportunity?

2. Our crisis in behavior. Old ways of doing things which seemed so right to our ancestors—and indeed may well have been right for them in their time—are now boulders on the road of our own pilgrimage. Take the fast-coming age of cybernation.

Can the church still teach that work is something that everyone must do at the penalty of not earning his keep? But what happens in a day of new technology when only a fraction of the labor force is needed to the work in mill, mine and office? What happens to our Protestant work ethic?

3. Crisis comes when our only response is to repeat the answers of the past.

Crisis in structure. Once a dedicated little band of people in "Buttonwood Corners" gathered under a white spire could live out a life together and a life of service to the community that touched the citizens of Buttonwood at birth and death, in sickness and health, at work and play. The local congregation had a full-orbed ministry.

Now Buttonwood Corners has become Buttonwood Manor, a booming suburb of people who work in the big city twenty miles away, play at the shore 200 miles away, are born and die in mass medical centers far from Buttonwood, send their children around the country to be educated in other mass centers of education. And even as they sit in their living-rooms at home, their eyes fixed on that oblong screened box in the corner, their choices on clothing, politics and hairdo are shaped by "somebody out there" a long way from the Buttonwood hearthside.

Our crisis comes when we expect the pastor and his little flock in Buttonwood Manor to do what his great-grandfather did so well in Buttonwood Corners.

Can that pastor today be a lone ranger? Can the ministry of Christ's church be carried on without partnership, teamwork, alliance with others who live out and tell these stories at those places of work and play, weakness and strength, learning and living, birth and death?

Can we afford to look back?

But why *do* we look back? Why did Lot's wife?

Lot's wife really did not trust in the Pilgrim God. She trusted herself more. Luther called it "incurvedness." Kierkegaard labeled it "shutupness." The Bible calls it sin.

The basic crisis—whether we are talking about Lot's wife, or Sodom and Gomorrah or a church in flight—is that things are going wrong side up. The only answer is to turn things right side up, or to make an about face as the New Testament puts it in its piercing word *repent*. Turn around!

Get with the one who marches at the head of line in the great Pilgrim Demonstration.

What Israel guessed at and hoped for the Christian sees "tangibilitated." God kept his promise. The expectation of an Isaiah for one who would carry our sorrows and be bruised for our iniquities is earthed in the "man of Nazareth." With the coming of this "Man," a new age opens up, an age of fulfilled promises, an age of hope in action. Yes, an age when the church itself is the first-fruits of the new Kingdom.

Come on, now! What does all that theological talk mean?

It means that a pilgrim looks at the world, and at the church, with a special set of eyes—looks at a beaten, bedraggled world and says "It *can* be different, and it *will* be different."

To believe that the God of Abraham is not a giving-up kind of deity, but a stick-to-it God is to be ready to stake your life on the things that God does.

God showed that a pilgrim people would not be deserted in the Great Happenings. Remember, Pentecost is one of them—the dynamic of the church, the new pilgrim Israel. He promised that where two or three pilgrims gathered in the divine name, there God is. And where the *presence* is there also will the power.

Now that is something!

We have an idea what that power is like from the Happening. It's revitalizing, renewing, resurrecting power. To believe that is to look at the church with new eyes of hope. No matter how backward-looking, inward-looking, and shut-up we are, God is not about to give up on us. We have a second-chance Pilgrim God. Repentance *can* happen. *New* thinking, *new* behaviour, *new* structures, *new* leadership are possible. Rebirth is real.

Blessing and honor and glory and power be unto God!

The signs are everywhere to be seen! A pope looks a shut-up people in the eye, goes over to a window and throws it open. A martyr dies, a movement begins, a sermon is preached, a book is written, a new fighting word is born in a bent-in Christendom: The world! "God so loved the *world!*" "You are the light of the *world!*" "Go into all the *world!*" Lot's wife looks in and back, but a pilgrim church looks forward and out.

This is a time of turning—turning from pre-occupation with the I, me and mine, from the heavenly hedonism which is always so concerned with my peace of mind, my soul, my needs, my church, toward the *other,* the neighbor, the one for whom Christ died. That is the mission of God: A turning-in serving, suffering love.

Talk is cheap. What does "being for others" mean? What is the local church in God's mission? How can my congregation get with God's mission?

A fair question—the *basic question* in the United Church of Christ in the years ahead. Fair and basic, as long as you are not asking for a bag of tricks, a package of gimmicks, that will guarantee "instant success."

We have no *product* to sell. But we do have a process. We invite you on a pilgrimage.

It's like one we are taking right now in this presentation. Its wheel of components include:

1. The congregation getting its sights squarely fixed on its purpose, its reasons for being, its identity, its basic belief about God and humanity, its vision of life and death, the church and the world;

2. Careful dissection of the time and place in which God has put the crises and challenges of belief, behavior, structure, and leadership within our own backyard and beyond;

3. An honest examination of just what the congregation has done to relate its belief to its past and present practices—self-study, self-assessment;

4. ACTION—doing right now what must be done in the light as vision;

5. Careful evaluation, checking and rechecking, to see if we are good stewards of the resources God has put in our hands and the vision he has lifted before our eyes.

The church is the Body of Christ and paradoxically also a very earthy institution. Because it is the latter as well as the former, it needs the best possible human savvy that can be mustered.

In fact, that is one thing we mean by the church maturing. We learn to *grow up* to the place where we stand on our two feet and use the brains God gave us. Surely, that includes using all the intellectual, physical and spiritual muscles he provides for us—the best in human ingenuity, planning and process.

But you know, and I know, that is not the whole story. The church is not just another human organization. Nor is the Christian believer a humanist who flexes muscles and flaunts power.

There is a final factor to take into account. Jonathan Edwards put it in memorable terms: *God does all, and we do all. God produces all, and we act all. For that is what he produces, viz our own acts. God is the only proper author and foundation; we only are the proper actors.*

This is a revision of a presentation given at the 1967 General Synod of the United Church of Christ in the author's role as the chair of the 1968–1969 biennial emphasis, "The Local Church in God's Mission." It appeared in the *United Church Herald,* vol. 10, no. 11(November 1962), 11M–13M. Used by permission.

## CHAPTER 12

# A Voice for the Voiceless:

## AN ABOVEGROUND UNDERGROUND NEWSPAPER

WOULD YOU BELIEVE—a town in which all three newspapers, the TV station, and a radio station are owned by the same family, where the news and views of the powerful get full airing and those of the powerless get short shrift?

Would you believe—a town in which the young, the black, the poor, the professor, the poverty worker, the church-in-world Christian and Jew banded together to publish their own newspaper, where the powerless took it into their own hands to "give voice to voiceless views—to print the unprinted news"?

The first is not hard to imagine. Indeed, 90% of America's communities have a monopoly press. The second is difficult to swallow, but it is beginning to happen. We tell the story of one "irrepressible weekly" in the small city of Lancaster, Pennsylvania, where the news monolith described in the first paragraph reigned until the recent birth of LIP, the *Lancaster Independent Press*. Its experience may be of some value as a laboratory for others planning their RIPs, PIPs, or NIPs.

Lancastrians read their newspaper as faithfully as their Bibles, and treat the former as much as "gospel" as the latter. A loose coalition of the community's powerless discovered this in the peace, poverty, and civil rights ferment of the decade in this Pennsylvania Dutch metropolitan community of 300,000. Often the editorials and the "news" stories were as unbalanced and destructive in these areas as the letters to the editor from the noisy right wing. The press gave the benediction to the *status quo,* with one important exception: The editor of the morning daily regularly took strong stands on civil rights concerns, locally, and nationally.

Shortly after several courageous editorials supported a plan to deseg-regate the city's junior high schools in the face of the fury of a thousand petitioners from white neighborhoods affected, a strange reshuffle took place in the editorial staff. A new name appeared on the masthead as managing editor—a former staff member of the evening paper—and the word was out that the regular editor had been relieved of effective con-trol of the paper. From that point on, what "liberal" noises had been made were silenced.

In the overheated months of 1968, stories in all papers appeared with increasing frequency about beatings, "riots," and shootings in which black militants appeared to be the culprits. Nothing was said about white motorcycle gangs that rode through the ghetto taunting black youth, nor was background given on known instances of white provocation, nor were the many grievances against police tactics in the black community aired. Local peace activists received particularly rough treatment in the media. Caricatures of the student revolution and the new breed of high school youth were plentiful. The Community Action Program came under regular criticism. Responsible coverage reached a new low in the fall of 1968 when several young, black militants were arrested for the murder of a white pedestrian, and the defense attorney pled for a change of venue using piles of news clippings which he rightly claimed had contributed to the inflaming of community passions. It appeared that it would be a repeat performance of *Murder in Paradise,* the book report-ing the strange Lancaster trial of a Franklin and Marshall College stu-dent who was executed in the 1950's for the murder of a local citizen. At that trial, the defense attorney also pled without success for a change of venue on the grounds of an inflammatory press. The black youth was more fortunate. Halfway through the trial, a visiting judge threw the case out of court because there was insufficient evidence to warrant contin-uing the prosecution.

During this period, talk about the press among civil rights leaders and churchmen took an increasingly serious turn. Restlessness with the sit-uation led three clergymen—the Rev. George Geisler of Trinity United Church of Christ, East Petersburg, and former chairman of the Social Action Committee of the Lancaster Council of Churches; the Rev. Allen Kroehler, director of the Seminary's Laboratory for Leadership and

Learning; and the writer of this article—to pay a visit to the editor of one of the country's leading, crusading small papers: the nearby York *Gazette & Daily.* Awed by the thought of starting from scratch, we thought the best that could be managed was a Lancaster edition of the York paper. However, similar overtures from Baltimore, Harrisburg, and Gettysburg had proved unproductive, and the editor advised us to launch our own.

After making some soundings among old allies in NAACP, ACLU, the peace movement, church leadership, potential new allies in the remnants of the Eugene McCarthy organization, the editor of the renewal center Encounter's newsletter (which served as a kind of clearing-house for information about community action), and Community Action Program (CAP) participants, an organizing meeting was called at the Laboratory for Leadership and Learning. Allen Kroehler's minutes read, "Twenty-four citizens of Lancaster County met September 18, 1968, to consider the need for more responsible news coverage. It was agreed that the need was urgent." Four task forces were formed to deal with purpose, layout, distribution, and fund-raising. Then began five months of daydreaming, brainstorming, wrangling, sifting, retreat and advance.

With the odd assortment of people that gathered around this venture—almost totally lacking in journalistic experience—the gestation of Lancaster Independent Press (LIP), was something to behold. Clergypersons found themselves training to be reporters, a seminary professor's wife became coordinator of photography, an RCA engineer became chief solicitor of funds, a housewife tried her hand at a TV column, an advertising executive took responsibility for making up crossword puzzles, an anthropologist took over distribution, and a history professor agreed to become the editor. Meanwhile, a dedicated but nervous attorney plotted the course through the anticipated legal and libel shoals.

There were also some professionals in this strange mix. A former editor of a local paper, now retired, met with us about technical matters, explaining along the way how he had put ventures like ours out of business. Another editor, from out of town, met with the planning committee to describe the hurdles in great detail and to advise us to quit before it was too late. Another counseled us that it was impossible to start without at least $500,000 on hand. A national communications executive advised us to have a radio program instead. Friends came and went in the five months of organizing. Some who were interested in the effort because of the chance for newspaper experience beat a hasty retreat when they discovered LIP's controversial bent. Members of the Students for a Democratic Society (SDS) appeared inquisitive at first, but soon concluded that nothing much could happen with a lot of middle-class, churchy types. Several of our early black militant supporters were jailed. Some CAP personnel disappeared after meditation on the Mann Act. An educational television station recorded a meeting with a view toward doing a documentary, but retired deciding the LIP venture was an improbable one. Survivors stumbled ahead.

By the first of the year, certain tangible signs appeared. The group agreed on a name and designed an appropriate logo—LIP with an intertwined interrobang—that found its way onto a six-foot banner and some newly printed stationery. The banner fluttered one Saturday over a workshop in Lancaster's oldest church building, Trinity Lutheran Church, in which 75 volunteers participated, sorting themselves into permanent committees and task forces for projected issues. A new headquarters was found—Encounter's three-story downtown building—after a Seminary administration, anxious about the tax status of its Laboratory building, asked LIP to move. A card was printed to solicit funds, with such optimistic categories as $500 for patron membership and $1,000 for life membership. The group acquired a treasurer, bonded him, and deposited its $234 in a newly established account.

Most important, the group finally decided who it was. The statement of purpose filed in the incorporation proceedings announced: "The Lancaster Independent Press is a nonprofit weekly newspaper published by Lancaster citizens for Lancaster citizens. Its purposes are to:

1. Publish news of local and national affairs that is not available to the average Lancaster reader—to print the unprinted news.
2. Provide a forum for opinion that is denied a public hearing—to give voice to voiceless views.
   LIP affirms the words, "Some men see things as they are and ask, why? I dream of things that never were and ask, why not?"

While this statement offers a broad, secular platform for all who are struggling for a more just and humane community, those of us who came to LIP because of our Christian commitments read it with lenses formed from those convictions. Thus, it speaks in Christian futurity idiom of a "shalom" in which all sorts and conditions will have a chance to participate meaningfully, echoing Martin Luther King's dream of society reconciled. It affirms the dignity of the "weak things of the world and despised," and seeks to be an instrument of the God who "casts the mighty from their seats and exalts those of low degree." It applies the Biblical realism about the corruptibility of absolute power to a monopoly media, and seeks to disperse it.

With its dreams and its $234, LIP moved into Encounter's downtown quarters. Borrowed typewriters, filing cabinets, chairs, and tables began to appear along with some very talented people, eager to help where they could. Among that number was a group of Volunteers in Service to America (VISTA) workers who promptly filled the positions of city editor, assistant cartoonist, and, as we were soon to discover, adventurous reporters. The spacious third floor "editorial offices" even began to look like a newspaper stereotype, complete with stagnant coffee cups, litter, and a chain-smoking editor.

In the first week of March 1969, 7,000 copies of LIP hit the streets of Lancaster. Of these, 2,000 were bulk orders to some forty churches that had been convinced by an articulate pastor that it was the kind of thing that renewal-oriented congregations should boost. Many were hawked for 10¢ per copy on the downtown streets, in suburban shopping centers, or sold door-to-door by the children of some of the organizers and by college students. Others were distributed outside of area high schools by the cub reporters who had helped to form the first issue on the subject of youth. An additional 1,400 were sent as free samples to a list of potential sympathizers, and the rest were distributed from Hawaii to Maine in a quest for outside support.

The excitement over the sheer "happenedness" of the paper tended to obscure, at first, some hard facts about its quality. Soon enough, our well-wishers and others pointed out that there was hardly any news in the first issue except a scoop picture of a steeple cross being placed on a local church. Also, for a paper that purported to be crusading, the posture seemed generally rather timid. There were, however, some in-depth articles on the youth of the black community, excerpts from the ACLU statement on civil rights for students, a story about high-school underground newspapers in the county, a calendar of events, a cartoon strip, and other items. The most popular feature seemed to be the centerfold poster with a striking picture of two smiling "flower children" on a park wall hovering a sedate, middle-aged couple on a bench below, with the signatures of many of the LIP workers and appropriate graffiti surrounding it.

The quality and the bite of the paper took a marked turn upward in succeeding issues, thanks to improved organization and feedback. A second issue on the housing theme had some hard-hitting commentary and data on slumlords, a story of discontent among both white and black poor over housing conditions, church involvement in housing efforts, a Puerto Rican column, and even two ads. The third issue, on peace, marked the expansion of the paper from 8 to 12 pages with such items as the story of Lancaster as the capital of the state because of the presence of several peace denominations, the personnel and operations of the local Selective Service system, and the growing militancy of the peace movement. The publication of unprinted news took on dramatic reality with a front-page story of a respected school board member who had been purged from the fall Republican slate because of his courageous vote several years previously for the integration of the junior high schools—a tale which has yet to appear in any of the conventional media. In a similar vein were interviews with the black attorney who defended the youth released from the murder trial for lack of evidence, and a local peace protester whose case for returning business reply cards with "Stop the war" on them had been dropped. To the Puerto Rican column was added one in Greek (as the LIP offset printing process enable it to photograph Father Alexander Veronis' Greek typescript letters, the word to the established media since has been, "Can you top this?"). The first comic strip was joined by a second, and now there were five ads.

Succeeding issues on such themes as local government and area higher education had studies of minority parties (Democratic and American Independent), an interview with a Birch Society leader and a black militant (both granted exclusively to LIP because it was not part of the "establishment press"), a column by high school students, reports of activities in the Jewish community, reports of student and faculty ferment in area colleges, and notes on the area educational TV. Ads now are numbered in the teens, and with subscriptions mounting toward the 500 mark and a regular press run of 5,000 copies, it looks like the newly employed editor, Lamar Hoover, may even get his meager salary on time.

When the names of LIP incorporators were published in the legal notices of the dailies in January, the city accepted the news with its customary, Pennsylvania Dutch reserve. Apart from our attorney receiving some good-natured joshing on lawyers' row, and several nasty letters expressing ire over the latest hobby-horse of the town's "radicals" (the group of incorporators included the president of the NAACP, and ACLU leader, a college professor, a businesswoman with a record of ardent civil rights activity, and a seminary professor), reaction was not discernable. After the initial issues, however, that picture changed.

LIP's research of racist pressure that prompted the dropping of the school board member earned the wrath of the local Republican machine. It evoked the same reaction from the Democratic establishment when it probed for bias and opportunism in the sidetracking of scattered-site housing plans and the treatment of welfare recipients. Interviews with the black militant and his lawyer which aired stinging criticism of county judicial procedures, jail conditions, and police practices made few friends in those precincts.

For some, the sheer existence of LIP, quite apart from what it said, raised blood pressures. The response of one woman at a church gathering where LIP was invited to explain its goals was not atypical. "How dare you!" she demanded. Indeed, to cast suspicion on the performance of the established press by starting a new paper is more than some elements of the Lancaster community can take. As the former president of one of the area's major industries put it, "It's subversive!"

Mild repression followed the rhetoric. Our first printer strangely withdrew his services the day the first copy was scheduled for the press. Our present printer, whose courage and commitment have led him to be our technical adviser as well, had certain trade privileges taken away the week he joined us. The proprietor of a drugstore, livid with rage after the third issue, ejected our professorial distributor and his bundle of fourth-issue copies. Organizers and editorial staff members regularly receive anonymous phone calls and letters.

Not all of the protests came from expected sources. Bulk orders from churches were greatly reduced. Why? Perhaps one incident reported by a pastor is a clue. When a leading layperson was asked at a board meeting to document activity, the best he could do was to exclaim, "Why he had a stack of LIPs in his office!" A middle-class black leader complained that LIP was trying to make heroes out of black criminals, and a local college chaplain looked over the list of activist sponsors and decided that his counseling duties were too time-consuming to allow for his participation!

Obstacles were not all of this nay-saying variety. Some had to do with the "newly discovered" sin of acedia. A Pennsylvania Dutch community happy with its comfortable standard of living for the majority was simply too absorbed in its TV, gardening, and weekend at the shore to bother much about the voice and concerns of the minority groups in their midst.

We have spoken of the enthusiasm and dedication of the organizing core. In concentric rings around it are supporting orbits of persons who have contributed significantly to the life of LIP.

The first circle is made up of the hundreds of charter subscribers who saw the desperate need for representing the unrepresented news and views. Taking out subscriptions of $2 to $10 each were citizens of an adventurous bent and those associated with various movements for social justice. Numbered among the first subscribers, although for somewhat different reasons, were various community political leaders who watched the phenomenon with no little interest.

Among the churches that began with LIP and have been of special, morale-boosting significance, one deserves special mention: the city's oldest and largest congregation, Trinity Lutheran Church. One of the first contacts the organizing group made in its brainstorming phase was with Dr. Wallace Fisher, the senior pastor and author of some well-known books on church renewal. Dr. Fisher gave the project his unreserved support. In addition to making available hundreds of copies of LIP on its literature table, the congregation runs regular ads and does an interpretive job with both the general public and some of the city's decision-makers. It is well to remember that when the newspaper takes a controversial stand on a local judge or a scattered-site housing program, it will be the participating churches and clergy whose locus is still within established Lancaster who feel the first shockwave. That is why there are not more Fishers and Trinitys. Fortunate is the community that has such prophets!

Except for an occasional dissenter, the black community was enthusiastic in its reception of LIP, particularly black youths and young adults who had regularly received a bad press. While the rhetoric of black separatism is popular among just these groups as in most urban communities, a functional camaraderie below the level of ideology was born around the operation and services rendered by LIP. This has tended to bear out the hopes of the founders to find new areas of black-white cooperation, based on the fact that each needs the other, to replace both the unities and disunities of old paternalisms and their backlash polarization.

Geographically on the furthest rim from the core are the out-of-town friends of LIP. Ranging from newspapers editors, church and secular—amazed to see the survival of the thing they forecast could never be born—through ACLU state officers, to OEO staff in Washington, planners in California, and Mennonite officials in Indiana, such counsel and support has been of great value. The largest delegation of extra-Lancaster support comes from United Church of Christ denominational leaders, agencies, and Conference executives.

As the sheer existence of LIP excites its antagonists so, too, does its factuality account for the interest and encouragement of its yea-sayers. It is living proof that the voiceless *can find their voice and claim their humanity!*

During a previous urban mission in Lancaster—the development of a network of freedom schools called Program in American Cultural Enrichment (PACE), and the subsequently successful struggle to integrate the junior high schools—Lancaster Seminary served as a think-tank attempting to sort out the components of effective action. The same kind evaluation procedure has already begun informally in the case of LIP. Here are a few preliminary observations on factors contributing to social change:

1. The momentum was built up by previous action in the community around such foci as Encounter (a downtown coffee-house renewal center), PACE, efforts to eliminate de facto segregation in schools and housing and other civil rights issues. Out of this, a loose coalition of people began to learn to work with each other. Also, their efforts were attended by some victories that convinced them that change could be effected.

2. The infusion of new blood into this mix contributes greatly, particularly high school students, young social workers, and black militants.

3. Related to the two above was what might be called the "McCarthy Phenomenon." This is more than a spill-over of the particular ex-Eugene McCarthyites. It is the emergence of a new, tough core of committed people in America who are willing to spend themselves for a humane society. Skeptical old-era politicians and other status quo types do not take into account this new readiness to "walk on water," and therefore, they vastly miscalculate its potential.

4. The "Bull O'Connor Effect." It is the presence and bumbling repressiveness of a monopoly media that invites and foments resistance to its actions and inactions.

5. The "Hatcher Factor." As the black mayor of Gary, Indiana, is bolstered in many ways by foundations, educators, planners, and government sources, so LIP's future is tied up with its long-distance counsel and support. This is why some of the bitterest diatribes of foes of social change are reserved for the "outside agitator."

6. The role of churchmen as catalysts, community accreditors, and providers of some organization and promotional savvy. In a pluralistic and secular society, church leaders cannot and should not attempt massive social change by themselves, for they are only a fraction of the community. But it is the secular Saul Alinsky who has discovered the clergy who "burn with a white heat," and the civil rights and peace movements that have learned to recognize kindred spirits among the renewal-oriented in the churches.

7. The piggy-back locally on issues of national import and momentum. The wave of concern about the need for a responsible media,

and the appearance of both underground and independent presses around the country.

8. The availability of a headquarters serving both practical and symbolic functions; in this case, Encounter.

9. The avoidance of the adventurism and sensationalism in sex and revolutionary rhetoric which plays into the hands of those looking for ways to undermine a critical press.

10. The nonjournalistic, but nonetheless professional skills of an array of volunteers: attorneys, advertising people, typists, photographers, writers, teachers, social workers.

11. The evolution toward a core of paid employees. As important as volunteers are, those who have worked in new forms of mission discover that summer vacations roll around, initial enthusiasms wear off, other challenges surface to compete. LIP is fortunate to have a paid editor, and also to recruit from the Voluntary Service Center at Pottstown. More will be needed.

We spoke in our opening paragraph about the believable and the unbelievable. Can the latter survive the former? Will this fragile new growth bear up under the predictable pressures from those for whom the voice of the voiceless is an embarrassment and an offense? Will the early zeal pass away? While no one is making firm predictions, new heart is taken each time the biweekly miracle recurs. The more daring make plans for thematic issues well into 1970. The Voluntary Service Center recruit has signed on for a year. LIP's home, Encounter, has lasted out the demise of many another coffee-house renewal center, and grown in new directions. Perhaps this latter survival is some indication that the tenacity of the Pennsylvania Dutchman, so long harnessed to horse and buggy commitments, can also be hitched to things of the future.

The two high school girls who write the youth column for LIP have captioned it "The Meek." We, too, believe that they shall inherit the earth.

(The Lancaster Independent Press continued to exist for several decades, then ceased publication with many of its goals achieved in the community.) A Voice for the Voiceless: An Aboveground Underground Newspaper *Journal* (Board for Homeland Ministries, UCC), Vol. 7, No. 11 (September 1969), 3–7. Used by permission.

## CHAPTER 13

# Public Education:

## A MISSIONARY MODEL

COMMUNITY EFFORTS IN NORTHERN CITIES to integrate the schools have slowed down from the peak years of concern, 1963–65. Both black and white have contributed to the decline in progress. Whites resist and flee to the suburbs; civil rights leaders currently emphasize the upgrading of the ghetto school; and black militants preach black identity and self-determination.

Quite contrary to such backward movement is the development of integrated education in Lancaster, a city of 60,000 in southeastern Pennsylvania. This chapter tells of that development and the role of the church in it during a period in the 1960s.

### What Happened?

When the wave of protest against de facto segregation was at its height in the early sixties, students at Lancaster Theological Seminary, especially those whose wives were teaching in the city schools, were drawn to look at their own local situation. Rather than importing diagnoses and prescriptions from other communities, they gathered a dozen schoolteachers together to inquire about the human issues in the Lancaster system.

Out of this exploration there emerged a proposal to establish a freedom school. Its purpose would be twofold: to demonstrate what racially integrated life and education look like, and to lift up the role of the African-American in the country's history and world culture. Both of these goals were being denied by racial isolation and curriculum deficiencies and distortions in the schools. After considerable planning and solicitation of support from civil rights and church groups, PACE was born—the Program for American Cultural Enrichment.

PACE began as a seven-week Saturday course for a control group of thirty-two fifth- and sixth-graders, half of them black and half white. The program used the best available curriculum materials produced by publishing houses alert to the freedom revolution, together with drama, music, crafts, and field trips to the location of the famous "Christiana riots" and stations on the Underground Railroad of pre-Civil War days. Leadership came from nearby Philadelphia and the United Church of Christ Board of Christian Education in the persons of the Rev. and Mrs. Percel Alston, and the Board's staff member in residence at the seminary, the Rev. Allen Kroehler, and his Laboratory for Leadership and Learning. PACE saw its role as demonstrating in miniature what the public education establishment could and should accomplish: integrated classes and teaching staff, training in effecting better human relationships, exposure to the facts about African-American history and culture that would both shatter white stereotypes and encourage a sense of self-worth in black children.

Participants and parents were so enthusiastic about their first year's experience that a second-year program was launched that enrolled 175 fifth-graders in eight classes held in church buildings around the city, and provided four adult courses on the freedom revolution and the issues of jobs, housing, and education. In an effort to give work to a black teacher displaced by southern desegregation, PACE developed a listing service for unemployed Southern teachers and obtained a full-time administrator for a three-month period from that source. It turned its data over to the school system with the hope that the administration would find the list useful when it needed personnel. The following year, PACE decided to concentrate its efforts in the ghetto schools and held another seven-week course for a group of eighty. By this time PACE had become a household word in the city and received from the Community Council the coveted "Community Betterment Award." But we are getting ahead of our story.

At the close of PACE's first year, there appeared in one of the newspapers a sensational report of a critical study that PACE had made of the bias in a sixth-grade social studies text used by the school system. For several weeks articles and letters, many originating from the school administration, filled the pages of the paper with defenses of the textbook in question. Some attacked PACE and the seminary for "meddling." Although PACE was not particularly geared for controversy, and many of its workers tended by nature to shy away from such furor, it nevertheless stood its ground and in fact mounted a stronger attack on the defects of the system. It became clearer from this confrontation that there was more to be done than lifting visions and developing educational models on the margin of community life. The public school system itself had to be addressed.

The following fall (1965) a PACE political action committee was formed. The group sought out the services of the Rev. Alexander Harper, newly appointed secretary for school integration on the staff of the United Church of Christ Council for Christian Social Action, as consultant. Harper's first advice was to form a broad-based community task-force that would address itself to the structural issues of public education. Thus ECC—the Educational Concerns Committee—came into existence, with representation from a wide spectrum of civil rights, church, and other community groups. The Rev. Claude Kilgore, who had just been called by the local Council of Churches as a metropolitan missionary with special responsibility in the ghetto, emerged as the natural leader of this task-force.

After much debate, ECC focused on the integration of the city's three junior high schools, with concomitant stress on textbook overhaul, minority teacher recruitment and placement, and upgrading of "special education." A carefully researched document on the need for racial balance in the city schools, together with a map design of how it could be attained at the junior high level, was drawn up by ECC members from Franklin and Marshall College in cooperation with Harper. ECC decided to channel the proposal through the education committee of the city-county Human Relations Committee in the hopes that support from this quarter would strengthen its presentation to the School Board. After heated debates, this committee whose membership included some school officials, adopted a slightly modified version of the original ECC document. This version called for commitment to an integrated school system and immediate implementation, but it did not formally endorse ECC's specific plan of redistricting the junior high schools.

The issue was now before the Board and actively debated in the press. Out of the discussion finally came a timid and ambiguous acknowledgment by the Board that there might be a problem, and perhaps it should be looked into. However innocuous this response, there was just enough there to indicate an opening for change.

In the succeeding months ECC mustered its forces, appearing in strength at each Board meeting. It kept up a steady drumbeat of public encouragement as well as protest of delay in integrating the schools. Civil rights and church groups gave support by a letter-writing campaign to the newspapers and by consultation with School Board members. The first hint of real progress came in the spring of 1966 when on recommendation of the administration the Board voted a major expenditure for the purchase of multiethnic textbooks in a variety of subjects and for new social studies textbooks revised by publishers in the wake of the freedom revolution. The textbook earlier in dispute was quietly dropped. On the heels of this, the Board went on record, with several vocal dissents, to launch "a modified open enrollment plan," granting voluntary pupil movement anywhere in the city, on the condition that it benefit racial balance in the elementary and junior high schools.

The fall saw a tiny delegation of sixteen students (twelve black and four white) apply for transfer under the open enrollment plan. ECC had resisted the plan, although it had succeeded in modifying it so that pupil transfer was permitted *only* for reasons of racial balance. But now ECC openly criticized the program as placing the financial and psychological burdens for restructuring the schools upon ghetto parents. The program really boiled down to abdication of responsibility by the administration and Board. ECC again began mass public appearances and testimony at Board meetings.

In December 1966, a picture appeared in one of the papers showing the school superintendent poised over a city map with a handful of pins ready for placement. Accompanying it was the announcement of an administration plan to redistrict the junior high schools.

In the opening months of 1967 things got lively on "Cabbage Hill," a Caucasian blue-collar district adjacent to the 7th ward whose junior high would be receiving African-American pupils, and part of whose youth would be transferred into the 7th ward junior high. A group calling themselves PET (Parents, Educators and Taxpayers), formed during early PACE days but so far ineffectual, suddenly took on menacing proportions. It managed to collect a thousand signatures opposing redistricting; it recruited hundreds for a protest meeting; and it sent a barrage of letters to the editor of one of the newspapers. One paper spoke gravely about the evils of the innovation. Another daily, which had given extensive and fair coverage to PACE-ECC affairs, came out for redistricting. Also endorsing the move with enthusiasm were the education committee of the Human Relations Committee, local chapters of the NAACP and of the Urban League (CORE and SNCC have no organizations in Lancaster), and community groups ranging from the Social Action Committee of the Council of Churches to the Great Books Club.

At a stormy School Board meeting in February 1967, held in a downtown auditorium to accommodate the crowd, members voted six to three to redistrict the schools according to the administration proposal, which involved the redistribution of pupils over a three-year period. Although the staggered time schedule modified ECC's original plan, the move was on the whole a striking advance in imagination and action for a conservative Pennsylvania Dutch city. Several months later a modest realignment of elementary school districts was quietly accomplished, on the grounds that a newly constructed school in the area necessitated pupil reshuffling. This rationale was offered by administration officials in addition to the need for racial balance for the junior high redistricting. Noting the importance of political factors in the school drive, ECC, together with NAACP, turned its attention next to the election of responsible school leadership. This new interest in politics got a cool reception from both political parties, and the petition to nominate black candidates was turned aside with the advice that "the time was not yet ripe." Angered by this paternalism, ECC and NAACP members (the latter organization could not formally endorse candidates) ran an African-American write-in candidate on the Democratic ballot in the spring primaries, much to the distress of the party machine, which was fearful of the retribution of its Cabbage Hill constituency. With a vigorous new sense of identity won by taking on a Goliath, ghetto residents canvassed the inner city, and set up and executed an ambitious election day get-out-the-vote drive for their candidate. By ECC tabulation, the write-in candidate got over half the votes garnered by regular party candidates, although the official tally fixed the number at about the quarter mark because of invalidation of numerous stickers that never found their exact location in the obscure writing slot of the voting machine. But no matter, the black community had found its voice.

In the succeeding months the ECC write-in candidate was appointed by the mayor to the Redevelopment Authority, and later serves as its secretary. Another PACE ECC Negro leader, a woman, was the first of her sex (but not of her race) to join the Housing Authority.

The battle is, of course, far from over. PET, now under the wing of the new rightist Constitution Party, has run candidates for School Board (though with small showings). Further, there is a strong possibility that the redistricting will be reviewed yearly, with campaigns mounted each time to scuttle it. However, the fears of white parents that black children will demoralize "their" schools have slackened in the early months of redistricting, and the superintendent himself has announced that all "is going very well." In fact, educators around the state are making increasing inquiries of the school staff to find out what the secret of such a progressive administration might be.

### How Come?

What indeed are the "secrets?" There are no secrets, but it is possible to pinpoint some factors that make community change smoother.

1. A dedicated team. The catalytic agent in the change process appeared to be the core of committed people willing to see the program through to a point of fruition. This kind of persistence and perseverance entailed "focus." It meant that other needs would have gone begging if they had depended for their basic support on this particular cadre of the concerned. This suggests an adaptation of the concept of "orders" to the social mission of the church. Rather than expecting everyone to do everything, it seems to make more sense to train teams of those ready for mission, each to

have its "portfolio" in one (or more than one) critical human issue, to whom others look as their tutors and representatives on that frontier. These same others of course, must make themselves available to participate in that venture when they are needed.

2. *The broad base of the team.* The representative character of the Lancaster Task Force meant that it had lines open to a variety of people and groups in the city. Church people by themselves cannot hope to effect significant social change in a pluralistic situation. The seed group was cross-cultural interracial, bipartisan, interfaith.

3. *Situational focus.* While the local effort reflected issues national in scope, abstract theories or ideology did not control the choice of concerns or the way they were addressed. The immediate needs of a particular eastern Pennsylvania community were kept in the foreground, and the methods used to meet those needs arose out of the particular ethos of that community.

4. *The outside "agitator."* Though a favorite scapegoat of bigots, north and south, the roving reformer is a crucial person in community change. Staff members of national Christian education and social action organizations were important sources of help to PACE and ECC. The timely coming of the national NAACP in the person of the district director (and references to the local problem in speeches by visiting Urban League dignitaries, including the national education director Frank Stanley, Jr., and Whitney Young himself gave hefty accreditation to local efforts. The national ferment of the freedom revolution that the visitors represented gave an air of familiarity to the issues fought out at home, so that the community was not totally unprepared for innovations sought by PACE and ECC.

5. *Establishment allies.* Not all the committed can or ought to be at the barricades in some, perhaps in most, such efforts. There are those in a position to make decisions or influence those who do. These people can play a crucial role as agents of change. A ranking conservative of one political party, who was on the School Board, as well as the president of the seminary, did grant work at key

moments. The editor of one of the city's newspapers, Redevelopment Authority staff members, people in social action organizations, courageous local clergy speaking the right word at the right time (and thus serving the validating function that Robert Spike speaks about in *The Freedom Revolution and the Churches*), local churches offering space in their buildings for PACE and other projects, lay organizations performing important shirt-sleeve tasks ranging from PACE canvassing to ECC-sponsored Board meeting attendance—all played vital parts.

6. *The emergence of black presence and power.* Although the spawning ground of PACE was a largely white seminary, the programs underscored black self-esteem. Philadelphia resource personnel at the beginning, and soon thereafter, the Southern administrator, and the local lay leadership were from the African-American community. Building on this momentum in PACE, ECC began with Negro leadership, basically middle-class in character, but soon developed strong grass-roots support and leadership in the ghetto paralleling a similar development in PACE. The weaving of its life into the day-to-day 7th ward fabric of drugstores, taverns, street corners, fraternal and church groups, and its door-to-door contact methods, established ECC's drive for integration as a natural part of the life of the area. The support given to the write-in candidate on short notice with no resources served notice to the party machinery that there was a new voice and spirit to be reckoned with in a part of town long considered powerless or manipulable.

7. *The resource role of whites.* Throughout the three-year struggle, whites saw their function as supportive and secondary. It came in the form of research through the academic channels of Franklin and Marshall College and Lancaster Theological Seminary, through interpretation to the white community and recruitment from it, and through general availability when needed and sought after by black leadership. In the context of a small city with six percent African-American citizenry with a ten percent school population, pragmatists both black and white were little attracted to the anti-coalition ideologies generated in large urban centers. But the motif

of leadership by African-American citizens of their own revolution was very much part of the Lancaster effort from its beginnings in the PACE training in black identity to its current struggle for black political power.

8. *A symbolic "headquarters."* PACE, ECC, and its allies tended to gravitate to "Encounter," a church-sponsored coffee house and renewal center. Here were held PACE exhibits on African-American art and history, ECC and PACE planning meetings, community forums on de facto segregation and textbook bias, and the original sessions initiated by the seminary students that set forth some of the movement's leading themes. In a later phase, Encounter became the location of "Freedom House," an NAACP-sponsored youth headquarters and program that made the center a natural gathering place for many in the 7th ward who came to take part in PACE-ECC thrusts. The liveliest use of Encounter came on primary election day, 1967, when the building served as nerve center of the write-in campaign, complete with the litter of handbills, coffee for the milling precinct workers, and radio election returns.

9. *The media.* By both accident and design, PACE and ECC had an interested and active press. The originality of PACE for the Pennsylvania German hinterlands made good copy for the three newspapers in the city. Controversy, editorials, and a boiling letters-to-the editor column gave the issues wide and constant exposure. And the more acriniony in the attacks of the conservative press and the PET group, the more espirit and solidarity developed in the ghetto.

10. *A think-tank.* The collection and interpretation of data, and reflection on the direction and meaning of the struggle were tasks done by area academic communities, including faculty and students at Franklin and Marshall and Millersville Colleges, but principally Lancaster Seminary. Although the seminary had no official connection with the movement (some of its sharpest critics were the few students who "were sick and tired of hearing about PACE and ECC"), students in Christian Ethics courses—which were predi-

cated on "reflection in the context of involvement"—took an active part in many of the phases, as did student spouses, who helped to initiate PACE and continued to work in it and the community confrontations on redistricting. The seminary's Laboratory for Leadership and Learning housed the PACE resources and later the PACE administrator. Some faculty and faculty wives gave unstintingly of their time, and the faculty as a whole performed an accrediting role on occasion with a public statement. The part the seminary president played on the School Board was noted earlier.

11. *Relation of core group to other rights groups.* Conceived from the beginning as ad hoc in nature, with heavy representation from other elements in the Civil Rights Movement, PACE and ECC sustained cordial relations with their allies. Support came at crucial moments from both local chapters and national staff of NAACP and the Urban League. The education subcommittee of the city-county Human Relations committee proved to be throughout a valuable sounding board and liaison agent on the outer rim of established Lancaster.

## What Does it Mean?

Two general observations may be made:

(1) Steps toward the elimination of de facto segregation, at the present so beset by difficulties in the large urban centers, may be within reach of smaller urban communities. (2) Coalition efforts are both a possibility and a necessity in this kind of a context. More specifically, the whole effort and experience teaches much about church strategy for social mission. Here are some lessons:

1. The church can make a difference in the struggle to humanize the structures of public education. In the Lancaster situation the work of laity and clergy ranged from approving the use of buildings for PACE activities and grinding the mimeograph and visiting PACE parents to church auxiliaries that showed up en masse at critical Board meetings and stands taken by preachers and council at the

height of controversy. Further, there was the use of Encounter as headquarters and the activities of national church staff members and the council of churches' missionary.

2. Rigid institutional patterns are not changed by exhortation and moral suasion, but by the responsible use of social power. The massing of ghetto sentiment, the public demonstration, the vocal stands of community groups and leaders, the power of the news media and the vote were important factors. (It should be noted, however, that there were some impressive exceptions, in which grasp of the facts *and* a sensitive conscience appeared to be at work.) The Christian view of sin, its depth and persistence, was borne out in this confrontation.

3. The massive hurts of the city, and the healing possible through effective action, should make the serving of human needs one of the mission priorities of the church in urban society. On Jericho roads, Samaritans first bind up wounds. The mission of the church is not exhausted in ministry to the neighbor, of course; but its calling to tell and celebrate the Christian story must always be fulfilled in the midst of the human ferment.

4. Mission is carried out in a pioneering relinquishing style. Thus the church is called to lift up a vision of healing (PACE as a tiny model of reconciliation and educational excellence in the race issue), then to try to stir the larger community to its own proper responsibility (ECC's prodding function), and then to fold its own institutional tents to move on to the next unseen and unmet need when the human community as a whole accepts its responsibilities (PACE's hope that it can work itself out of a job).

5. The church is called to address the corporate structures of the city, in this case the public school system and the political machinery. Its claim arises from the simple mandate of a neighbor love that seeks to use the most effective means at hand to heal human hurt. The New Testament recognition of the Lordship of Christ over the principalities and powers is further confirmation of this ministry. The pluriform nature of church mission means that decisions have to be made about what structures are viable.

6. Theology comes alive in the heat of mission. Laity and clergy, students and faculty, grew in their understanding of the biblical themes of the work of Christ in the world, the nature of sin, the principalities and powers, and the eschatological signs of hope in history. And the quality of worship and the meaning of faith itself was not left untouched. The Teacher is found in his classroom in the world.

7. Church people must be prepared to pay the cost of sharp community conflict: economic reprisal, acrimonious attack in the press, threats of violence and their occasional implementation, the anonymous phone call and letter, jeopardy to the institutions to which one is attached, the cold shoulder in established circles, both church and secular. These, however, are small irritants compared to the larger sacrifices faithful people are called to make on other terrain.

Shortly after the School Board vote on redistricting, Encounter sported a new graffiti wall, inviting philosophical scribble from its visitors. It was christened by an NAACP militant with a large-lettered, "HOPE?"

Sober hope, that is the idiom of faith. Along with a future-oriented generation, it looks forward to the shape of things to come. Aware as it is of the frailty of every human advance, it nevertheless believes with Martin Luther King that human beings have a right to dream. And it points to, and works within, the historical harbingers of a better world that beckons from out ahead. Those who have taken part in the birth-pangs of something important to the people of a small city believe they have seen such a portent.

Public Education: A Missionary Model, *Second Fronts in Metropolitan Mission* (Grand Rapids: Eerdmans booklet from *Reformed Journal* articles, 1968), 17–30. Used by permission.

## CHAPTER 14

# Social Ethical Decision-Making in the 70s

JUST HOW CAN YOU GO ABOUT the business of translating your social dreams into reality? Can you?

The business of social ethical decision-making is no easy task, especially for Christian visionaries. Their final reference point is an elusive one, "at the End of history." The fulfillment of shalom is always out ahead of any particular conceptualization or realization of it. How then do you make decisions about the rightness or wrongness of particular social actions?

## WHAT DO WE DO WITH THE VISION?

For one set of visionaries in the Church this is not a real problem. Perhaps by dialogue with them, we can get a little clarity on what is, for the rest of us, a very ambiguous situation.

The absolute pacifist is the kind of dreamer who believes that if cheek-turning, second-mile nonviolent shalom is the way of the Kingdom, it is also the way we should act right now. To bring it in (the Kingdom), you do it now. And you can do it; there is no gap between what can be and what will be.

### Package it?

Such perfectionist ethics sets a rigorous pace for the rest of Christianity. It keeps our sleeping consciences awake and restless with anything less than the highest moral standard. But we have to clarify one important point: the function of a dream. Is it a code that can be applied literally to our day-to-day behavior, as the absolute pacifist assumes? Or, is it an otherworldly vision designed for angels that has no relevance to the here and now, except in some rare circumstances when you can find a few angels or saints?

Neither. The dream cannot be packaged and exported form "heaven" to "earth," as perfectionists maintain. Why not? Cheek-turning, second-mile self-abnegation is indeed responded to in kind in the Kingdom of God. Love elicits love, and shalom happens. That is the purity of which heavenly dreams are made. Where God is "all in all," love triumphs. Things are different on earth. The line is drawn between the two by a lethal factor, "sin." Because this stubborn human incurvature makes its home in our midst, cheek-turning love does not automatically produce shalom. Innocence gets regularly slaughtered. Perfect *agape* ends up on a cross. Particularly so when it steps onto the turf of the principalities and powers where "immoral man" becomes even more "immoral society."[1]

### Dismiss it?

While dreams cannot be transported simplistically onto our terrain, neither can they be rocketed into some extra-terrestrial nowhere land. Not biblical dreams. They have to do with things that most intimately concern us here and now—peace, healing, reconciliation. The Kingdom of God is the world at its best. It's the City of God that our human city is meant to be. So Christians pray. "Thy Kingdom come on earth . . ." and set up signs that point from one to the other. The dream becomes especially compelling in just the area about which pacifist feel so strongly, war. The instruments of war have become so formidable today, and the planet-shattering possibilities so horrendous that visionaries are being listened to again by the soberest of people.

### Translate It

If dreams are to take on some semblance of reality in day-to-day affairs they have to do it on the inhospitable terrain of a sinful world. This means finding a way in, scaling a vision down. Such a translation process involves the development of ethical norms that are kindred to the Kingdom of love, but are in touch with the realities of our human kingdom of hate. The experience of both the Christian community and the race at large has generated this kind of moral wisdom—general guidelines for behavior that presuppose our self-aggrandizing tendencies and the conflict of chaos that comes in their wake. They include justice, equality, freedom, order. The sections in the Decalogue that have to do with human conduct are other such rules of the game. These "natural laws" are important data in the Christian decision-making process.

Together with this general counsel, there are certain institutions authenticated in the Christian tradition which both reflect something of the heavenly vision yet also take into account human sin. Thus, marriage mirrors the unity of the divine life itself, but also serves, as Luther puts it, as a "dike" against chaos that could be introduced into the human community if sex impulses were not responsibly channeled. Again, the state expresses the human life together for which we are intended, but does it by an institutionalized force made necessary by the potential disaster of unrestrained conflicting ego interests.

## THE ROLE OF THE CHRISTIAN COMMUNITY

In addition to the perennial norms, the Christian community has sought constantly to refine and update its moral lore. In councils formal and informal, in laboratory testing in the infernos of its time, certain consensus points tend to surface about issues in the common life. Thus in an era of thrust for the civil and human rights of black, poor, young, and women, there emerge "middle axioms" that do their work in Christian teaching and preaching, scaling the abstraction "justice" down to political, economic, and social rights due to particular people. And further, the Church may anguish over and research a highly specific moral issue, such as the legitimacy of the war in Vietnam, and risk corporate judgment and action about it. The positions taken by a General Synod or Christian Social Action Council on capital punishment, gun control, ABM, international economic development, South African banks, and selective conscientious objection are examples of the responsibility of the Church to come down out of the stratosphere of general principles and help Christians make their way on the streets of daily decision. And the way the Christian Church works at these specifics is in community, not as moral Lone Rangers. The more specific such corporate judgments are, the more risk of error and the more chance of disagreement among constituents. But a faithful Church has to risk that specificity and controversy or become irrelevant. It does so with modesty about its pronouncements, knowing its own fallibility, and also its own sin.

## THE INADEQUACY OF CONTEXTUALISM

We have spent some time on the role of the community in social ethical decision-making because our native rugged individualism regularly censors out this dimension of the moral task. Not only is this true about irate parishioners who resent the Church's taking stands on social issues. It pertains as well to sophisticated modern theories of ethics such as the popular "contextualism." It is true that everyone must finally do their own deciding in their own context. But there are more data to be fed into choosing then neat "faith and facts," or "love and the situation" as formulas suggest. On one side, there is eminently more than a "benevolent will" out of which faith and love act; there is also a rich historical and cosmic dream which provides the reference point for decision. And on the other, together with the situational data, there is a community's reflection upon it.[2]

## THE REJECTION OF TRADITIONAL ETHICS

The resistance to communal ethical wisdom is related to the use made of it by traditional ethics. For the latter, moral mandates were "absolutes," "laws" handed down by the Great Lawgiver which were to be "obeyed," much as children paid obeisance to a paternal autocrat. Such ascendancy-submission patterns of religious thinking have come in for drastic criticism all along the line of Christian doctrine, from our conception of God to our understanding of the role of the clergy. "Big daddy is dead."

The death of the father-figure can be interpreted in two different ways. It can mean the elimination of the Factor that formerly played the role of tyrant. Thus the all-powerful Deity that kept us submerged is annihilated by the "death of God theology." Or the pretentious Mother Church which claimed to be the sole ark of salvation is rejected by a secular Christianity which declares: to join the world is to join the church! Or again, a moral law interpreted as unquestionably fiat is dismissed and in its place is put the formula, "Love plots the course according to the circumstances."[3]

## THE ALTERNATIVE

There is another way to down old tyrannies without constructing new ones. It is the way of dialogue in which old paternities die, and are born again as companions and colleagues. The God of suffering love takes the place of the oriental Potentate; the servant church replaces the solemn matriarchy; the community's moral wisdom comes as counsel instead of command.

To take the community's counsel seriously in the area of social action means that a congregation or an individual confronted with a contemporary issue has to do some homework. As a member of the Body of Christ, the first move is to see whether there is anything in the Body's memory bank about that question. Have the "fathers and mothers, brothers and sisters" (the past and the present community) done any research on it, or come to any conclusions about it? If a person takes seriously membership in a particular communion, or the holy universal church, for that matter, the bodies set apart for such research will be consulted—the Council for Christian Social Action, General Synod, National Council of Churches, World Council of Churches, Second Vatican Council, etc. These will not be orders that have to be obeyed, but the reports coming in from an accredited R& D division that have to be taken seriously, argued with if need be, and, if rejected, done so out of superior insight or more finely honed ethical sensitivity. No one is an island—including no Christian. Our mainland is our faith community. Its bell tolls for us, too.

## ELEMENTS IN DECISION

We began our reflection on social action in the 70s by talking about the biblical dream of shalom as the fundamental point of orientation for moral decision-making. Have we really been faithful to the Bible by focusing on this one Vision? What about the countless pieces of moral advice scattered through the pages of Scripture? Look, it says in the Old Testament that usury is a sin. Saint Paul declares that women should wear hats in church. And the early Christians pooled all their financial resources. Don't we have to abide by these ideas too?

## THE COUNSELS OF THE BIBLE

Indeed some of these counsels might be studied with a good deal of profit, for they often rise from a passion for justice and a care about persons—the prohibition of usury, and the common life of the primitive Church, for example. But as the most fundamentalist interpreter of the Bible will be quick to tell you when confronted by that last matter of Acts 2:44–45, moral practice grows out of the peculiar needs and conditions of the times. And circumstances change. Therefore, specific moral routines of another age, which might have served an important purpose then, do not necessarily do so now. "New occasions teach new duties." While it is true that some of the specific moral counsels of the Bible are as fresh as ever, particularly those crystallized into more formal codes such as the Decalogue ("Thou shalt not kill" is as timely as the struggle against capital punishment and war), in general, moral particulars have to be worked out ever anew within the faith community.

## FACTS AND THE FINDINGS OF THE SCIENCES

In executing this task as a community, or in personal decision-making, solid familiarity with the circumstances is crucial. The best methods of gathering and sifting data therefore become important parts of Christian decision-making. In a complex society, the resources of sociology, psychology, political science, and more recently as we approach the awesome question of the control of human life, physics and molecular biology, are fundamental partners in making responsible social ethical decisions.

## THE POSITION OF THE DECIDER

At the center of the data-gathering task is the positioning of the decider. Crucial choices about the issues of war and peace, black and white, rich and poor, cannot be made from twenty rows up in the grandstand. We get the lay of the land by walking on it. Alexander Miller in describing where the best theology is carried on once said, "The safest place for the theologian is in the midst of the social struggle." The same thing is true about any Christian who wants to find his or her way in the knotty moral problems of modern society. Christian decision-making takes place in the setting of involvement. Our teacher will be Christ himself who is found where the hungry are fed, the naked clothed, and the prisoner visited (Matt. 25:31–46). The fundamental context for Christian social action, therefore, in the words of Bonhoeffer, is "to participate in the sufferings of God in the world."

## NOTES

1. See Reinhold Niebuhr's later comments on his early work *Moral Man and Immoral Society in Man and His Communities*. (New York: Scribner's, 1965), p. 22.

2. For a detailed analysis and evaluation of this problem in situation ethics see Gabriel Fackre, *Humiliation and Celebration: Post-Radical Themes in Doctrine, Morals and Mission*. (New York: Sheed and Ward, 1969), pp. 53–67, 209–251.

3. Joseph Fletcher, *Situation Ethics*. (Philadelphia: Westminster Press, 1966), p. 143.

Social Ethical Decision-Making in the UCC, *Social Action*, Vol. XXXIV, No. 4 (December 1969), 23–30. Used by Permission.

## CHAPTER 15

# September 11:

## ON BINDING UP WOUNDS AND RESISTING THE POWERS

JESUS WEPT (Lk. 19:41). Tears rolled down the face of God for Jerusalem, and today God weeps for New York. Deity was there at Ground Zero. And we, too, are called to that place to participate in the sufferings of God (Dietrich Bonhoeffer). Where there is the slaughter of innocents and hurt of such magnitude, our first ministry is to bind up wounds and thereby keep company with Christ. And to reach out in compassion as well to Arabs—Arabs who are Muslims, Christians, and followers of other faiths. They and the other peoples of the Middle East and South Asia had no part in this atrocity and also suffer from unreasoning hate.

The response of the United Church of Christ so far has shown that it understands the call to minister to the neighbor in need. The outpouring of prayer and care has been overwhelming, moved by the love of God. But do we also know what to do with the wrath of God? One of our great United Church of Christ theologians of an earlier era was not so sure. H. Richard Niebuhr indicted liberal Protestantism for teaching "a God without wrath who brings humans without sin into a kingdom without judgment through a Christ without a cross."

"Judgment" here has to do with holding the perpetrators responsible for this atrocity. Their suicide bombing was not a passport to paradise but a passage to the Great Judgment where they will answer for their sin before a righteous God. And their sponsors will give an account as well to the world's community of conscience, gathering now to bring terrorism to justice. And what of our own share in the judgment of God for an American hubris so graphically symbolized by the Babel-like proportions of our towers? Are we free of all guilt of the horror that happened? What is it about us that evokes the hate of so many of the world's poor? Dare we listen to Jeremiah's thunderbolts as well as Jesus' weeping?

We must learn to put together both the tough and the tender love of God. We get some help from yet other forebears who had to work out a Christian response to the terrorists of their day. In 1941, the Reformed theologian Karl Barth wrote a letter to Christians in Great Britain as bombs were falling on their cities. He reminded them of Good Friday but also of Easter morning, when God's definitive answer to the world's crucifiers was Resurrection (Col. 2:15). That victory assures the coming of the final reign of God, where every flaw shall be mended and absolute justice done. Because Jesus Christ has risen from the dead, Barth wrote, "the world in which we live is no sinister wilderness where fate or chance hold sway, or where all sort of 'principalities and powers' run riot unrestrained. . . ." That resurrection faith empowers us to "come to grips spiritedly and resolutely with these evil spirits." And, he added that "we shall not regard this war . . . either as a crusade or as a war of religion . . . [but] as a large-scale police measure which has become absolutely necessary in order to repulse an active anarchism."[1]

Much to ponder here.

Reinhold Niebuhr, another United Church of Christ giant of that earlier day, also has some counsel for us. Like Jeremiah, he was unsparing in his criticism of his nation's arrogance. He called for penitence for our sins and urged the making of peace as our controlling vision. But he pressed home, as well, the distinction that had to be made between tyranny and democracy and the need to defend the legacy of freedom and justice for all from the perils of the hour.

Our challenge in a United Church of Christ that prides itself on being a "just peace church" (and rightly so) is to deepen the meaning of that self-definition. No peace is worth having that does not bring the guilty to justice and, thus, our mandate to "resist the powers of evil." We do so with penitence and a passion for peace, confidant of God's presence in both trial and rejoicing and the coming of that Realm that has no end. And, with the reminder to ourselves that what counts most is the Word about who God is and what God does, more than preoccupation with who are in our justice-doing and peace-making.

Unless the Lord builds the house, those who build it labor in vain.

Unless the Lord guards the city the guard keeps watch in vain

—Psalm 127:1

## NOTES

1. Quotations from Karl Barth, *A Letter to Great Britain from Switzerland* (London: Sheldon Press, 1941).

Binding Up Wounds and Resisting the Powers, *O God, Tender and Just: Reflections and Response after September 11, 2001* (United Church Press, 2001), 46–47. Used by permission.

## CHAPTER 16

# Evangelism and Social Action:
## Either/Or?

THE TITLE "EVANGELIST" APPEARS after the names of a number of entries in the archives of New England Congregationalism. The biography of one records his commissioning to found three churches "in the interior counties." Another is credited with "abolishing atheism in southern Iowa." Another is described as instrumental in the conversion of a large number of the inhabitants on one of the Sandwich Islands.

The histories of these evangelists mention some other interesting facts: one started the first abolition society in his territory; one was what we would call a "community organizer" on the most agitated social issue in his location—temperance; one was a leader in the struggle against the exploitation of Polynesians by the sandalwood traders of the mid-Pacific.

This wedding of evangelism and social action sounds like an anachronism because the divorce of the two has become commonplace in much contemporary church life. So much so that the great-grandchildren of these Congregational pioneers have to be reminded of the faith of their fathers and mothers. The assumption of separation is now so deep-rooted that the best-known evangelist of our time, Billy Graham, can sever the tie with one swift stroke: "I am a New Testament evangelist, not an Old Testament prophet."

What are the grounds for the historic union of evangelism and social action, and what is the nature of this bond? The alliance is based on kindred purposes and a common biblical root. Let us examine each.

*Evangelism* is the joy and task of sharing the tale of the deeds of God. It is telling the story of what God did, is doing, and will do to fulfill the vision of a world reconciled, *shalom*. At its center is the evangel, the

Good News that the powers of sin and evil have been overcome in the life, death, and resurrection of Jesus Christ. Evangelism is the communication of this *kerygma* to those who haven't heard it—therefore, getting the story *out*.

Evangelism, however, is a specific kind of storytelling, one that connects the biography of God with our own autobiography. The saga of God does not let us alone. It upsets, exhilarates, and calls for decision and commitment. It wheels us about from one direction to another, a turn *epistrophe, metanoia* we describe as conversion.[1] Evangelism, therefore, is getting the story out that turns people around.

*Christian social action* takes its stance from the story. Its fundamental reference point is the ultimate vision of shalom toward which the narrative thrusts, that realm of God in which swords are beaten into plowshares, wolf and lamb lie down together, the lame walk, the blind see, the naked are clothed, the hungry are feed, the prisoner is liberated, justice is done, and peace is made. Social action is one expression of *diakonia,* servanthood, the human deed that witnesses to the divine deed, that Kingdom in which all tears shall be wiped away, and there shall be the liberation and reconciliation of all things. It is that form of diakonia that deals with "the principalities and powers," the systemic, structural forces that seek to kill the dream. Social action is: the struggle to bring social power to bear on social issues and institutions in the light of the vision of shalom.[2]

## ACTION EVANGELISTS

Why have New Testament evangelists engaged in the business of Old Testament prophets? The answer is found in the story the evangelist has to tell. It is the saga of the acts of God moving toward a world liberated and reconciled. How can such a tale be told without pointing to that kingdom? "The end pre-exists in the means," says Emerson. Most of all this is true for Christian storytellers. The great end toward which the story moves, one which has entered our history in Jesus Christ, must be manifest in the witness of the evangelist. A deed of shalom is integral to a word about shalom. The *medium* of acts of liberation and reconciliation testifies to the *message* of liberation and reconciliation.

How clearly this can be seen in the evangelism of the first evangelists! The chronicle of their work is not called the *Talks* of the Disciples but the *Acts* of the Apostles. From the first evangelism sortie after the birth of the church (Acts 3:1–10) to the close of the books of Acts, the first apostles of the Good News demonstrated their message in deeds of healing as well as words of hope. And this act of evangelism, action evangelism, was viewed by them as a divine accreditation of their mission as well as an imperative for it. The signs and wonders of shalom in which bodies as well as souls were liberated from the powers of evil were seen to be confirmation by the Holy Spirit of the word they preached.

In the long history of evangelism and mission the Holy Spirit has empowered evangelist successors to Peter and Paul, Priscilla and Tabitha, to both do *and* tell the Good News, to so unite word with deed that the witness becomes a word-in-deed.[3] *How* they manifest this empowerment to heal bodies as well as souls varied according to the gifts and challenges of time and place. That they were called to do so was never in question. On some occasions storytellers bound word to deed after the fashion of William Booth's social service/evangelism. On other occasions doing and telling became partners in the social action/evangelism of Toyohiko Kagawa. Throughout, the great redemption in which bodies as well as souls, society as well as selves, were liberated and reconciled, was attested to by the word-in deed witness of Acts evangelists.

The partnership of doing and telling was set forth in a manifesto of United Church of Christ pastors in a time when word and deed seemed to be going their separate ways.

"In Jesus Christ the man of Nazareth, our crucified and risen Lord, he has come to us and shared our common lot." In him, hope happens and *shalom* comes to be. The powers of evil meet their match, mercy covers our guild, and the future is opened. A new people is born to celebrate the deeds of God and to participate in the Spirit's ever-fresh stirrings of liberation and reconciliation. That Body is turned toward the future looking for the new things God will do, and the time when his full Kingdom will be. "Blessing and honor, glory and power be unto God!" Evangelism is the sharing of this tale of hope. For the United Church of Christ it is a special kind of sharing. As the Word became flesh and dwelt among us, so an authentic human word about God must be embodied. More than word *and,* true Storytelling is word *in* deed—speaking in the midst of doing. We testify to salvation not in tent or temple but *on the road* in our own journeys toward freedom, justice, and peace. We believe in action evangelism, and seek new ways and models of marrying word and deed.

—The Deering 1972 (UCC) Conference on Faith
and Its Corporate Expression

## OF "PRINCIPALITIES AND POWERS"

In the Acts charter of evangelism faithful witness to the Gospel takes the evangelist regularly into the arena of the "principalities and powers." Thus Peter and John encountered the power structure, a political-military-ecclesiastical complex, which, taking offense at both their words and deeds, jailed them. How often in the history of evangelism has this same scenario been acted out. Thus in the annals of the German Reformed Church in America appears this record of an evangelistic effort among native Americans by a group from Bethlehem, Pennsylvania: "In proportion to the success of the mission among the Indians grew almost a wicked prejudice against it, and opposition to it, among the white settlers of the province. . . . The loss the whites sustained in not having the Indians under their control, as formerly when they were accustomed to taking unlawful liberties and advantages of them by defrauding them of their just due for labor, by imposing liquor upon them . . . was considered by them a serious loss. . . . In ascribing the cause of the change in life and morals of the Indians to the missionaries, they sought by every stratagem to get rid of them. . . . All kinds of false changes were brought against the missionaries. They were accused of being enemies of the government; as being secret papists and traitors; as being in alliance with the French in Canada to furnish arms and ammunition to fight the English. In December, 1744, they were brought before the magistrate for examination; and still later, they were cited to appear before the governor himself . . . at length such oppressive laws were passed in reference to them, and such restrictions laid upon them, that they could no longer care for their missionary work. In the beginning of the year 1745, they were compelled reluctantly to leave the convert-ed Indians to themselves; and Mr. Rauch and his companions, not with-out insults from the mobs on the route, found their way back to Bethlehem."[4]

The apostles' expectation of the imminent closure of history preclud-ed the careful strategizing and organizing we associate today with social action. Our engagement with power structures is executed in a different frame of reference, one that must dissociate the calendar error of the evangelists' apocalypticism from the perennial relevance of their escha-tology. The continuing impact of the vision of the coming *shalom* means that we in our time are called and empowered by the Holy Spirit to do deeds of *shalom* with the resources and perceptions God gives us in this context. These resources and perceptions press us into the same arena of the principalities and powers to call them to accountability before the lordship of Christ and the judgment of his kingdom. One of the most powerful contemporary currents of this kind of eschatological evangel-ism that calls powers and principalities, as well as persons, to repentance is found in Third World mission theory and practice. In Latin America, for example, it can be seen on a spectrum that runs from the Protestant Orlando Costas to the Roman Catholic Gustavo Gutierrez.[5]

Does Christian social action reach toward evangelism in the same way that witness in word fulfills itself in company with deed? The Acts par-adigm would certainly suggest it. The proclamation of the story comes on the heels of an act of *shalom* (Acts 3:11–26), and in the midst of the court confrontation with the powers that be (Acts 4:5–12). Why should Christian mission press us beyond a Wordless deed as much as beyond a deedless Word? There are two reasons:

The first has to do with the grounds for Christian social action: wit-ness to the vision of *shalom* is at the center of the story told by the evan-gelist. Social action gets its mandate from the kingdom of God, and, by the power of that future working in our world, sets up signs and point-ers to the liberation-and-reconciliation-to-be. As testimony to this ful-fillment, seen in its fruits first, Jesus Christ, the Christian activist is con-strained to say *why* these deeds are done. At the very least, those engaged in social action should be "ready to give reasons for the hope that is in them." And when they become agents of the Spirit's miracle of humanization, today's activists, as Peter and John, are called to interpret the social act, and thus tell the story.

The second reason bears upon the fulfillment of the intentions of social action itself. A few years ago Joseph Hromadka, the Czech theologian, reported a new interest by Marxists in the Christian faith. The Marxists told him that socialism had solved to their satisfaction the problems of systematic injustice. However, they found that the human beings in the new society appear to be so subject to corruptions and apathies that the system itself was being endangered. So, they expressed curiosity about how the Christian community changed *persons*, and asked Hromadka to lecture to them at the University of Prague on the subject of prayer.[6]

## STRUCTURAL CHANGE NOT A GUARANTEE

Structural change does not of itself guarantee a new society. The tiny tower of the human spirit is rooted in, but rises above the social, economic, and political systems with which change agents deal.[7] The impulses emanating from that spirit can either subvert or enhance the changes affected by social action. They can also empower or erode the drive of social action. Therefore, a form of mission that addresses itself to those spiritual heights (and depths) should be seen by the action agent as an important ally in the task of social action. An evangelism that changes persons is companion to a social action that changes structures.

The opening to evangelism in the mainstream churches in the 1970s is related to a growing realization of these two factors. Denominations that had plunged into socially-oriented mission in the 1960s experienced resistance to this thrust by many in their constituencies. Some of this resistance sprang from a demonic racism and war-mongering and had to be faced down. Some of it, however, rose from ignorance of the Word that spawned the social deed. And some of it was the result of an uneasiness that the Word itself had been censored from mission by overzealous activists interested only in the deed. As a consequence, there emerged a concern for a more full-orbed mission that blended faith and action, word and deed.

To this response to the church's silent majority was added a developing awareness by social action protagonists of the insights noted by Hromadka. Basic social change in our society requires changed persons as well as changed structures. (The perversion of this new sensibility also occurred in the wholesale retreat into neomysticism and neopietism by a significant number of 1960s activists). Out of the convergence of this consciousness-raising with regard to the personal dimension and a rediscovery of the interpretive word, there grew a variety of endeavors to bring together evangelism and social action.

## SINGULARITY AND UNITY

The partnership in the process of formation cannot violate the integrity of each commitment. Paul viewed the church as a body with many parts (I Cor. 12, Eph. 4, and Rom. 12). Now, as then, some have the spirit's gift of evangelism, some are healers, some prophets. This the grain of truth in the Graham bifurcation noted above. There is a unique function of telling the story that turns people around. And there are people who have a talent and call to exercise this gift. There is a special function of encountering prophetically the powers, and doing deeds of mercy and justice. And there are people who have a talent and mandate for this social action. Some are tellers and some are doers.

But if we are faithful to the holistic vision of Acts then we must affirm that neither of these functions can be fulfilled unless it is joined by the other. The deed must buttress the word of the evangelist for the story to go forth with power. And the word must support the deed of the social actor for the story to be done in its completeness. Indeed, the special gift of the teller will be in the foreground in evangelism, and the unique talent of the doer up front in social action. But the environment for each is constituted by the witness of the other.

The maturation of each ministry entails the growth of the evangelist toward the capacity to do as well as tell, and the activist toward the ability to speak the word as well as enact it. This is the message of I Corinthians 13, which call the gifts described in the twelfth chapter beyond their particularity into loving interrelationships with, and learning from, the other parts of the Body of Christ. The goal of such interpretation is the kind of evangelist and activist described in Acts, who bring healing, prophecy, proclamation, and the call to commitment together.

Most of us have a good deal of growing to do. We are still children who see the goal of full stature in Christ (Eph. 4:13), the call to full mission, but find it all we can do to exercise the gift we do have. Growth from our infant witness means, in its earliest stages, first steps toward the other members of the body. The simplest one is the decision to honor the differing gift of another. The evangelist who affirms the presence and role of the activist, the activist who accepts the importance and gift of the evangelist.

"You do your thing, I'll do mine," is not venturing far out, but it is a movement beyond an old polarization in which one denied the significance of the other, and sought to exterminate the other. Beyond this minimal act of mutual accreditation there is the reaching out for partnership in mission. Thus an evangelism task force and social action commission in a congregation, or state conference, or national church, can join together to plan for ways in which each can undergird the work of the other. The achievement of a giant step in growth would be the mutual fructification that equips each with the gifts of both so that evangelism and social action are carried out according to the Acts rhythm of the apostles.

The holism of the first apostles is grounded, finally, not only in their Gospel but also in their Lord. Action evangelism and evangelical action take their pattern from the incarnate Word, Jesus Christ. Here is the deed of God that is one with the word of God. Word-in-deed mission has its source in the Word made flesh. The Incarnation itself is manifest in the career of Jesus in which acts of healing, encounter with the powers and principalities, proclamation of the Good News, and call to decision are fused together. Thus in the central chapter of the Christian story, the enfleshment of God in Jesus Christ, and its expression in the saga of that Nazarene, is laid the groundwork for that gestalt of mission lived out by the apostles in their time, and sought by us in ours.

## NOTES

1. For a detailed study of the meaning of conversion see Gabriel Fackre, "Conversion," *Andover Newton Quarterly*. Vol. 14, No. 3 (January 1974).

2. Themes developed in three essays in *Social Action*, Vol. XXXVI, No. 4 (December, 1969).

3. A formation of the meaning of "Word-in-deed" evangelism is found in "A Statement of Commitment" worked out by a group of clergy and lay evangelists in 1972. It appears in *Evangelism for a New Day*, edited by Frances Eastman and Theodore Erickson. (New York: United Church Board for Homeland Ministries, 1972), pp. 28–29. It is the premise underlying the *Evangelism Training Manual*, a six session training program for lay evangelists in a local congregation (New York: United Church Board for Homeland Ministries, 1974), mimeograph, developed by grassroot evangelism leadership in the United Church of Christ. When the word "evangelism" is used in this article it has reference basically to this kind of peoples' evangelism activity, clergy and lay, rather than to the professional evangelist.

4. Henry Harbaugh, *The Fathers of the German Reformed Church in Europe and America*, Vol. I (Lancaster: Sprenger & Westhaeffer, 1857) pp. 383–384.

5. See Orland E. Costas, *The Church and its Mission: A Shattering Critique: from the Third World*, and Gustavo Gutierrez, *A Theology of Liberation*, translated by Sister Caridad Inda and John Eagleson (Maryknoll, New York: Orbis Books, 1973).

6. Described by Donald Miller in Allen Miller, editor, *Reconciliation in Today's World* (Grand Rapids: Wm. B. Eerdmans Publishing Co., 1969) p. 28.

7. The tower figure is Reinhold Niebuhr's. See his *Nature and Destiny of Man*, Vol. I. (New York: Charles Scribner's Sons, 1945) pp. 17, 157 and *passim*.

8. Attempts to put word and deed together are to be found in the *Evangelism Training Manual* mentioned previously, the *New Life Mission Manual* produced by the Board of Discipleship, United Methodist Church (Nashville: Tidings, 1974), and *Resources for Developing and Evangelistic Life Style* from the American Baptist Churches (Valley Forge, PA, 1972).

Evangelism and Social Action: Either/Or?, *Engage/Social Action*, Vol. 2, No. 11 (November 1974), 6–14. Used by permission.

CHAPTER 17

# Evangelism For Our Day

THE SHELVES OF SHOPPING-MALL bookstores bulge with revelations of the latest guru and swami. TV features the popular series, "Religion in America." Long lines form at theaters showing the current film on sorcery, exorcism, the supernatural. Why this new fascination with religion?

## Spiritual Hunger

Many are drawn to the cult and occult because science and sobriety seem to have failed them. A world that believed in laboratories and factories, pragmatism and politics, appears to have produced ecological disaster and energy crises, poverty and inflation, wars and Watergates. "If we can't trust the cold machinations of the West, then we'll try the warm mysteries of the East"—so it is said.

Behind the thirst for mystery is the quest for meaning. The recent decades of scientism and secularity silenced gnawing questions like the one put in the mouth of Judas in *Jesus Christ Superstar:* "I only want to know...." I want to know about life and death, divine reality and human destiny, the stubbornness of evil and the possibilities of hope. The answer of the secular city, "no comment," is no longer sufficient.

To those who hunger for mystery and meaning there comes a response from the church: "We have a Story to tell!" There is some Good News about life, death, and destiny.

There is food for those starved for hope. It is not exotically packaged like the sweetmeats of a faddish neomysticism. But it is solid nourishment. As D.T. Niles put it: "Evangelism is one beggar telling another beggar where to find bread."

## Time for a Change

There are some other things happening that shape the church's fresh determination to "get the Story out." Weariness with wickedness in high places, and low places too, makes us say, "It's time for a change!" We need new visions and new decisions, new beings, new persons.

We've had an era of people who were "turned on." Now we need people who are "turned around." That's the meaning of conversion. Converts are those who have done an about-face, turning from darkness to light, from the idols of Mammon and power, from the gods of arrogance or apathy, pride or lust, to the God of mercy and justice who shone in the face of Jesus Christ. The converted are those who not only see the Light but who see *in* the Light the wretched of the earth, and seeing, set about to serve the neighbor in need.

To crave change, to hope for changed lives and a changed community, is to be open to the promise that the Story we have to tell will turn people around. Evangelism today is the response the church is making to the anguished awareness that it is time for a new direction.

## State of the Church

Dissatisfaction with the state of the church as well as the state of the world contributes to the evangelism imperative. Discontent with the church is nothing new; we have just been through a period of drastic self-criticism. But now it has to do with questions of survival. The membership curve of mainstream Christianity has plummeted sharply. How many more losses can the churches sustain before they disappear from one community after another?

Evangelism, for many, is the rising consciousness of this state of affairs and a growing will to do something about it. Evangelism seeks new growth for the church as well as new direction in life.

Why evangelism today? It is a response to the hunger for faith, the need for change, and concern for the future of the church.

These developments and yearnings are the "outward and visible signs of an inward and spiritual grace." I believe that the human response to the needs of the hour is made possible by the fearful and wonderful working of the Holy Spirit. The lively Presence is at the bottom of the restlessness in the world and the stirrings in the church. As the evangelism thrust of the early church was empowered by the Spirit that descended on the apostles at Pentecost so today the winds and fires of that same Spirit are moving today in our midst.

We shall track here the footsteps of the Presence. And you will have your own testimony to the Power in your place. With Paul we confess about the signs and wonders of evangelism, "It is I, yet not I, but Christ. . . . "

## WHAT IS EVANGELISM?

There are almost as many definitions of evangelism as there are evangelists. Actually this is not so bad because evangelism is many-faceted. But it is important to understand the unique quality of evangelism that distinguishes it from other aspects of the church's life.

Let's start with the root of the word *evangel* itself. That means "Good News." To the first Christians who used the term it meant the announcement of what God did, is doing, and will do to bring humanity, nature, and God together. It is the Story of the deeds of God from creation to consummation, with the highlight on its central chapters: Bethlehem, Galilee, Calvary, and Easter—Jesus Christ. Evangelism is getting that Story out.

But that tale-telling is no conventional chronicle. It is a report that can't be turned off casually like the evening newscast. It upsets, exhilarates, wounds, heals, liberates, reconciles. It changes things. It converts. It turns people around.

Evangelism, therefore, in a broad sense that includes a variety of practices, is: Getting the Story out that turns people around. Wherever that kind of an event takes place, evangelism is happening.

### "Acts" Evangelism

The book of Acts is our charter for evangelism. It recounts the activity of the first Storytellers. A look at the way Peter and John, Priscilla and Tabitha, Stephen and Paul, carried out their mission will help us to do ours.

The determination to get the Story out presses us back to our Storybook, the Bible. But learning from the apostles about evangelism is more than mechanically repeating what they did and said.

The Holy Spirit has been moving in the church and in the world for 2,000 years, always teaching us fresh ways to carry out the mission they launched. We must, therefore, listen for the special Word to us that comes through the first-century words, one that will guide us in our time and in our way to do what they did in theirs.

The rhythm of apostolic evangelism emerges in chapters 2, 3, and 4 of Acts. Let us follow that drama.

Before evangelism could happen in the early church the disciples had to be transformed into apostles. They had to be turned around from inward-looking nostalgia for their departed Lord to outward-thrusting, future-oriented mission with him. Acts 2 describes this about-face. It came not by boot-strap pulling but by the surging winds of the Holy Spirit. Shaking knees were strengthened and self-doubts disappeared as God poured fire into the apostles.

There are two lessons for us. One is that evangelism begins with empowerment. The momentum for getting the Story out comes from the winds of God. Whether evangelism happens—yesterday and today— depends on the movement of the Spirit. We pray for its power and celebrate its upwelling!

Another lesson from the Pentecostal birthday recorded in Acts 2 is that evangelism depends on a ready state of pre-evangelism in the church. Before we can get the Story out we have to "get it together."

There is a fundamental task of nurture to be done within the church if the people of God are to be empowered for mission beyond the walls of the church.

Faithful, lively preaching and teaching, deep and powerful prayer and worship, dedicated stewardship, thoughtful planning and responsible organization, a caring and sharing Christian community—all are instruments of empowerment that the Spirit uses to prepare us for the evangelism thrust beyond the doors of the congregation.

*Deed*

"One day Peter and John went to the Temple. . . . There at the Beautiful Gate, as it was called, was a man who had been lame all his life." (Acts 3:1–2, Today's English version) After the birth of the church at Pentecost, two evangelists found themselves in the marketplace, facing their first test. New Testament evangelism takes place "outside the gate."

In their path they find a strange challenge for those equipped with a Story to tell: a body to be healed, a deed to be done. Here, the very title of the book we are reading comes clear. It is not "The Talks of the Disciples," but "The Acts of the Apostles." The evangelists have a Story to be done as well as told; they perform an act of mercy for a broken body.

And it is a miracle. Peter and John are resource-less in the fact of the plea ("He begged them to give him something. . . . I have no money at all. . . ." Acts 3:3, 6) and have no standing in the eyes of the world ("They were ordinary men of no education" Acts 4:13). But they risk thinking the unthinkable thought that God wills the lame to walk, the blind to see, that the naked to be clothed, the hungry fed, the prisoner liberated. And they do the un-do-able with the power God gives the powerless.

The same Spirit works in today's evangelists who are part of a church that the world thinks is of no account. This free Spirit is not bound by the methods of Peter and John, but has worked miracles of healing and hope for 20 centuries through many ways and means. While the *how* explodes in variety, the *what* is the same yesterday, today, and tomorrow: Evangelists are instruments of the Spirit who bring wholeness (shalom) to bodies as well as souls.

*Word*

As the lame man leaped up, "the people were amazed." And Peter said, "Why are you surprised?. . . . The God of Abraham, Isaac and Jacob…has given divine glory to his Servant Jesus" (Acts 3:12–13).

In the midst of the deed the Word tumbles out. Peter told the Story of the God who moved in judgment and mercy from Exodus to Easter, who acts to make the wounded whole, and who will finally bring all things together. Evangelism is sharing the Good News. Peter and John got the Word out about the deeds of God because they had been captured by the saga themselves.

Evangelists today also will be propelled to get the Story out when they, too, have first been able to get the Story straight. Preparation for evangelism in our churches means putting ourselves where Peter and John were, discovering with them the acts of God in the march from Egyptian slavery to the promised land, in law and prophet, in Mary's cradle, on the Galilean seaside, at Golgotha's dark hour, on Easter's bright morning. Evangelism will happen when we become friends again with that old, old tale.

Getting the Story out, for us as for the apostles, means putting it in the language and setting of those to whom we speak. How we translate the narrative, the way we do it, will be shaped by the Story and in which God places us, the terrain of our time and place.

## Call

Getting the Story *in* is the hoped-for result of getting it *out*. The Holy Spirit makes this connection when a hearer says, "Yes, *the* Story is *my* story."

It takes place when the horror of Calvary is not only a catalogue of the evils of humanity, but when its reality strikes home and I confess, "God have mercy upon me a sinner!" "I was there when they crucified my Lord."

And it happens when the unfolding drama of redemption reaches our own inner depths and we can exult, "Thanks be to God who has given us the victory through our Lord Jesus Christ!"

The task of evangelism includes the enabling of connections between the biography of God and our own autobiographies. That is why Peter brought tale-telling down to earth: "Repent and turn to God" (Acts 3:19).

Here is a call to reorientation, to conversion. And the full turn of conversion meant not only turning in faith and hope to Christ, but also turning in love to the neighbor in need and to membership in the Body of Christ.

## Confrontation

"Peter and John were still speaking to the people when the priests, the officer in charge of the Temple guards, and the Sadducees came to them. They were annoyed. . . . So they arrested them and put them in jail . . ." (Acts 4:1–3).

The New Testament evangelists bumped up against the power structure of their day—one that happened to be a political-military-ecclesiastical complex. And it was not a pleasant encounter.

What prompted the confrontation? Two things:

1. "They were annoyed because the apostles were teaching that Jesus had risen from death. . . " (Acts 4:2). The powers of night do not like to hear it is dawn. The game is up for them; they do not control the future. And the powers of death fight back against life.

2. "If we are being questioned today about a good deed done to the lame man. . . " says Peter on the day of the trial (Acts 4:9). The power to do the deed of liberation was confirmation that Jesus Christ was Lord, that the future was open and no longer closed by the rulers of this world.

Authentic evangelists will be led by their words and deeds, by their Word-in-deed, into the arena of powers well as of persons. They will be confronted by society as well as selves. And they will not be afraid to disturb the peace of the principalities and powers, and take the consequences. Evangelism is not the sale of cheap grace; evangelism understands the cost of discipleship.

## Growth

"But many who heard the message . . . about five thousand" (Acts 4:3). While the VIPs were being turned off, the VLPs (Very Little Persons) were being turned around.

"Acts" evangelism produces results. For a long time we've been afraid to say this. We accepted uncritically the half-truth, "God wants us to be faithful, not successful." No doubt about it. Faithfulness will cause controversy and give us scars. But we have good reason to believe that God will, at the same time, bring to birth children of light.

Church growth is the promise of faithful planting. We dare to look for the green shoots that can spring up from the good seed of our sowing. And we pray that God "will give the increase."

## Life Together

"As soon as they were set free, Peter and John returned to their group. . . .When they finished praying, the place where they were meeting was shaken. They were all filled with the Holy Spirit and began to speak God's message with boldness. . . . The group of believers was one in heart and mind. No one said any of his belongings were his own, but all shared with one another everything he had. There was no one in the group who was in need" (Acts 4:23, 31–32, 34).

The Christian community itself is part of the witness to the Good News. Its proclamation and celebration of the Word are the environment in which the Spirit moves to empower the evangelists and to nurture those who have been won to the faith. Caring and sharing and stewardship among its members represented an evangelistic witness that evoked from the ancient world the tribute, "See how those Christians love one another!"

Evangelism today includes the same kind of "body language" that the early church manifest. Its own institutional signals are a crucial witness to the Story we have to tell. As an apostolic evangelism rhythm begins with an outer Word-in-deed, so it climaxes with the inner Word-in-deed of Christian life together.

## THE PARTS AND THE WHOLE

In Paul's letter to the congregation at Corinth he delighted in the variety of gifts that the Holy Spirit had given the church (1 Cor. 12). In the same way today God gives us a great array of talents and dispositions in the enactment of evangelism. Some are gifted in word, some in deed, some in the personal call, others in gathering new members, and still others in making the congregation a house of great hospitality,

While Paul honored variety in the church, he also prayed and pleaded for unity. He affirmed that no single gift represented the whole of God's bounty, that each was but a part, an organ of the full Body of Christ, the church (1 Cor. 12). Each found itself within the whole as, together, the many parts worked in love (1 Cor. 13). The same is true of our gifts. They best fulfill their role when they are teamed together.

So it was in the evangelism rhythm of Peter and John who "put it all together." This wholeness of witness of the first evangelists had its origin in Jesus himself, for his pattern of mission was exactly that of doing, telling, calling, confronting, gathering, and sharing, and the empowerment of that mission in the descent of the Holy Spirit.

Putting it all together in evangelism is going the full route with Peter and John and keeping company all the way with Jesus Christ. God gives us our part in this process and calls toward the vision of the whole.

Action Evangelism for Our Day, *AD: United Church of Christ Edition,* Vol. 3, No. 11 (November 1974), 28–31. Used by permission.

# PART FOUR

# Retrieving, Believing in the Midst of Caring and Doing

## CHAPTER 18

# Theological Soul-Searching in the United Church of Christ

S OME CALL THE MOOD ONE OF "ferment" (Avery Post, President of the UCC), others "turbulence" (*Seventh Angel*), still others a challenge to the "theological disarray" in the United Church of Christ (*Christianity Today*).

The theological dynamisms current in the United Church of Christ make it a laboratory for learning how a Church can both be open to the mandates of mission and unity and at the same time preserve its theological identity and some doctrinal coherence. The denomination, a conjunction of for somewhat diverse streams of Protestantism— Congregational, Christian, German, Swiss and Hungarian Reformed, and the part-Lutheran and part-Reformed Evangelical Synod of North America—has grown up in the twenty-seven years of its life in the midst of major theological and social upheavals. Reflecting its origins and formative years, the United Church of Christ has been deeply involved in social issues, open to cultural questions, an advocate of justice for marginalized groups and active in peace movements. These diversities and directions have brought the charge that the Church in its national expression is essentially a social action group, subject to the influence of one or another current ideology, and that its local congregations are the home of "a pallid but personable faith" (*Time*).

How to hold together the "world-formative" (N. Wolterstorff) character of its Reformed tradition, and the world-drenched nature of its recent history, with its historic rootage in scriptural authority and creedal and covenantal bonding—that is the question. Right now the United Church of Christ is in the middle of this kind of serious soul-searching. What follows is a chronicle of that quest from the perspective of one participant-observer.

## POST-60s SEARCHINGS

The present self-inquiry has long roots. From the beginning, these heirs of Jonathan Edwards, the Mercersburg theology and the Niebuhr brothers have never been devoid of theological concern, as evidenced by the widely used Statement of Faith of 1959, thoughtful Christian education programs, liturgically rich worship books, and strong ecumenical involvement, all concurrent with a passionate social witness.

However, signs of burnout after the activist 60s, concern about the reduction of mission to only its deed dimension, and worry about the acculturation of its message brought the beginnings of a new theological agenda. The meaning of mission became a natural early focal point. The church's Board for World Ministries began to explore its understanding of mission with a task force inquiry on evangelism, and the development of a statement of its dual nature as deed *and* word. In a similar vein, its Board for Homeland Ministries, having declined to participate in the nationwide Key 73 evangelism campaign, held a summer conference at Deering, New Hampshire in 1972 to examine its responsibilities in sharing the faith. Participants seized the initiative and produced the Deering Statement of Commitment that fused the social imperatives of the 60s with the faith sharing mandates of the 70s. Influenced by current action-reflection modes of theology, the Statement spoke of word in deed, the word of faith linked inextricably with deeds of mercy and justice. This grassroots movement, supported by BHM resources, developed extensive materials and training programs using "story" as its theological metaphor—"getting the story out."

Parallel with these outreach settings for theological recovery were inreach developments in the church's Office of Church Life and Leadership (OCLL). Seeing a growing interest in congregations in exploring ultimate questions, OCLL instituted a "faith exploration" program in which small gatherings were encouraged to share their doubts, hopes, and convictions, and move ahead on their spiritual journey. OCLL also gathered a group of pastoral and professional theologians in the mid-70s who issued a call for "Sound Teaching in the United Church of Christ," one that sought to integrate social witness and faith commitments.

Significant impetus was given to theological consciousness-raising in the UCC by two grassroot movements that emerged in the late 70s: BTL and UCPBW. BTL—the Biblical-Theological-Liturgical group, the "BTL Club"—was born at an anniversary celebration of the Evangelical Synod of North America, one of the streams of UCC history, in September, 1977. Organized by a local church pastor, Frederick Trost, the gathering (some in it) concluded that the time had come to work more aggressively on the biblical, theological, and liturgical tasks represented by these and other forebears. Developing a membership throughout the Midwest and East, BTL has met yearly to hear papers on Authority in the Church, Baptism, Eucharist, the Augsburg Confession, and the proposed new UCC worship services. An East Petersburg Statement was issued in 1979 criticizing the captivity of churches to bourgeois values and calling the UCC to its biblical and christological standards. Trost, in these years leader of the Wisconsin Conference of the UCC and convener of BTL, also founded an occasional journal, No Other Foundation, bringing theological and homiletical resources together for UCC clergy. The most significant contribution of BTL to date may be its sponsorship of the Craigville Colloquy, an event to be described in connection with the vigorous activities of 1984.

The United Church People for Biblical Witness (UCPBW) was formed in April, 1978 at a convocation of UCC clergy and laity who questioned the influence of contemporary values and ideology on a human sexuality report prepared for the UCC General Synod of 1977. Behind that lay a perceived erosion of biblical authority in the denomination. Similar concerns had been expressed earlier by a small group of conservative evangelicals, organized as the Fellowship of Concerned Churchmen. Led by Barbara Weller in its early years, with pastors Gerald Sanders and Martin Duffy as key associates and Donald Bloesch and Royce Gruenler as important theological resources, the UCPBW sought to make its influence actively felt on UCC policy through committee representation and Synod resolutions on the one hand, and an educational venture within the denomination on the other. The latter has included the production of an alternative resource on sexuality, *Issues in Sexual Ethics,* and a journal, *Living Faith,* with its commentary on denominational issues and theological essays, and a study guide on controverted UCC issues, *Affirming our Faith.* I shall treat its Dubuque Declaration and reorganization in 1984 subsequently.

Responding to the vocal presence of the UCPBW and noting its numerical growth in the United Church of Christ (with estimates as high as 50,000) in this period, another group of UCC members established a counter organization, Christians for Justice Action, which seeks to press the social issues it believes UCPBW neglects.

## 1983–84: YEARS OF FERMENT

Nineteen eighty-three was marked by an acceleration of theological activity that prompted talk of a "movement" or "theological renewal" (Executive Council statement) in the United Church of Christ. Aforementioned groups showing continuing signs of vitality and new manifestations were to be seen:

1. BTL scheduled its yearly meeting at New Brunswick Seminary in New Jersey in conjunction with clergy and seminary people from both the United Church of Christ and the Reformed Church in the United States to discuss the Mercersburg theology, a sacramental and ecumenical tradition shaped by 19th century theologians Schaff and Nevin. On that occasion a new organization alongside BTL was founded, an ecumenical Mercersburg Society. In the days that followed, many of the New Brunswick attendees journeyed to Washington, D.C. to join the UCC delegation in the mass demonstration marking the twentieth anniversary of Martin Luther King Jr.'s March on Washington for justice and peace, showing the linkages between social and biblical commitments envisaged by this kind of theological renewal.

2. After a determined effort up to and including the 1983 General Synod to air its views on sexuality and inclusive language, with little apparent result in the councils of the Church, the UCPBW constituency reviewed several scenarios for reorganization, looking

toward possible broader alliances and more impact on denominational decision-making. At a November board of directors meeting, the Dubuque Declaration was drawn up, asserting biblical authority (in the infallibilist rather than the inerrantist tradition), loyalty to the Nicene Creed and faithfulness to the theological commitments in the Basis of Union and Preamble of the UCC Constitution. The new organization proposed was named the Biblical Witness Fellowship.

3. With some overlap with the BWF in its constituency, a Fellowship of Charismatic Christians founded in the 1970s continued to make its presence known and concern felt in the denomination through its publications and national meetings on renewal.

4. Theologians involved in the development of the "Sound Teaching" document (Fred Herzog, Walter Brueggemann, Douglas Meeks), together with others on the faculties of the seven UCC related seminaries (Barbara Zikmund, Max Stackhouse, Susan Thistlewaite, etc.), believing the time had come to raise serious questions about the lack of theological clarity in the United Church of Christ, circulated a statement among that group, signed in the end by thirty-nine UCC teachers. The statement, "A Most Difficult and Urgent Time," declared that judgment on "worship resources, language practices, life-style and modes of accountability in the Church appeared to be "made, . . . on grounds of 'pragmatism,' 'liberalism,' 'conservatism,' 'pluralism,' which are inappropriate to the church of Jesus Christ . . . postures (arrived at) happenstance without the discipline and guidance offered to us in our theological tradition." The appeal was sent to the Executive Committee of the UCC with the urging that some serious theological grounding be sought for the policy and direction of the Church.

5. Decisions made by the Church at large or action taken by its agencies with clear theological import evoked wide discussion and controversy within the Church. Among them: a) A new set of services for the worship, sacraments, and rites of the Church, long in the making by a task force of OCLL, was published in 1983 and began to be tested throughout the Church. Attention was given in these

services to the classical traditions in liturgy, on the one hand, and on the other hand an effort was made to render virtually all the language of liturgy in inclusive terms. b) The Executive Council that acted then for the Church between Synods entered the lists by voting approval of an inclusive language version of the UCC Statement of Faith. Debates about inclusive language and its theological import were fueled by the concurrent release of the National Council of Churches lectionary readings that went further than UCC inclusivist proposals. c) Responding to the 1979 General Synod call for direction on Disciples-UCC union talks, the joint steering committee put forward the plan "Shared Life: A New Approach to Church Union" with proposals for common life and work as a matrix for decision-making on merger. The prospect of this union and the way toward it contributed to the growing theological discussion with special reference to the nature and mission of the church. Increasingly vocal opposition was heard from those with more organic views of the Church (especially in former Evangelical and Reformed areas) who felt these would be put in further jeopardy by Disciples polity and practice, and by others who argued that preoccupation with the mechanisms of merger would spend energies that should be devoted to mission.

6. An UCC-EKU (Evangelical Church of the Union in Germany) Working Group, sponsored by the United Church Board for World Ministries, became increasingly active in the publication of materials on the theology of the UCC. In 1983 and 1984, in its UCC-EKU Newsletter, it published essays from representatives of the seven UCC-related seminaries on various theological topics (authority in the Church, the teaching office, the confessional nature of the United Church of Christ, the Trinity and inclusive language, etc.) Those papers were in turn critiqued by faculties in other seminaries and then shared with EKU counterparts.

7. Sensing the ripeness of the moment for more official action on the theological front, the Office of Church Life and Leadership (OCLL) in 1983 launched a church-wide program to facilitate theological dialogue among the membership. The OCLL staff invited thirteen UCC persons representing a spectrum of interest and constituencies

to spend a year thinking through what such a denomination-wide effort would entail, identifying issues, possible areas of agreement and tasks to be undertaken.

8. The deans of the seven UCC-related seminaries put in motion a proposal to create a theological journal of and for the denomination.

9. Ethnic and minority groups in the United Church of Christ organized around advocacy issues joined together to form COREM (Council on Racial and Ethnic Ministries) to give voice to their perspective on both action questions and the widening theological discussion. Similarly, women's caucus groups throughout the United Church of Christ focused on rights issues have had to deal with theological questions (ordination, inclusive language, etc.) propelling them increasingly into the explicitly doctrinal arena. The organizing of a Coordinating Center for Women in Church and Society in the United Church of Christ and annual national women's meetings has provided a forum for these growing concerns.

Winter meetings of one or another segment of UCC leadership hosted by Florida constituents, are becoming a sounding board for denominational policy. In February of 1984, a joint gathering of Conference executives, agency heads, and denominational officers aired the question of "a theological centerline" in the United Church of Christ with Roger Shinn, drafter of the original UCC Statement of Faith, reflecting on this issue and responses from feminist, black, and evangelical perspectives. In a separate meeting of the executives of the 39 UCC Conferences, Disciples-UCC proposals for steps toward union—the "shared life" approach—were critically reviewed and a larger shadow cast over the future of these negotiations. An even more negative response to the prospects of this union was given at another winter meeting of UCC pastors from larger congregations with a signed protest from them and others appearing in the denominational information journal, *KYP*, as a "Committee for a New Alternative."

The faltering Disciples-United Church of Christ conversations are not a measure of UCC ecumenical commitments, to judge from other theological signs in 1984. The ten denomination project in unity, COCU, continue to enjoy wide tacit support in the United Church of Christ, although there was no vigorous campaign right now for it. The *Baptism, Eucharist and Ministry* (BEM) document produced by the Faith and Order Commission of the World Council of Churches was currently being discussed throughout the Church with agreements regularly expressed on the Baptism and Eucharist sections, but questions posed about its failure to honor adequately the ministry of the laity, and the too-priestly cast given to the pastoral office. Nineteen eighty-four also saw the discussion of the Lutheran-Reformed document of agreements and challenge, *Invitation to Action,* in which dialogue UCC was represented, and Called to Witness to the Gospel Today, an invitation from the World Alliance of Reformed Churches to respond to its theological concerns. A revitalized Council on Ecumenism actively discussed these proposals and made a public plea in KYP for support for the ecumenical agenda.

Nineteen eighty-four was a year of transition for the United Church People for Biblical Witness-Biblical Witness Fellowship. The reorganizational proposals of its Board were confirmed, and the Dubuque Declaration was endorsed at a meeting in Byfield, Massachusetts attended by 400 members and observers from around the country. Responding to criticism that it represents a potentially schismatic movement in the United Church of Christ, the leadership declared that it was in for the long haul, saw positive signs of theological renewal throughout the church, and was more determined than ever to press vigorously for its issues.

Questions of piety and spirituality, regularly intertwined with theological matters, emerged in their own right in the spring of 1984. A "spirituality network" was officially formed with a call for reinvigorated personal piety and public worship with appropriate theological undergirding. And a "Third Order of St. Francis—United Church of Christ" (chartered in 1983) began to gain momentum.

## CRAIGVILLE, 1984

The Craigville Colloquy represents, in the writer's view, the clearest expression of the direction, mode and possibilities of current theological soul-searching in the United Church of Christ. With neither budget nor staff, in fall, 1983 BTL and the Mercersburg Society issued a call for a grassroots assembly on UCC theological basics, with the 50th anniversary of the Barmen Declaration as background, prevailing upon the Craigville Conference Center in Massachusetts to house the event. The invitation generated twenty pre-Colloquy discussion groups around the country seeking to identify elements in a statement the Colloquy might make about the UCC theological frame work. On May 12, 1984, 160 people from California to Maine to North Carolina arrived, with the largest numbers from New England, Pennsylvania, and the Midwest. With its focus on the teaching premises of the United Church of Christ, and, therefore, the responsibilities of the teaching office, participants included pastors, local and regional (the latter being State Conference Ministers), with some seminary faculty and students, laity in leadership, and national executives, including the President of the Church, Avery Post, who was on a "theological sabbatical." Forty women were present in leadership roles and as participants. Many of the partisans in recent theological disputes were on hand, representing a variety of points of view concerned to make their voices heard, running from evangelicals in BWF and sacramentally-oriented Mercersburgers through UCC leadership figures and theological centrists to feminists and political activists.

With a sixty-page notebook of pre-Colloquy reports in hand, the participants met in twelve working groups to further clarify the themes that might appear in a Craigville statement, one determined in a plenary session to be "epistolary" rather than a formal declaration, since a "Letter to our Brothers and Sisters" reflected better the along-sided spirit and form that were sought. Feeding into the process of theological reflection were a series of presentations on the four traditions that formed the United Church of Christ—Congregational ( Joseph Bassett), Christian (Willis Elliott), Evangelical (Fred Trost), Reformed (John Shetler)—the ecumenical challenge (Diane Kessler), the Third World Context (Orlando Costas), the UCC theological trajectory (the writer), and a report from the President on responses expected of the UCC from various ecumenical entailments. An intense theological discussion about these issues was carried on in the setting of six worship services.

After plenary reports and discussion of the working groups, the material was turned over to a drafting committee formed in the self-select, "theology-from-below" mode at work in UCC theological renewal, with five members chosen by lots from a volunteer pool of thirty, with two "poets" added, Fred Trost the Colloquy convener, and the writer. The committee worked eight hours through the night presenting its results in a plenary session that debated and modified the text, voting it in the end, 141 to 1, with a standing ovation and doxology.

Developed according to the rhythms of worship, the letter moves from praise through confession and assurance to affirmation and thanksgiving. Its goal is the clarification of first principles—the assumptions behind what the United Church of Christ is and does. In the section on authority, it lifts up the UCC constitutional commitment to a christological center of the normative prophetic-apostolic testimony of Scripture (showing parallels with the Barmen Declaration), with the creedal and convenantal heritage of UCC faith honored in its relative role, and it declares the task of reinterpreting that faith in ever-fresh historical and cultural settings. In doctrinal content it speaks of the UCC's trinitarian framework of faith, citing the narrative sequence from creation to consummation, with its center point in the life, death, and resurrection of Christ (a framework familiar to UCC members through its Statement of Faith). It speaks of a sacramental life in Baptism and Eucharist, and holds to the importance of both the pastoral office and the ministry of the laity. The letter acknowledges some of the unresolved issues in the denomination from polity to morality, but forcefully affirms the UCC commitment to justice and peace and the covenantal ties that bind the members of the Body. Following Barmen, it ventures some specific rejections, ranging from the issues of "self-liberation" and relativism to racism and sexism, and, again following Barmen, disavows the ideologies of both left and right, and concludes with a doxology.

As important as the agreements reached in the Letter was the Craigville process. From invitation through pre-Colloquy discussion to the exchanges at the Colloquy, accent was placed on self-activated, theologically energetic participation. No official "line" was laid down, and no pattern of representation was demanded (either confined to or dominated by one theological perspective, or determined by proportional representation of advocacy groups). Does the Spirit work best in such an open-ended venture? Can there be a *sensus fidelium* as the matrix of sound theology? The vitality of the exchange among diverse groups and the remarkable consensus that developed are strong arguments for trust in this kind of forum. Those with heavy axes to grind will, of course, be suspicious if the result does not include their conclusions. The Colloquy assumed that the United Church of Christ is a Church of Jesus Christ in which the Spirit lives, a Spirit who will let light and truth break out when the ways of the Spirit among the people of God are honored.

The reception and sequel events are a measure of the UCC quest and hope for theological identity and integrity. Recognizing the significance of a theological framing for which the United Church of Christ had not often been known, the media gave Craigville wide coverage with long articles in the *Boston Globe,* a Religious News Service report, *Christianity Today* and *Christian Century* coverage and front-page stories in United Church of Christ-related organs *KYP* and *Seventh Angel.* Many UCC members committed to the Church's justice and peace agenda but troubled by its theological unclarity and developing polarization in its ranks, responded enthusiastically to a statement of first principles and an apparent consensus on the biblical and christological basics by the otherwise diverse constituencies present at Craigville. A number of letters and testimonies from leaders in other denominations and in the larger Christian community expressed appreciation for UCC commitment to biblical authority and classical faith, assuring continuing linkage with the ecumenical movement. Evangelicals in the United Church of Christ, including BWF leadership were on the whole pleased with the sections in the Letter that declared UCC commitment to biblical authority and the hope it represented for coming together of partisans around matters of basic framework.

Critics soon appeared. A Boston Feminist Dialogue group was formed to assess the Craigville letter and raised questions about the weight given to biblical authority, traditional theological formulations and matters of inclusive language (the Letter was scrupulous in its use of inclusive language but employed the baptismal formula "In the name of the Father, and of the Son and of the Holy Spirit" to affirm the ecumenical Christian usage in this binding rite). On the other hand, one editorialist criticized

Craigville for taking up issues in a denominational context that belonged more appropriately to an ecumenical setting. Some evangelicals were unhappy about a view of biblical authority that appeared to be limited to faith and morals and made a place for "ever new light and truth," a position which they judged contrary to the necessary conception of inerrancy. On the other hand, some advocacy groups and activists were concerned that more explicit positions on current ethical issues from a nuclear freeze to the abortion debates were not included.

A long critique by Al Krass in *Seventh Angel* faulted the Letter for its "blandness," failing therein to condemn specifically such evils as "the social and economics policies of Reaganism," and judged that the Colloquy was the product of aging middle class male clergy and seminary professors seeking to reassert their authority in the United Church of Christ after a season of contextual theology, much like the restrictiveness of the John Paul II era in Roman Catholicism vis-à-vis Küng and Gutierrez. Some from denominations with more dogmatic definitions thought Craigville's theological assertions too minimalist. Others felt that the openness of the UCC was imperiled by any attempt to bring up theological premises, including the elemental one found in the UCC Preamble to the Constitution.

The Craigville event is having its own immediate institutional effects—widespread study of the Letter in congregations and pastors' groups, and the planning of two subsequent events: a May 1985 BTL-Mercersburg meeting in Chambersburg, Pennsylvania, responding to the WCC proposal, "Toward Confessing the Apostolic Faith Today," the World Alliance of Reformed Churches, and the Lutheran-Reformed dialogue agendas, and a September 1985 church-wide Craigville II on the critical questions of Scripture/Word in the United Church of Christ (organized by a diversity of theological active groups, official and unofficial). Even more, it has accelerated the theological soul-searching we have traced here, accenting a special dimension to that process, the work of "theology from below:"

> pastors and people of the UCC making their views and concerns
> known, especially as they are concerned with grounding the witness of
> this Church to justice and peace in the soil of biblical authority and
> classical faith.

# THE CRAIGVILLE LETTER

*Grace and Peace*

On the 50th anniversary of the Barmen Declaration we have come together at Craigville to listen for God's Word to us, and to speak of the things that make us who we are in Christ.

We praise God for the theological ferment in our Church! When such life comes, and light is sought, we discern the Spirit's work. The struggle to know and do the truth is a gift of God to us. So too are the traditions that have formed us—Congregational, Christian, Evangelical, Reformed, and the diverse communities that have since shaped our life together. We give thanks for the freedom in this family of faith to look for ever-new light and truth from God's eternal Word.

Thankful for the vital signs in our midst, we know too that our weaknesses have been the occasion for God's workings among us. To make confession at Craigville is also to acknowledge our own part in the confusions and captivities of the times. The trumpet has too often given an uncertain sound. As the people of God, clergy and laity, our words have often not been God's Word, and our deeds have often been timid and trivial. Where theological disarray and lackluster witness are our lot, it is "our own fault, our own most grievous fault."

Yet we trust God's promises. Mercy is offered those who confess their sin. Grace does new things in our midst. Blessing and honor, glory and power be unto God!

In our deliberations we have sought to honor the ties that bind us, and to learn from the diversities that enrich us. We gladly speak here of the affirmations we can make together, and the judgments we share.

*Authority*

Loyal to our founders' faith, we acknowledge Jesus Christ as our "sole Head, Son of God and Saviour" (Preamble, Para. 2, *The Constitution of the United Church of Christ)*. With Barmen we confess fidelity to "the one Word of God which we have to hear and which we have to trust and obey in life and death" (Barmen, 8:11). Christ is the Center to whom we turn in the midst of the clamors, uncertainties and temptations of the hour.

We confess Jesus Christ "as he is attested for us in Holy Scripture" (Barmen, 8:11). As our forebears did, we too look "to the Word of God in the Scriptures" (Preamble, Para. 2). Christ speaks to us unfailingly in the prophetic-apostolic testimony. Under his authority, we hold the Bible as the trustworthy rule of faith and practice. We believe that the ecumenical creeds, the evangelical confessions, and the covenants we have made in our churches at various times and places, aid us in understanding the Word addressed to us. We accept the call to relate that Word to the world of peril and hope in which God has placed us, making the ancient faith our own in this generation "in honesty of thought and expression, and in purity of heart before God" (Preamble, Para.2).

## Affirmation

According to these norms and guides, we call for sound teaching in our Church, and so confess the trinitarian content of our faith. Affirming our Baptism "in the name of the Father, and of the Son and of the Holy Spirit" (Matthew 28:19), we believe that the triune God is manifest in the drama of creation, reconciliation and sanctification. Following the recital of these mighty acts in our Statement of Faith, we celebrate the creative and redemptive work of God in our beginnings, the covenant with the people of Israel, the incarnation of the Word in Jesus Christ and the saving deed done in his life, death and resurrection, the coming of the Holy Spirit in church and world, and the promise of God to consummate all things according to the purposes of God. In the United Church of Christ we believe that the divine initiatives cannot be separated from God's call to respond with our own liberating and reconciling deeds in this world, and thus to accept the invitation to the cost and joy of discipleship.

## Church

Our faith finds its form in the Christian community. We rejoice and give thanks to God for the gift of the one, holy, catholic and apostolic Church, gathered by the Holy Spirit from the whole human race in all times and places. That Church is called to share the life-giving waters of Baptism and feed us with the life-sustaining bread and wine of

Eucharist; to proclaim the Gospel to all the world; to reach out in mission by word and deed, healing and hope, justice and peace. Through Baptism the Church is united to Christ and shares Christ's prophetic, priestly and royal ministry in its servant form. We rejoice that God calls some members for the ministry of Word and Sacrament to build up the Body and equip the saints for ministry in the world. We rejoice that God calls the laity to their threefold ministry, manifesting the Body of Christ in the places of work and play, living and dying.

We confess that although we are part of the Body in this Church, we are not the whole Body. We need always seek Christ's Word and presence in other communities of faith, and be united with all who confess Christ and share in his mission.

## Polity

We confess our joy in the rich heritage of the Congregational, Christian, Evangelical, and Reformed traditions and the many diverse peoples who compose the fabric of the United Church of Christ. We are a "coat of many colors" and we give thanks for this diversity. We affirm the value of each voice and tradition that God has brought together and that our unity in Christ informs our faith and practice. In these days together, we have been reminded of the search for unity amidst the marvelous diversity in the United Church of Christ. We acknowledge that our diversity is not only a precious gift of God but that it is sometimes the source of hurt, frustration and anger.

God is gracious. Through God's grace we are able to embrace in forgiveness and to reconcile divisions. In covenant we are continually being called to be present to and for one another. In covenant we are being called to acknowledge that without one another we are incomplete, but together in Christ we are his Body in which each part is honored.

We have not yet reached agreement in our discussions regarding the governance of the Church. We acknowledge a need to develop further our polity; to hold together in mutual accountability all the various parts of our Church. We affirm that the Christian community must conform its life and practice to the Lordship of Jesus Christ and dare not heed the voice of a stranger. We affirm that in the United Church of Christ the

Holy Spirit acts in powerful ways as the communities of faith gather for worship and for work, in local churches, in the Associations, in the Conferences, in the General Synod, and in the Instrumentalities and Boards. As a servant people, the prayer on the lips of the Church at such times is always: "Come, Holy Spirit!"

## Justice

We have not reached agreement on the meaning of peace with justice. We confess, however our own involvement with the injustices present in our society. We acknowledge our need to embody God's eternal concern for the least and most vulnerable of our neighbors. This shall require a renewed commitment to the study of the biblical teachings on justice and a fresh determination to do the things that make for peace.

We invite you to join us in reconsidering the meaning of Jesus' call and the summons to the Church to preach good news to the poor, proclaim release to the captives, enable recovery of sight to the blind, set at liberty those who are oppressed, and proclaim the acceptable year of our Lord.

Where justice is compromised and the rights of the weak sacrificed to the demands of the strong, the Church is called to resist. Christ stands along side those deprived of their just claims. We pray for ears to hear God's voice resounding in the cries of those who are victimized by the cruel misuse of power. God's tears are shed also amidst the indifferent. We share with each of you the ministry of reconciliation. We ask you to consider thoughtfully the meaning and implications of this high calling in the world God loves and to which Jesus Christ comes as the embodiment of hope, the messenger of love, and the guarantor of the divine intention that the bound be set free from the unjust yoke.

In response to the witness of the Holy Scriptures and the example of Jesus Christ, we beseech our government at every level, to be steadfast and persistent in the pursuit of political, economic, and social justice with mercy and compassion. We are of a common mind, inviting you to join us in the urgent pursuit of those longings which compel a just peace in the nuclear age. Where justice is withheld among us, God is denied. Where peace is forsaken among us, we forsake Christ, the life of the Church is compromised, and the message of reconciliation is gravely wounded. Let us bear witness to the truth in this.

*Ambiguities*

We acknowledge with joy that new light is yet to break forth from God's Word. This bright light is a gift for the nurturing of our lives as Christians. At the same time, it is our experience that this vision of the Church is often blurred and incomplete. "For now we see through a glass, dimly" (I Cor. 13:12). Where our vision is unclear and the voice of the Church uncertain, we are urged not to indifference or compromise, but to our knees; to repentance, to prayer, and an earnest quest, seeking together the way of Christ for us.

We acknowledge with gratitude that in Christ every dividing wall of enmity or hostility is broken down. How do we celebrate this when we are tempted to ignore, avoid or resist some members of the community? Is not such resistance a contradiction of love of neighbor? As brothers and sisters in Christ we are summoned to address one another with humility knowing that our words and actions are subject to the judgment of God. Are we not to trust God to reconcile divisions among us, and when there has been separation or hurt to lead us back to one another as a shepherd searches for the flock? Can we afford to be any longer apart from the promise of the Gospel? Are we not to live this promise in the brilliant light of God's redeeming ways with us? God is faithful and just. Trusting in that faithfulness and the enormity of divine grace, surely we may bear the tension of the paradoxes of salvation not yet fully realized.

*Rejections*

Ours is an age of a multitude of gods and we are tempted on every side to cling to a false message and a false hope. This is a dangerous path and it is no stranger to any of our congregations. Idolatry can tempt us and lull us to sleep; it offers us false comfort and false security. We ask you to consider with us the idolatries of our time and to reject all that denies the Lordship of Jesus Christ.

We reject "the illusions of self-liberation" (WARC, II, 2, p. 12). With the framers of the Barmen Declaration, we reject the false teaching that there may be "areas of our life in which we would not belong to Jesus Christ, but other lords; areas in which we would not need justification and sanctification through him" (Barmen, 8:15).

We reject the racism and sexism that demean our lives as those created precious in the sight of God.

We reject materialism and consumerism that put things in place of God and value possessions more than people.

We reject secularism that reduces life to its parts and pieces, and relativism that abandons the search for truth.

We reject militarism that promises "security" by means of a nuclear balance of terror, threatening God's creation with destructive "gods of metal."

We reject identification with any ideology of the right or the left "as though the Church were permitted to abandon the form of its message and order to its own pleasure or to changes in prevailing ideological and political convictions." (Barmen, 8:18).

We reject cultural captivity and accommodationism as well as the notion that we can turn aside from the world in indifference, for we remember that "the earth is the Lord's and the fulness thereof. . ." (Psalm 24:1).

We urge the Church in each of its parts to prayerfully consider the meaning for our times of Paul's admonition in Romans 12:2 ". . . Do not be conformed to this world but be transformed by the renewal of your mind, that you may prove what is the will of God, what is good and acceptable and perfect." Pray that God will help the United Church of Christ discern the things we must reject as well as the things we must affirm, that to which we say "no" and that to which we give our glad assent.

## Life Together

For the health of the Church and the integrity of our witness and service, we urge clergy and laity to gather in timely fashion for prayer, study, and mutual care. We encourage the mutual support of clergy for one another in their ministry, and ask the theological faculties to maintain communion with students beyond the years of their formal study. We ask Church and Ministry Committees to nurture Christian love and concern for seminarians during the course of their preparation for ordained tasks in the Church. We hope that retreats and periods of rest, reflection and spiritual renewal will become part of our life together in each Conference, and that the teaching ministry might be affirmed by laity and clergy to the end that our congregational life and our mission be anchored deeply in Scripture and informed generously by the urgent realities of our time.

*Doxology*

To the truth of the Gospel that has sustained and emboldened the Church in each generation, we too say "yes." With grateful hearts, we affirm the gift of faith present in the United Church of Christ—evangelical, catholic, and reformed—which we are being called to live out in these fragile and bewildering times.

While the way ahead is not always clear to us, we dare to hope and rejoice, believing that we be long to our faithful Saviour, Jesus Christ, our "only comfort in life and death" (*Heidelberg Catechism*, Ques. 1). We seek to hold together worship, discipleship, proclamation and service, Word and world.

As our forbearers have done, we too declare that we shall tread this path with all who are "kindred in Christ" and "share in this confession" (Preamble, Para. 2). We invite you to walk with us in this way.

In Christ
The Participants in the Craigville Colloquy,
Craigville, Massachusetts, May 16, 1984

The Craigville Colloquies have been annual events, now one week in length, Craigville XXII in 2005 being on the topic "Christ Will Come Again. Reclaiming Eschatology.

Theological Soul-Searching in the United Church of Christ, *TSF Bulletin*, Vol. 8, No. 4 (November–December 1984), 5–9. Used by permission.

## CHAPTER 19

# Does the Center Hold?:

## "Confessing Christ" in Year Ten

"CALLS FOR CHANGE IN THE UCC" read the December 1, 1993 *Christian Century* news story. Whence these rumblings in the mainline denomination that traces its ancestry to a mix of Pilgrim forebears and immigrants German and Swiss? Are the biblicists busy again calling us away from today's frontier issues and even toward schism?

The fifteen names on the September 1993 letter that prompted the story did not quite fit the picture. Numbered among them were loyal UCC pastors, four state Conference Ministers including, at the time, the only two African-American leaders serving in this position in the denomination, a handful of faculty from the Church's seminaries, all of these with long histories of involvement in the social action agenda of the UCC, Biblical issues yes, and more. Responding to a denominational call for discussion of the Church's purposes, it declared, "We are deeply concerned . . . that the commitment to 'listen for God's Word in Holy Scripture' and 'in our rich heritage' is often neglected in our Church. We view this indifference to Scripture and debilitating amnesia as a threat to the Gospel. Central to our Church is its trinitarian faith in Jesus Christ as Lord and Savior, grounded in the authority of Scripture and faithfully expressed in the ecumenical creeds and in the confessions and covenants of our Reformation tradition, as well as in the theological standards of our Constitution, Statement of Faith, symbol, and the living witness of our Church." The point: let's attend to the theological basics that ground our social witness, and not take our signals from the culture's fads and fancies.

The letter sent to 450 on the mailing list of the Craigville Theological Colloquies, an earlier grassroots venture launched at a UCC Center on Cape Cod in 1984, brought 400 pastors to day-long meetings in New England, Pennsylvania and Wisconsin, to discuss the concerns expressed in the letter. From those gatherings was born the "Confessing Christ" movement in the United Church of Christ, now asking itself whether those "changes in the UCC" have happened, or can happen.

While this is the tenth anniversary of Confessing Christ, it is part of a longer trajectory from what was called in the 1970s "the theological ferment in the UCC." Confessing Christ's lineage began in 1977 in the living room of Pastor Frederick Trost at the close of a hundredth anniversary celebration of the founding of the Evangelical Synod of North America in the St. Paul's UCC congregation he served. (The Synod was founded in 1871, but adopted the name in 1877. The Missouri Synod Lutheran Church dates its origins from the same congregation in 1847.) A group fresh from that event agreed that the theological excitement manifest there, especially against the backdrop of its perceived absence in the United Church of Christ of that period, should be perpetuated in some more enduring form. Thus was founded the "Biblical-Theological-Liturgical Group" that held the first of a series of conferences on the historic teachings of the UCC, a 1978 two-day gathering at St. Paul's Church on Holy Communion, followed by one in Massachusetts on Baptism. Best remembered by the Church-at-large, however, was the manifesto from this "BTL Club" (a playful distinction from the infamous "PTL Club" of Jimmie and Tammie Baker), at its May 1979 conference on "Authority in the Church," the "East Petersburg Declaration," one that protested:

—The techniques of management and manipulation on which we have relied in the Church that have elbowed aside biblical preaching, sound theological teaching, living worship and sacrament;

—the latest wisdom of this world that regularly beguiles us from our fundamental norms of Scripture and Tradition;

—our captivity to the comforts and idolatries of a bourgeois Protestantism that shuts our eyes and closes our mouth before mis-

ery, tyranny, and untruth. Sisters and brothers this bondage must not
be! As pastors and teachers . . . we own again this common
covenant—to listen only to the one Word, Jesus Christ; to tell only
this story of the liberating and reconciling deeds of the triune God.

BTL continued to hold periodic conferences that echoed these concerns, one notable such event being in the spring of 1983 at New
Brunswick Seminary focused on the World Council of Churches' document, Baptism, Eucharist and Ministry. On an evening during that conference, the attendees gathered in the living room of the seminary president, Howard Hageman, and in a meeting convened by Frederick Trost
voted to establish "The Mercersburg Society," whose purpose was to
carry forward the christological, sacramental, and liturgical traditions of
John Williamson Nevin and Philip Schaff, nineteenth century teachers
at the Mercersburg seminary of the German Reformed Church (now
Lancaster Theological Seminary). Their "Mercersburg theology" was a
movement historian Sidney Ahlstrom describes as pioneering ecumenism in North America.

The pre-history of Confessing Christ continued with a May 1984
assembly of one hundred-sixty UCC clergy and laity at the aforementioned Craigville Theological Colloquy I, marking the fiftieth anniversary of the Barmen Declaration. The conference was jointly sponsored
by the Biblical-Theological-Liturgical Group and the Mercersburg
Society, and was preceded by 23 working groups around the country
asked to identify the essentials of UCC teaching as related to the concerns of Barmen. The colloquy produced a "witness statement" drafted
by a committee of five chosen by lot to depoliticize the process, with
two other members assigned by the colloquy planners. The result was a
declaration picked up by the wire services as newsworthy, being count-
er-evidence to the stereotype of the United Church of Christ as uncon-
cerned about doctrine or having "little interest . . . concerning a pastor's
religiosity, biblical faith, evangelism, emphasis on spiritual renewal or
liturgy," as a *Time* story described the United Church of Christ ["A
Pallid but Personable Faith?" *Time,* Sept. 29, 1980, 85]. After confessing
their own complicity in the theologically lackluster condition of their

denomination, the signatories went on to call for "sound teaching in our Church" re-affirming the IJCC Preamble to its Constitution:

> Loyal to our founders' faith, we acknowledge Jesus Christ as the "sole Head of the Church, Son of God and Savior". . . . With Barmen we confess fidelity to "the one Word of God which we have to hear and which we have to trust and obey in life and death". . . . Christ is the Center to whom we turn in the midst of the clamors, uncertainties and temptations of the hour . . . .

And underscoring the trinitarian deeds of God declared in the UCC Statement of Faith:

> We celebrate the creative and redemptive work of God in our beginnings, the covenant with the people of Israel, the incarnation of the Word in Jesus Christ and the saving deed done in his life, death and resurrection, the coming of the Holy Spirit in church and world, and the promise of God to consummate all things according to the purposes of God. . . . We believe that the divine initiatives cannot be separated from God's call to respond with our own liberating and reconciling deeds in the world, and thus to accept the invitation to the cost and joy of discipleship.

As Confessing Christ had an ancestry in these earlier efforts to rejoin Word to deed, it was also, surely, influenced by the over-all "theological tumult" in the United Church of Christ of the 1970s and 1980s (as it was called by a Presbyterian publication), including a 1978 "Call for Sound Teaching in the Church" by a group of UCC thinkers amid the manifesto by "the Seminary 39" (many of the UCC faculty in the Church's seminaries), "A Most Difficult and Urgent Time"; and then from a group to the right, the 1978 organization of "United Church People for Biblical Witness" that became in 1983 the "Biblical Witness Fellowship," and one from the left, the formation in 1980 of the organization, "Christians for Justice Action." Given its stand for the full-orbed faith pressed for by its predecessors and embodied in the UCC's founding documents, it was sympathetic to the call for sound teaching and troubled by the same things identified by the seminary teachers, and agreed about the importance of both the personal and public witness stressed by one or the other latter movements. But it wanted to place all these concerns more firmly in continuity with historic faith and in the framework of ecumenical commitment.

UCC officialdom knew that Confessing Christ was not to be caricatured as a pietistic retreat or schismatic withdrawal, given the activist history and denominational loyalty of the signers, but shortly after its founding public misgivings were expressed. UCC president, Paul Sherry, responding to charges of theological indifferentism, told a Cleveland newspaper reporter that "The UCC has not lost its theological foundations." John Thomas, then the denomination's ecumenical officer in a 1994 AP story on Confessing Christ questioned the movement's plan to formulate a catechism for use in UCC congregations, stressing the theological diversity within the denomination. Conference executive Donna Schaper wrote in a Christians for Justice Action publication that its own leadership was "more comfortable with 'following Jesus' than 'confessing Christ.'" Advocacy groups with one or another agenda made their objections known as well, troubled by the invitation letter's desire to give voice to the "often-silent center" of the Church.

"Center" did become a rallying cry for Confessing Christ, but in a more theologically-oriented sense than just a location distinguished from left-right culture war categories. Its literature speaks of a three-fold meaning. The word points, first and foremost, to "Christ the Center," reflecting Dietrich Bonhoeffer's usage, the denomination's own name and the language of the Barmen Declaration, "Jesus Christ, as...the one Word of God"; then to the "centralities" of the trinitarian faith embodied in the UCC' s confessional and covenantal heritage and its shared ecumenical faith—and then to the center as a bridge spanning the left-right chasm of the day in both church and culture, a meeting place for serious and joyful theological work among otherwise alienated partisans against the background of the Center and the centralities.

Now eighty Confessing Christ consultations later in eight regions of the country, six books and booklets and five Occasional Papers, a newsletter *Joy in the Word!* and a daily prayer and reading discipline sent out to fourteen hundred on the Confessing Christ mailing list, an

Internet Web site with papers and resources and a ten-year running Internet discussion with tens of thousands of daily notes, Confessing Christ has given evidence of its effort to carry out its goals, now embodied in a Statement of Principles built around the Preamble to the UCC Constitution:

> *Confessing Christ* is an invitation to joyous theological reflection and serious theological work throughout the United Church of Christ. Confessing Christ affirms faithfulness to the one Word of the triune God, Jesus Christ, which we are to hear and which we have to trust and obey in life and in death.
>
> *Confessing Christ* is committed to listen for God's Word in the Holy Scriptures of the Old and New Testaments and in our rich theological heritage. Central to the United Church of Christ, which baptizes in the name of the Father, Son and Holy Spirit, is its faith in Jesus Christ as Lord and Savior. This faith is grounded in the authority of Scripture and is expressed in the ecumenical creeds, in the confessions and covenants of our Reformation traditions, in the Preamble to its Constitution, and in the prayers, worship and public witness of the Church.
>
> *Confessing Christ* embraces the responsibility of every generation in the Church to make this faith its own.

The subjects of the many consultations, attended by groups that range from fifteen to one hundred fifty, most in between, often a day in length but also for two to three day periods, have run the gamut of theological and ethical issues. Among them have been: "Word and World: Christ and Culture at the End of the Century," "Catechism: A New Old Way for All Christians?" "Genetics: Review of UCC Statements," "The Baptismal Formula," "Authority in the Church," "Re-forming the Christian Life," "What Does it Mean to Take the Bible Seriously?" "How Can the Church Reclaim Tradition without Succumbing to Traditionalism?" "Incarnation: In Christ was Life and the Life was the Light for All People," "How Can We be a People of the Book in a Video Age?" "Who is Jesus Christ for Us Today?" "What Does the UCC Believe?" "If the

Church is Broken, How Can it Be Fixed?" "Preaching Christ in Advent . . . Lent," "The Cambridge Platform," "Dancing at the Savoy (Declaration)," "The Jesus Seminar: Another Voice." Consultations of a bridging sort include dialogues on "Same-Sex Marriage?" with spokespersons pro and con and an ecumenical observer; "What is the Theology of the New Century Hymnal?" with Confessing Christ member critiques and responses by the hymnbook publisher and editorial board members; a series of ecumenical conferences—Lutheran and Reformed on the then-proposed North American Formula of Agreement, Lutheran-Roman Catholic-Reformed trialogues on various subjects including the Lutheran-Roman Catholic *Joint Declaration on the Doctrine of Justification,* "One Path to God: No Salvation Outside Christ? No Salvation Outside the Church?" "Living and Preaching in This Strange New Time," "The Moral Crisis in Our Churches"; an Episcopal SEAD-CC joint meeting, "Jesus Christ and Culture-Christianity"; gatherings with overseas leaders from the Evangelical Church of the Union (EKU), the Evangelical and Reformed Church of Honduras, the Church of the Rhineland and others on such topics as "Confessing Christ in a Post-Christian Era," "Justice, Peace and the Integrity of Creation," "Confessing Christ in a Global Community," "Christianity: Balm of Peace or Bomb of Violence."

Confessing Christ publications include two volumes by Pickwick Press, *How Shall We Sing the Lord's Song?* (a series of essays critiquing *The New Century Hymnal,* edited by Richard Christensen, with responses by its producers) and *When I Survey the Wondrous Cross,* a work on the Atonement by Richard Floyd. Books published by Confessing Christ itself include *He Comes the Broken Heart to Bind,* a series of essays on 9/11 edited by Frederick Trost, the initial papers of its organizing meetings, and a booklet "Revelation and Re-Imagination." The Pennsylvania regional CC group worked for many years to carry out the original hope of producing a catechism, and in 2001, through the determined leadership of Pastor Deborah Rahn Clemens, *Pass Along the Faith* was published, questions and answers against the backdrop of both contemporary issues and the Heidelberg Catechism. One Pennsylvania CC pastor, Christopher Anderson, produced his own humorous update, *The Revised Heidelberg Catechism: A Joke Book.* And in a nice bit of irony and perhaps humor too, John Thomas, now current president of the UCC, whose comments on catechism are mentioned above, addressed the 1997 assembly of the Evangelical Lutheran Church of America about to vote on a Formula of Agreement with three Reformed communions, is said to have given added theological credibility to the United Church of Christ by beginning his remarks quoting as UCC teaching the famous first question and answer of the Heidelberg Catechism.

The consultations and publications have been overseen by a National Steering Committee that meets twice a year and occasionally by phone conference call, and by regional steering committees in Wisconsin, Pennsylvania, New York, Massachusetts, New Hampshire, Connecticut, Maine and California. All is by volunteer labor and by regional ventures largely financed by participant registration, except for a national administrator, originally James Gorman, who launched the busy CC Internet discussion groups in 1993), paid $3000 out of a national budget that has run about $10,000 a year, with a big assist in mailing from the Mission House Center at Lakeland College, founded, in part, at the initiative of the Wisconsin Confessing Christ group. The national convenors have been Wisconsin Conference Minister, Frederick Trost, until his retirement in 2001, and more recently, Penn Southeast Conference Minister, Russell Mitman who was succeeded by Professor Lee Barrett of Lancaster Theological Seminary.

To return to the *Christian Century* caption, has Confessing Christ actually changed anything in the United Church of Christ? As there is no formal measuring rod, the evidence is anecdotal, some strong, some weak. In the former category, fairly convincing is the ecumenical impact the movement has had. Not a few of its leaders were influential in both preparation for and implementation of the 1997 Lutheran-Reformed Formula of Agreement (FOA), including presence in the four-year study, *A Common Calling* that laid the groundwork for the FOA; hosting Confessing Christ meetings with Lutherans on the FOA; joint ventures by ELCA bishops and UCC Conference Ministers associated with Confessing Christ, notably in Wisconsin and Southeast Pennsylvania; representation on the present national UCC committee to carry out the FOA. Indeed, more than a few Lutherans have said that the Confessing Christ movement showed a face of the United Church of Christ it had not seen heretofore, especially with reference to its charters and official documents that expressed the denomination's ecumenical faith. In the same vein, but less widespread, Roman Catholics, taking part in Confessing Christ consultations on the Joint Declaration on the Doctrine of Justification, *Dominus Iesus* and other issues, also testify to their fresh awareness of UCC theological commitments, not apparent in the denomination's public portrayals.

Again, on matters of testimony that changed not only the perception of the United Church of Christ, but determined affiliation with the denomination, have been the many avowals of both pastors and congregations that they continue in the United Church of Christ because of the presence and witness of Confessing Christ. In sections of the Church where "the establishment" pays little attention to foundational Christian doctrine, or has minimal recourse to biblical norms in taking positions on the issues of the day, more than a few UCC clergy and congregations either retreat to islands of local autonomy, consider departing the denomination, withdraw their monies from national, or take up a hostile stance toward everything that proceeds from "Cleveland" (UCC headquarters). Confessing Christ resists schism in any of these forms, urging giving to the United Church of Christ at large before any contributions are made to Confessing Christ, takes active part in regional and national boards and committees, and has had in its leadership UCC Conference Ministers, including the chair of the national Council of Conference Ministers. It counsels restive congregations to "hang in" with the United Church of Christ and make their witness as a loyal opposition. An early case in point was the invitation of Confessing Christ leaders to appear before the annual meeting of the Calvin Synod, the Conference of Magyar congregations then considering departure from the United Church of Christ because of perceived theological adventurism, an appearance that eventuated in its bishop serving for a period on the Confessing Christ National Steering Committee. More recent was the 2003 requested appearance of a National Steering Committee delegation before the leadership of the largest and one of the oldest UCC congregations in New England that was in the midst of a year-long study to decide whether to leave the denomination (an appearance of three Steering Committee members, preceded the week before by the president of the national Church and the state Conference Minister concerned about such a major loss). The congregation in question, at that time by a very close vote, decided to stay, and the pastor is in conversation with the Steering Committee about future relations with Confessing Christ, including hosting a consultation on the Trinity.[1]

For all its effort to honor its UCC home, it speaks a firm "No" when it judges actions within the Church to be at odds with the United Church of Christ own professed convictions and historic faith. When suggestions were made by some in the national offices that the theological Preamble to the UCC Constitution, cited regularly in the UCC's ecumenical negotiations in order to establish its ecumenical credentials, was out of date and should be revised, and the symbol of the UCC with its cross and crown above the world altered because of its triumphalist imagery, Confessing Christ let its voice be heard. On a more general note, concerned that theology was not given its due in Church and Ministry Committee interviews of prospective ordinands, it wrote to all these "gatekeepers" in the denomination urging attention to UCC theological standards. Its first major effort of this sort was a strong protest of aspects of *The New Century Hymnal* published by one of the Church's instrumentalities. While affirming some of its freshly-written hymns and those of new ethnic background, Confessing Christ resisted the efforts in the hymnal to stretch the call for language inclusivity to the point of altering the theology of classical hymns on matters of the Trinity, Christology and other basic Christian teachings in order to satisfy the self-determined standards of the editorial committee. Hence its volume, *How Shall We Sing the Lord's Song?* More recently, a denominational program, "God is Still Speaking" with a slogan borrowed from Gracie Allen, urging that we not put a period where a comma belongs, suggests that open-mindedness to the new is the UCC signature, the past being the problem to be transcended by our "cutting edge theology . . . [that] puts us out there alone." ("Who We Are," God is Still Speaking Web site, www.stillspeaking.com) The Confessing Christ National Steering Committee, also celebrating the famous counsel to Pilgrims of Pastor John Robinson in a statement to the "Comma" sponsors reminded them that his rightful urging of us to look for "more truth and light" breaking forth was from God's "holy Word," and thus normed by Jesus Christ as attested by Scripture. The Committee asked the sponsors to cite not only the sentence from the UCC's Preamble to its Constitution about making the faith its own "in each generation," but also its context that stipulated it to be "the faith of the historic Church expressed in the ancient creeds and reclaimed in the insights of the Protestant Reformers," the faith of a Church that "acknowledges as its sole Head, Jesus Christ, Son of God and Savior."

Does the following show the influence of Confessing Christ? The reader must decide. It introduced the word "confessing" into the mainline Church picture in 1993. Later, several self-described "Confessing" movements came into existence and held a major conference in the Fall of 2002. However, Confessing Christ was neither invited, nor chose to attend, wary of the schismatic overtones and focus on culture-war rather than doctrinal issues that seemed to characterize the sponsors. As it turned out, a group of well-known theologians wrote to the assembly to urge the role of loyal opposition, rather than flight, and attention to the deep theological questions in mainline Churches. These have been the orienting views of the UCC's Confessing Christ movement since its inception, and they continue to be so.

With the mixed picture of Confessing Christ, can the changes sought by Confessing Christ really come about? The grounding of the Church's social witness in its professed theological commitments; the United Church of Christ, a pioneer in ecumenism, with an affirmation of its historic ecumenical faith rather than one that "puts us out there alone"; the practice of a declared "inclusivity" in which the largest New England UCC congregation can be welcomed and recognize itself in UCC self-definitions; a Church known for its honoring personal faith as well as social witness, evangelism as well as social action; a denomination with a public face that includes its theological vigor as well as its eagerness to be associated with one or another culture-war issue; a Church in which contemporary "experience" serves as a catalyst that discloses fresh dimensions of historic Christian faith not as a control that dismisses core belief as constricting? The difference between wishful thinking and hope is the presence of some portent of the latter. Yes, here and there a change to be seen in the aforementioned directions, yet small and fragile. While the penultimate future is ambiguous, Confessing Christ is confident that the ultimate Future is not.

# NOTES

1. The congregation in question, First Church of Christ, Wethersfield Guild, Connecticut, voted in 2004 to leave the United Church of Christ. Confessing Christ co-planners honored their original commitment to hold the ecumenical Trinity Conference several months later at Wethersfield Guild although they were never urged by the UCC officially not to do so. The conference was attended by one hundred UCC, Lutheran, Presbyterian, Greek Orthodox, and other pastors with papers given by theologian Ellen Cherry, Robert Jenson and the writer.

"Confessing Christ" at Year Ten, unpublished paper. Used by permission.

## CHAPTER 20

# Mercersburg in the Twenty-first Century

THE 20TH ANNIVERSARY OF THE Mercersburg Society prompts, some vivid memories of our founding: an image of the living room of Howard Hageman on the campus of New Brunswick Seminary, 30 or so of us seated in a circle, taking that vote to continue in the late 20th century the witness of Nevin and Schaff. Pastor Fred Trost was presiding, as the then leader of the "BTL Club"—the Biblical-Theological-Liturgical Group (in contradistinction to the infamous PTL Club of the Bakers). BTL with its interests in the sacraments and ecumenism was something of a trajectory toward the new Society converging with the Worship Convocation in which John Shetler was such a key figure. And of course, the cluster of other movements with similar or parallel interests that grew up under the impetus of the Mercersburg Society—the Craigville Colloquies, the Mercersburg Society being co-sponsor with BTL of its first historic gathering in 1984, the Confessing Christ movement that was proposed at Craigville Colloquy X in 1993, the Order of Corpus Christi and more. All things to celebrate on this anniversary!

But what of the future? Not just the future of the Society, but of the vision of the 19th century Mercersburg movement in the 21st century? The Mercersburg Society came to be out of the theological ferment of that time, twenty years ago. The occasion at New Brunswick coordinate with its founding was a consultation sponsored by BTL on the Faith and Order document, *Baptism, Eucharist and Ministry*. The focus of the meeting was the sacramental and doctrinal substance of classical Christianity. Its background was concern about the fads and frenzies of the day in mainline denominations, the worry that such ideology might overwhelm these centralities in our tradition. The same matters are still with us, and thus the continuing timeliness of Mercersburg's commitment to them, and for that matter, the commitment of all the evangelical catholic stirrings in ours and other denominations. This year's focus on the Heidelberg Catechism and the recent republication of Nevin's *Mystical Presence* are cases in point.[1] But I believe there is an organizing principle for the sacramental, doctrinal and christological accents that was hinted at in our founding, but now needs higher visibility in the new context of the 21st century. It is nothing new to the historic Mercersburg movement, and was, in fact, the gleam in the eye of Nevin and Schaff and I believe still is, as they look down on us from the heavenly ramparts.

The eminent church historical Sidney Ahlstrom pointed to it when he said that "the most creative manifestation of the Catholic tendency in American Protestantism was the movement of theology and church reform which flowered for two or three decades after 1840 in the German Reformed Church."[2] By "Catholic tendency," Ahlstrom meant the drive toward the universal church. Our Mercersburg mentors spoke of it in their theology of history as the coming to be of the "Church of John," what they called the church of "love," that was the transcending union of the "Church of Peter," representing "hope," and the corrective Reformation "Church of Paul," representing "faith."

This Nevin/Schaff gleam in the eye is *ecumenism* in its profoundest sense, the answer to Christ's prayer that we all be one as the Father and the Son are one. However, more than a few church pundits declare the ecumenical movement to be, right now, in serious trouble. That judgment is made even by some of its friends. For example, Michael Kinnamon, recent executive Secretary of COCU, and long-time ecumenical insider struggles with its problems in his new book, with its revealing subtitle: *The Vision of the Ecumenical Movement: And How it Has Been Impoverished by its Friends,* remarking, "Over the past eighteen years, I have come to realize that the ecumenical movement . . . is not in good shape."[3] For example, major ecumenical bodies—the National Council of Churches, the World Council of Churches— ironically, appear to have turned from the goal of fundamental church unity to other agendas— the pressing political, social and economic issues of the day or the challenge of interfaith matters. The executive secretary of the WCC, Conrad

Raiser, seems to give his blessing on such, calling for a "paradigm shift." And closer to home, and personally painful to me was the decision just made by our Massachusetts Confessing Christ Steering Committee to terminate our four-year effort in Catholic-Lutheran-Reformed collegiality, as attendance at our yearly events had dropped from a high of 150 to last month's 33 folk gathered for what appeared to be a compelling subject, especially so given the problems of the Boston archdiocese, "The Moral Crisis in Our Churches" (note the "our" as we included Protestant clerical promiscuities as well). But the energy was not there for busy pastors, who, I am told, only will come out for matters of "practical Christianity."

But it was not always so for "busy pastors." One of the busiest was Douglas Horton, known to many as one of the outstanding leaders of ecumenism in the twentieth century. Theodore Louis Trost has written an excellent book, titled, *Douglas Horton and the Ecumenical Impulse in American Religion*[4] just out this year. Is it any accident that a Mercersburger like "Ted" would have the eye to see that ecumenical impulse? From his earliest days, Douglas Horton, as a pastor, through his deanship at Harvard, his leadership in the Faith and Order Commission of the World Council of Churches, his role as one of the architects of the United Church of Christ, his being veritable dean of the ecumenical observers at Vatican II— embodied the paradigm of Christian ecumenism in the 20th century. But must we say that he also represents a *lost* "ecumenical impulse" in the Christian churches today?

For all that, consider this manifesto just published: *In One Body Through the Cross: The Princeton Proposal for Christian Unity*.[5] Here are some people who want to return ecumenism to a central place on the church's agenda, one built on solid christocentric faith and order foundations. These 16 theologians meeting for three years decided to put their call in the words of the 1961 New Delhi Assembly of the World Council of Churches, the mandate to make visible the already given unity of the church,

> as all in each place who are baptized into Jesus Christ... are brought by the Holy Spirit into one fully committed fellowship, holding the one apostolic faith, preaching the one Gospel, breaking the one bread . . .[6]

In fact, Kinnamon, the very friend of ecumenism who bemoans its sad state appeals to the same assembly and to just those words with the same passion for recovering the vision. Indeed, Ted Trost makes the case that Douglas Horton's work in the Faith and Order Commission of the WCC was a factor in this New Delhi vision of ecumenism as "one bread, one baptism, one ministry."[7]

Surely you will recognize in this sentence from New Delhi echoes of something earlier. Who planted the seeds in this country for such a call for the unity of Christians; baptized into Jesus Christ; holding the apostolic faith and preaching the one Gospel; and breaking the one bread?

Ironically, there is no mention of Mercersburg in the Princeton document. However, I cannot help but believe that some of the signatories and sponsors—Geoffrey Wainwright, George Lindbeck, William Rusch, Mark Achtemeier (Lancaster Seminary's Paul and Elizabeth Achtemeier's son), Michael Root, Carl Braaten, Robert Jenson and others involved in this manifesto—know of Mercersburg's pioneering role in setting the Church's sights on that goal.

And the 1961 New Delhi assembly itself? I was a UCC alternate delegate to that meeting, having attended the first assembly at Amsterdam in 1948 and the second at Evanston in 1954 with my spouse, Dorothy. However, the regular UCC delegates did not get sick and there was no UCC money to send in the second team as well, so I never made it to the assembly! Robert Moss, of blessed memory, then president of Lancaster Seminary and on the first team, did bring home a consolation prize for me, the emblem of that assembly, now on proud display in a cabinet of memorabilia. With Bob at New Delhi, and Horton too, friend of George Richards and knowledgeable about the tradition, the witness of Mercersburg was not unheard at this landmark meeting with its ecumenical message for that century and this one. Of course, regarding Horton, we must ask whether or not his ecumenical impulse came from his view of it as instrumental to a moral passion for the reconciliation of a warring and unjust world, one that could play out as well in the establishing of a center for world religions at Harvard, and similar peace-making efforts, rather than from a Mercersburg sense of obedience to John 17:21 as such, seeking this Christian kingdom of unity first, and all other things following. This is a question that I think is in the back of Ted's own mind as he reviews the ecumenical Horton.[8]

Yet we must ask, is the Princeton group a voice crying in the wilderness? Is a Mercersburg call for an apostolic faith unity of the church catholic a pipe dream in the twenty-first century? The difference between hope and wishful thinking is this: some signs present right now of the anticipated future. There are such portents of the coming Kingdom of catholicity, I have seen them myself, and you have too. The 1997 Formula of Agreement of Lutheran and Reformed Churches is North America, reflecting the 1983 Leuenberg Agreement of Lutheran and Reformed Churches around the world, is a solid sacramental and theological unity in the Mercersburg tradition. It was hard to come by, as some of you know who were active in bringing it to be. Indeed, the Society planted a few seeds of its own when it had Lutheran theologian Carl Braaten as speaker at one of our meetings, giving him a glimpse of the evangelical catholicity which preceded his own evangelical catholic self-identity. The FOA is based, not on a theological indifferentism that marks too much ecumenism, but on hard-won doctrinal agreements, including sacramental ones kin to Mercersburg thinking on the real Presence.[9] (A personal aside on the influence of Nevin subtly at work in agreements like this and possible future ones. Here is a note from Robert Wilken, chair of the board of the Center of Catholic and Evangelical Theology, on which this Mercersburger also serves, and onetime active participant in these negotiations, "Thank you for your review of Nevin's *Mystical Presence* in the current issue of *Pro Ecclesia*. He was one of my inspirations while studying under James Hastings Nichols." Parenthetically, it was Nichols, interpreter of Mercersburg to another generation who put two of his other students, my wife and I, in touch with Nevin and Schaff and counseled us to join the Evangelical and Reformed Church in 1950.)

Another small sign of twenty-first century hope for the Mercersburg vision is the multilateral agreement reflected in the "COCU Consensus" that undergirds what is now the present manifestation of COCU, Churches Uniting In Christ. Our own John Shetler has been a firm voice supporting COCU through all its ups and downs. We'll see where this next step of CUIC goes. It needs our support.

Yet another portent of things to come in the Mercersburg vision is the 1999 Augsburg Accord, the groundbreaking Lutheran-Catholic Joint Declaration on the Doctrine of Justification. While this doctrine did not have the prominence of the doctrine of Incarnation in the Mercersburg scheme of things, the reaching out of the Lutheran Churches to the Roman Catholic Church, and vice versa, is very much of a piece with the movement of the Church of Peter and the Church of Paul toward the Church of John. It is interesting to note that this agreement on justification was, in fact, made possible, by placing it in the framework of a larger Reformation-Roman Catholic convergence on a trinitarian-christological reading of justification, exactly a Mercersburg accent. I argued just that as accounting for the agreement in a recent Yale dialog with Cardinal Kasper, George Lindbeck and others.[10] Here is the key sentence in the *Joint Declaration:*

> The foundation and presupposition of justification is the incarnation, death and resurrection of Christ. Justification thus means that Christ himself is our righteousness in which we share through the Holy Spirit in accord with the will of the Father.[11]

How can we not believe that Nevin and Schaff were smiling down on the city of Augsburg on October 30, 1999?

The genius of Mercersburg is that its ecumenism is based on the christological core so central to all the significant new movements manifest along today's ecumenical frontier. This is also Kinnamon's view with an appeal to the vision of its modern founders such as Visser't Hooft, Nathan Soderbloom, William Temple, Suzanne De Dietrich: we are already in unity for it is Christ who has brought us together by baptism into his one Body, an invisible ontological gift given that now becomes our task to make visible. We don't create it, as it is already here by the grace of Jesus Christ. The Lutheran-Reformed Formula of Agreement puts it this way (so cited by Kinnamon): unity begins not conditionally with an "if...then," but unconditionally with a "because...therefore."[12] Kinnamon also commends this agreement, incidentally, for the formula, "mutual affirmation and mutual admonition," that is, an ecumenism in which we realize that we do need the gifts that other traditions bring in order to have the fullness of the Body, a I Corinthian 12 catholicity, again precisely what our Mercersburg forebears had in mind.

Christology is inseparable, also, from Mercersburg's stress on the real Presence of Christ so much a partner in the ecumenical advances of the day as in the BEM document, and connected with the importance of the ordering of ministry, yet another Mercersburg emphasis. Once again, Mercersburg's stress on catechesis and thus doctrine, is another key factor in the kind of ecumenism espoused by the Princeton Call, the New Delhi Assembly, and the bilateral and multilateral advances. So when we lift up 21st century ecumenism as the legacy of Mercersburg, it is that kind of ecumenism which is christological, trinitarian, sacramental and liturgical.

If the accents of Mercersburg, not to mention its influence, are alive and well in the twenty-first century, what implications does that have for this Society in the twenty-first century? Could the Society, for example, help to implement the cascade of suggestions made by the Princeton Proposal? I mention some of its suggestions:

a. Seminaries should hire faculty and leaders actively committed to the ecumenical vision of New Delhi.

b. Where there are formal agreements in full communion, every effort should be made to actually implement such, rather than leave them in bureaucratic limbo as is often the case. (The Penn Southeast Conference of the UCC and especially the commitment of its Conference Minister, Russ Mitman, in working with the ELCA bishop in cross-pollinating UCC and ELCA congregations and pastors is a good example of this. Sadly, I'm not sure that kind of thing is widespread.)

c. Efforts in ecumenical witness and service should be pushed forward, Instead of sheep-stealing or solo denominational programs, joint evangelism is needed. Already, we do a lot in partnered social service and social action. An earlier UCC slogan seems as apt as ever in all departments, "Do nothing separately that you can do together."

d. Princeton says, "When baptism is mutually recognized, it should be plain in the manner of administration."[13] My guess is that this is warning about deviant formulas which, in the effort to be inclusive, undercut the standard language of "Father, Son, and Holy Spirit," rendering those so baptized as entered only into that congregation and not into the church catholic.

e. Then there are a series of injunctions for those who are desperately needed to make ecumenism a reality—initiatives by the Roman Catholic Church following the lead of its pope; involvement of evangelicals and Pentecostals who have too often been sectarian and have thrown stones at ecumenism; initiatives by the Orthodox Churches, avoiding the temptation to be standoffish.

f. And very close to home, paying attention to the congregation around the corner or down the street, and doing with them things that are better done together than separately.

All these are suggestions to which the Mercersburg Society and its members could well give aid and comfort. Let me put a few in specific terms vis-á-vis the Society in the 21st century:

1. Could its meetings and projects better mirror the ecumenical vision? Of course, the Society's membership is, to a small degree, a reflection of that, including UCC, RCA, ELCA, Episcopal, Christian UUA. Why not broaden that base significantly and thus embody the vision of the Church of John, with many more parts of the Body of Christ in its membership? One way to facilitate that is to make sure the meetings of Mercersburg include participants of other traditions in the program with invitations out to the constituencies they represent. Also, choose topics that deal with the ecumenical challenges and advances of the 21st century. Again, issues of the *New Mercersburg Review* could be devoted to cutting edge ecumenism of the 21st century.

2. Support of the "Church of John" means participation of Mercersburg members in events that embody the vision. For example, Craigville Colloquy XX (the Society co-sponsored Craigville I, as noted) is on the subject "Christian Solidarity in a Fragmented World: How Can We All Come to the Table?" featuring WCC Faith

and Order executive secretary, Thomas Best, and other ecumenical notables from the churches of Peter and Paul. Again, it means solid support for our ecumenical officers. We could not ask for a better one than the UCC's Lydia Veliko and she needs all the help she can get. And again, regarding the United Church of Christ, support for the seven-volume Living Theological Heritage which is shot through with the influence of Mercersburg and reflects exactly its concerns, theological and ecumenical.

3. It might mean devoting programs, Review pieces, Web site focus to the solid doctrinal issues about which Mercersburg founders were interested, showing linkages to ecumenical advances. This 2003 meeting on the Heidelberg Catechism is just such a model of serious theological attention to classical teaching.

4. It surely means support of the ecumenical relations our various churches have with other bodies, such as the Formula of Agreement, Churches Uniting In Christ and the like.

5. It means battling in our own denominations for the christological, doctrinal, and sacramental teachings so integral to Mercersburg, and resisting the cultural ideologies by which our mainline denominations are so easily seduced. In the 21st century that includes providing an alternative to popular forms of worship so like the "new measures" that our forebears resisted. And it has to do with challenging the sectarianism of the left or the right, the self-congratulation that announces that we are the only ecclesial body doing the right thing—whether it be on culture-war issues such as gay-lesbian agendas or interpretations of theological programs such as "God is Still Speaking," that ignore the fact that God has already spoken in Christ, Scripture, and tradition. The Preamble to the UCC Constitution has it just right on this point when it speaks about "making this faith" its own in every generation, "this faith" being, "the faith of the historic church expressed in the ancient creeds and reclaimed in the basic insights of the Protestant Reformers."

   An example of the need to "resist the powers" as it relates to the baptism issue mentioned by the Princeton Proposal, might be for

Mercersburgers in the Connecticut Conference of the UCC to ask its leadership why the United Church of Christ is the only mainline denomination that declined to participate in the ecumenical baptismal certificate (Roman Catholic, Protestant) because it could not endorse the trinitarian formula. Ironically, our own UCC Book of Worship uses just that formula: "I baptize you in the name of the Father, and of the Son, and of the Holy Spirit.

## CONCLUSION

How many challenges to the Society and its members to witness to the ecumenical faith of our forebears in this the 21st century! We have a mission to share our charism with the church catholic. And we are not alone. We have allies in that mission, and momentum toward it. With a good heart and a confident hope. . . indeed the Heidelberg Catechism's only hope and "comfort, in life and in death". . . let us join our Lord in the long march toward the land of the Church of John.

## NOTES

1. See my review of *The Mystical Presence: A Vindication of the Reformed or Calvinistic Doctrine of the Eucharist,* Augustine Thompson, O.P. ed., (Eugene, OR: Wipf and Stock Publishers, 2000) in Pro Ecclesia Vol. XI, No. 4 (Fall 2002), 494–496.

2. Sidney Ahlstrom, *A Religious History of the American People* (New Haven: Yale University Press), 615.

3. Michael Kinnamon, The Vision of the Ecumenical Movement and How It Has Been Impoverished by Its Friends (St. Louis: Chalice Press, 2003), 2.

4. Theodore Louis Trost, Douglas Horton and the Ecumenical Impulse in American Religion (Cambridge, MA: Harvard Theological Studies, 2002).

5. Carl E. Braaten and Robert W. Jenson, In One Body Through the Cross: The Princeton Proposal for Christian Unity (Grand Rapids: William B. Eerdmans Pub. Co., 2003).

6. *Ibid.,* 6 11.

7. Trost, *op.cit,* 211.

8. 8 ,13, 61, 111.

9. See Keith F. Nickle and Timothy F. Lull, eds., *A Common Calling: The Witness of Our Reformation Churches in North America Today* (Minneapolis: Augsburg Fortress, 1993).

10. "A Reformed Perspective on the Joint Declaration of the Doctrine of Justification," in Ecumenical Perspectives on the Joint Declaration (Collegeville, MN: Liturgical Press, forthcoming, 2003).

11. The Lutheran World Federation and the Roman Catholic Church, *Joint Declaration on the Doctrine of Justification English Language Edition* (Grand Rapids: Wrn. B. Eerdrnans Pub. Co., 1999), 15.

12. Kinnamon, op. cit., 18 quoting from *A Common Calling: op.cit,* 57.

13. In One Body Through the Cross *op.cit.* 49.

Mercersburg in the 21st Century, *New Mercersburg Review,* forthcoming. Used by permission.

# Epilogue

A S BEFITS THE NARRATIVE CHARACTER OF UCC belief, and its expression in caring and doing, this series of essays is framed in a prologue and epilogue. These concluding remarks trace the journey taken, and observe its relationship to the actual history of the United Church of Christ.

The Parts reflect to some extent the emphases that marked the decades of UCC history. For many years, the Church, indeed, had "Biennial Emphases" that took into account the pressing issues of the day. As chair of the Policy Committee of the 1968–69 Emphasis on "The Local Church in God's Mission," I saw up close how the denominational leadership sought to alert its constituency to the signs of the times as it read them.

While the chapters that constitute Part I were written at a later period, the first era of UCC history was occupied with articulating the convictions that the four uniting streams held in common, making possible such a union. Belief was, of necessity, to the fore. Such was reflected in the drafting of the Basis of Union, the Constitution and the UCC Statement of Faith. Moving past this birthing time were kindred ventures such as the creation of a UCC theological commission, the periodic gathering of all the UCC affiliated seminary faculties to discuss doctrinal issues, the publication of books and booklets stating UCC beliefs, the producing of new confirmation and Christian education material for a united Church as well as volumes on the heritage of the uniting traditions. In this earliest period also, reflecting the influence of the "neo-orthodoxy" of the times, new trends in liturgy and the design of worship space, accents in some parts of the church on the sacraments, and the influence of the newly founded World Council of Churches Faith and Order foci, preaching and teaching in the UCC gave much attention to "what we believe."

Both concurrent and subsequent to the era stressing belief was the caring for our ecclesial life together, the ecumenical impulse and rationale of the United Church of Christ. Ecumenism flourished in such matters as the UCC's founding of course, but subsequent to that, its participation as one of the first four Churches in what was to become the nine-denomination Consultation on Church Union, now Churches Uniting In Christ. A UCC ecumenical officer, the president of the Church and designated representatives, played an important part in affiliating the UCC with various unitive efforts such as the dialogue and developing "full communion" agreements with the Evangelical Church of the Union and the Disciples-United Church of Christ and Lutheran-Reformed conversations. Notable also was UCC presence at the Second Vatican Council in the person of UCC leader Douglas Horton considered by many the most important ecumenical observer on that occasion and author of the multivolume Vatican Diaries. Though distinguishable as interfaith, rather than intra-Christian ecumenism, UCC outreach to the Jewish people had begun also during this period, best remembered for UCC theologian Reinhold Niebuhr's writing on Jewish-Christian relations. The essays here as outreach in caring for the ecumenical and interfaith "other" represent developments of that earlier period though written at a later point of fruition and decision.

Part III represents yet another era in UCC history, the "doing" that comes forcefully to the fore on the heels of the earlier accents. Some of the essays here attempt to hold together believing and doing, or integrate the local church into the mission to the world challenging its dismissal by some then-current advocates.[1] Other chapters describe UCC-inspired and supported confrontative experiments in "secular mission" during the action-oriented 60s. And yet others are theological and social-ethical frameworks for addressing issues of moment. Part IV deals with the period in UCC history in the 80s and 90s when concern to retrieve the believing foundations for caring and doing found expression in the formation of grassroots movements, a brief history of early such efforts appears here as well as commentary from within two such movements. The concluding chapter echoes the refrain through-out this volume, the hope that the ecumenical "life together" of which the United Church of Christ is paradigmatic may show itself, as well, in the mutual affirmation of believing, caring and doing.

## NOTES

1. See the writer's canvass of the critics in "The Crisis of the Congregation: A Debate," in D.B. Robertson, ed., Voluntary Associations: A Study of Groups in Free Societies Essays in Honor of James Luther Adams (Richmond: John Knox Press, 1966), 275–298.